THE ORIGINAL LOUISVILLE SLUGGER

OLD JUDGE CIGARETTES Goodwin & Co., New York.

Praise for *The Original Louisville Slugger*

"An impressive feat of research about an underappreciated guy."—Brad Balukjian, author of *The Wax Pack: On the Open Road in Search of Baseball's Afterlife*

"Newby has written a quality book. Readers will walk away not only knowing more about Pete Browning but inspired to learn more about other baseball figures from the era."—Ralph Carhart, author of *The Hall Ball: One Fan's Journey to Unite Cooperstown Immortals with a Single Baseball*

"There is nothing like old-school baseball, and Pete Browning personifies that. The best book on nineteenth-century baseball I've ever read."—H. Foley, host of the *Are You Garbage?* podcast

"Baseball is a game full of myths, legendary figures, and tragic stories. With this wonderfully woven biography of the original 'Louisville Slugger,' Tim Newby artfully combines all three."—Lee Kluck, author of *Leave While the Party's Good: The Life and Legacy of Baseball Executive Harry Dalton*

"Readers will be drawn in by the exploits of a player who does absolutely belong in the 'too weird to live, and too rare to die!' wing of baseball lore."—Sean J. McLaughlin, coauthor of *The Finest Place We Know: A Centennial History of Murray State University, 1922–2022*

"The colorful tale of Pete Browning is a reminder that the beating heart of baseball is the people who play and watch the games. Through Newby's telling, we see the rules and the industry of the national pastime grow up around Browning. Browning's rise and fall are depicted with compassion and humor, illuminated against a backdrop of a complex nation stumbling its way toward the twentieth century."—Clifford R. Murphy, author of *Ink: The Indelible J. Mayo Williams*

"Pete Browning is an iconic outlaw from baseball's early wild years. He is vividly brought to life in all his hard living and hard swinging glory by Tim Newby in *The Original Louisville Slugger*. Through the story of Browning's life, insight into the baseball of that era and the tone of the times is revealed, and the essence and beautiful simplicity of baseball captured."—Jim Riggleman, former Major League Baseball manager

"Pete Browning, the original and inimitable Louisville Slugger, comes fully to life in this fast-paced, historically informed, and deeply researched book. Determined to uncover the real Browning, Tim Newby's nuanced and engaging biography takes full account of his subject's stunning propensity for self-promotion and drunken debauchery, his debilitating physical and mental demons, as well as his amazing hitting prowess during a short but legendary twelve-year professional career. This is a must-read for every baseball and sports fan, as well as anyone interested in powerful, memorable human stories that are brilliantly told."—David Wrobel, author of *America's West: A History, 1890–1950*

The Original Louisville Slugger

THE LIFE AND TIMES OF FORGOTTEN BASEBALL LEGEND PETE BROWNING

TIM NEWBY

A note to the reader: Some of the quotations in this volume contain outdated and racially insensitive language. The original terminology is included to provide full historical context for the events under discussion. Discretion is advised.

Scholarly publisher for the Commonwealth, serving Bellarmine University, Berea College, Centre College of Kentucky, Eastern Kentucky University, The Filson Historical Society, Georgetown College, Kentucky Historical Society, Kentucky State University, Morehead State University, Murray State University, Northern Kentucky University, Spalding University, Transylvania University, University of Kentucky, University of Louisville, University of Pikeville, and Western Kentucky University.

Editorial and Sales Offices: The University Press of Kentucky
663 South Limestone Street, Lexington, Kentucky 40508-4008
www.kentuckypress.com

Cataloging-in-Publication data available from the Library of Congress

ISBN 978-1-9859-0084-4 (hardcover)
ISBN 978-1-9859-0085-1 (paperback)
ISBN 978-1-9859-0087-5 (pdf)
ISBN 978-1-9859-0086-8 (epub)

This book is printed on acid-free paper meeting the requirements of the American National Standard for Permanence in Paper for Printed Library Materials.

Manufactured in the United States of America

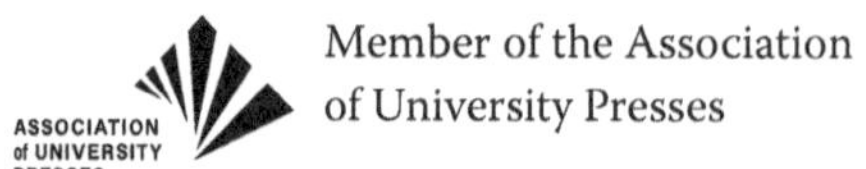

Contents

Introduction

Man, Myth, Pete

Professional baseball and the history, myth, and legend that pervade it are often guided by statistics. We measure the greatness of players by those numbers. We understand the game through those numbers. We argue with friends and fellow fans about those numbers. Numbers tell the story of the game and can shine a light on unknown or underappreciated players. For example, in the 150-year history of Major League Baseball (MLB), just over 20,000 players have appeared in at least one game. Among those players, only 27 have won three or more batting titles. Only 20 have hit .400 or better in a season. Only five rookies have won batting titles. Only four players have won batting titles in multiple leagues. And only one player has done all that, and it is not who you expect. It is not Babe Ruth or Willie Mays or Lou Gehrig or Hank Aaron or any of the other legends of the game. It is Pete Browning, a powerhouse hitter from the nineteenth century who laid waste to many pitchers but whose name is not familiar.

In addition to his on-field accomplishments, Pete is recognized as not only the namesake but also the genesis of the famed Louisville Slugger. He owned the first custom-made bat turned out by what became the Hillerich & Bradsby Company, sparking a revolution in the design and production of baseball bats. Pete was also a hitter of generational talent. His skills with the bat made the difficult art of hitting a baseball appear easy. Over his 13-year career, he won three batting titles and finished in the top three nine times. He led the league multiple times in many other statistical categories, including on-base percentage (OBP), slugging, on-base percentage plus slugging (OPS), games played, hits, doubles, and total bases, and he regularly finished in the top three for home runs and runs batted in (RBIs). These statistics rank him as one of the top players of his generation, one of the premodern era's greatest hitters, and among the game's all-time greats, yet curiously, he has been excluded from the Baseball Hall of Fame. Even with more in-depth baseball scholarship examining the history of the game, Pete has been completely ignored as a serious candidate. In the nearly 90 years the Hall of Fame has been recognizing players, not a single vote has ever been cast for Pete, with no clear explanation as to why.

His numbers tell only half the story. Pete was larger than life. He was known as the Gladiator, Line 'Em Out Pete, the Old Warhorse, He of the Red Eye, the Prince of Bourbon, and, early in his career, simply Long Pete Browning. He was loud, boisterous, and cocky and lived life to the extreme. For Pete, baseball was all-encompassing. Conversations with him were chock-full of nothing but baseball. He continually talked about the game, theorizing on new ways to improve his hitting. When not on the field, Pete happily held court in local saloons, recounting his glories to his fans. Baseball was his identity. A teammate once said of Pete:

> Of course I know that they tell some rather queer stories about Pete and although some of 'em can be said to be a little hard on him, they do not convey a fake impression of his character. Browning would sooner play ball than eat pie and outside his profession, if you want to call it that, he doesn't care for anything. He lets the events of the day slip by him without a single comment and I believe if there was a war in the country tomorrow, he would ask who was leading in the race. In fact, if he had to quit playing, he would die of a broken heart in a month.[1]

Pete was an old-style hitter, as he liked to swing away. "It's my place to hit 'em out," he asserted. "I'm not a bunter."[2] Throughout his career, as he strode to the plate lugging one of his immense bats, he whispered words of encouragement to it, wetting his right forefinger as he reached under his hat to plaster the long, loose hairs to his brow before unleashing his mighty swing. That swing was "always an object of worry to opposing pitchers" and one of the most feared of the nineteenth century, as it led to some of the most statistically dominant seasons of the era.[3] It was also a threat to many a third baseman. "I have come pretty near killing several third basemen," boasted Pete. "It makes 'em shaky when Old Pete goes to the bat. They know he pulls 'em around third and they don't like it."[4] The *Washington Post* wrote, "There were shortstops and third basemen more intent on protecting their shins from one of his scorching grounders than they were with throwing him out at first and when the Gladiator came to bat the outfielders went back to the fence."[5]

Pete was the Paul Bunyan of nineteenth-century baseball, as the stories and myths surrounding him grew to epic proportions. The *Atlanta Constitution* claimed that Pete "knocks two or three balls so far every season that they are never found."[6] Stories of Pete's legendary bat control were embellished over the years with a flourish of imagination, adding to the slugger's legacy. In a game in 1888 against Cincinnati and pitcher Lee Viau, Pete, who was an expert at fouling off pitches until he got one he liked, fouled off 12 in a row. Zach Phelps, one of the owners of the club, stood up and shouted, "Stop that nonsense Browning and smash the ball." Pete, never one to do what he was told, fouled off the next pitch in the direction of Phelps in the owner's box. The ball whizzed past Phelps and tore through the hat he was waving in his hand. Pete stepped out of the box, looked up at Phelps, and yelled, "Well, I smashed it boss!"[7]

These stories became even more unbelievable after Pete retired. Many of the tall tales were perpetuated by Pete himself, who was a good storyteller, although his stories often stretched the fabric of the truth a bit. One can only imagine Pete in a social media world, where his legendary postgame rants and diatribes could reach millions.

Pete was famous for saying he kept the carpenters busy all season with the number of balls he drove through the outfield fence, proclaiming, "Old Pete, he sure did git his bingles in this day. He done druv' one of 'em clar thru the center field fence."[8] In his typical braggadocious manner, he called a home run he hit in 1882 in an exhibition in Atlantic City an "all-around the world hit" that was still going. Over the years, that home run was remembered as a shot that "cleared the fence and landed in the ocean 100 yards beyond."[9] This representation of Pete's power was no exaggeration, as he regularly launched balls that staggered belief.

This image of Pete as a superhuman who bashed balls all over the planet became a common theme in the Browning mythology. "There was no ball player then or since who could drive the ball so great a distance as could this queer genius," insisted the *Butte Miner* in 1908. "He was known as the hardest hitting man in the world. Not you understand, on account of the number of hits that he would make, but on account of the terrific manner in which he would strike the spheroid and the distance he would send it, after landing on it."[10] According to one story, Pete got ahold of a low fastball around his knees and launched it through a big load of hay stacked on the farm behind the field. It didn't "drop to the ground until it struck the next county, where it was found embedded in a brick wall about a foot deep."[11]

Sportswriters of the era romanticized his trips to the plate and wrote about them in glowing terms. One recalled, "The Gladiator was careful in picking out a stick" before unleashing a swing with his "black hickory," sending the ball "on a line to the left field seats" for a home run.[12] When Pete's bat met the ball, the result was rarely an infield hit, where he beat out the throw to first base by a nose or scampered to safety on a Texas League blooper that landed just out of the outfielders' reach. Pete's hits were the real thing—doubles and triples—made even more impressive given the poor quality of baseballs at the time. They were the same size and weight of modern baseballs, but with a rubber center as opposed to cork. This made it much harder to drive the ball for distance. Generally, only one ball was used throughout a game, and balls hit out of play were retrieved and reused. By the end of the game, the ball was a mushy mess, stained with dirt and tobacco juice and with the stitching coming apart, making it difficult to see, let alone hit it any distance.

In 1905, long after he retired, Pete's legend with the bat was not diminished. The Louisville newspaper continued to sing the praises of the hometown hero, calling him "a natural batsman of vast ability and supreme self-confidence. He quaked before no pitcher. The smoothest curve or the fastest delivery were all the same to him. Carrying a huge bat, far heavier than they wield in these degenerate days, he would stride to the plate, pick out one that suited him and whang that leather with a crash that could be heard three miles away."[13]

In the premodern era of few fences, large fields, no gloves, and poor fielding, players were far more likely to get on base simply by putting the ball into play rather than swinging away. Players did not want to risk striking out with big swings, especially in ballparks where the odds of an out-of-the-park home run were limited by distant or nonexistent fences. Instead, players choked up on the bat and relied on a more contact-oriented approach at the plate. "Sacrifice hitting is becoming more common in a winning team than long drives," explained the *Louisville Courier-Journal* in 1888. "A manager would rather have in his team a good sacrifice hitter than a man who drives out long hits. A man who can bunt the ball and make a sacrifice hit is worth four sluggers who hit the ball occasionally, and will win twice as many games."[14] In that era of controlled contact hitting, Pete's display of power was frightening, yet it belies how truly skilled he was at the plate, where he was regularly hailed for his instinctive approach.

Modern baseball has become a seemingly statistics-driven science, with launch angles and exit velocities all the rage and hitters having determined that fly balls are better than ground balls. But it was not a regular topic of discussion among baseball minds in the nineteenth century. In 1885 the *Courier-Journal* was ahead of its time when it published a brief article discussing the best angle at which to hit a baseball: "A scientific investigation has developed the fact that the ball must be struck at an angle of 23 degrees to send it the furthest possible distance."[15] This is in line with modern thinking, which has determined that the best hitters in MLB tend to smack lots of balls with launch angles around 25 degrees.

Pete thought about hitting above all else. "He goes to bed with it uppermost in his thoughts, and takes singles, doubles, and triples for breakfast, dinner, and supper," wrote the *Cincinnati Enquirer.*[16] One of the thoughts he expressed over the years was that left-handed pitchers should be banned from the game. The reasoning for this radical change was mostly a personal one, as Pete sometimes struggled to hit southpaw hurlers.

To Pete, baseball was an art, and batting was his passion; he was a maestro with the bat. When he left the field, the game was not over for him. He continued to talk about batting, theorize about batting, come up with new ideas about batting, and dream about batting at night. He was remembered for the pleasure the simple yet difficult act of hitting a baseball brought him. One teammate said, "I never saw a player who liked to hit the ball like Pete Browning. One day when the Gladiator made three hits, it was next to impossible to hold him in the carriage coming away from the park. Old Pete was like one intoxicated with joy. He would sing, laugh, and hailoo at everybody on the street."[17]

Hitting was a personal endeavor for Pete, and he cared more about getting hits than about winning the game. "Batting was his forte and his fad, and his temper after a game was reckoned by the number of hits he had made, regardless of the outcome of the game."[18] Pete performed best in crunch time, when the team needed him most. "If he failed to make a hit at the time of need he would have tears in his eyes and bitterly bewail his misfortune," wrote sportswriter Jack Boyle in 1910. He "only thought of his hits and the glory of making them."[19] He was so consumed with his batting average that he was known to update and calculate his statistics on the cuffs of his shirts during games, later transferring them to a book where he kept notes on all his at-bats (dispelling the myth that he could not write). Once, when traveling from Boston to New York by boat, a violent storm broke out. Pete, fearing the worst, put on his life preserver and wrote his name and batting average on his stateroom door, ensuring that his statistics would not be forgotten, even if he was.

In 1888 teammate John Kerins told Pete to "brace up in center" because he was "playing a rotten fielding game." Not surprisingly, Pete's response was flippant. "Oh, damn the fielding," he said, "look at my batting record," as he held up three fingers—the number of hits he got in that day's game.[20] Another night he was spotted out on the town having a grand time when a fan asked him about the team's tough loss that day. "It was great," answered Pete, "I got four." When the fan asked him the score of the game, Pete responded, "I dunno what the score was, but I got four hits." Then he sauntered out of the room with his long, swinging gait that was so familiar to baseball fans.[21]

During games, he was known for his intense concentration at the plate, patiently waiting for the perfect pitch. His concentration was no doubt aided by his poor hearing, which blocked out the noise of the crowd and heckling from opponents. Pete approached his hitting with a fierce intensity. When an outfielder galloped to the fence and pulled down one of his mighty drives, Pete regarded it as a personal insult and would "glower at the offender like a baffled tiger."[22] "One time he was at the bat when I was catching," recalled Sam Trott of the Baltimore Orioles:

> He knocked a stinging ball right out in close right field and in running from the plate to first hurried his bat around back of him. The heavy thing struck me on the knee and very nearly put me out of the game. I, of course, expected him to apologize when he got back from the bases, but when at last he came in, and I spoke to him, what do you think he said? An apology? Why not a bit of it. "Everybody gets out of my way when I get

> going," he said, as if it were the most natural and rightful thing to say.[23]

Pete could also turn his ire and fierce intensity on umpires, as "it fairly broke his heart to strike out or to be called out on strikes."[24]

Pete's prowess on the field was often overshadowed by his drunken exploits and personal struggles off it. He was a champion consumer of bourbon and wrestled with his demons publicly. Louisville Colonels owner and manager Mordecai Davidson once claimed, "If that man would keep sober, he would be the greatest ball player living. He has the best eye for a ball that I ever saw, and unless he is drunk on the grounds his playing is not affected, not even by a spree the night before."[25] Davidson's statement was not entirely true, for no matter how well Pete played when drunk and hungover, his performance suffered. One can only speculate how great Pete might have been if he had not squandered so much of his time and talent on the bottle. He was suspended multiple times throughout his career for his behavior and developed a reputation for being unmanageable, tainting the perception of him as both a player and a person.

In addition to his battles with the bottle, Pete was known for numerous eccentricities. He drank Tabasco sauce and washed his eyes with buttermilk, claiming both improved his ability to hit a baseball. He named his bats after biblical characters and took meticulous care of them until they had exhausted the number of hits he believed each one possessed. During games, he refused to slide into base and stood perched on one foot while playing defense. Many of those eccentricities can be traced to an untreated ear infection in childhood that rendered him basically deaf by the time he was an adult. Many of the comedic yet sad shortcomings that defined Pete's life were likely attributable to mastoiditis, the devastating ailment that robbed him of his hearing, deprived him of an education, eroded his professional skills, and turned him into an alcoholic. For Pete, taking the field was a daily struggle to overcome the constant, often debilitating pain in his head (whether from his physical condition or a hangover).

Pete's recognition as one of the premier players of the nineteenth century is often clouded by his larger-than-life personality. His unconventional life both on and off the field is surrounded by legend, with much of it coming from Pete's own mouth. He was a "picturesque story-teller" who could "recite an endless number of pithy anecdotes about 'Petey.'"[26] He was famous for arriving by train in a new city and announcing to everyone on the platform that he was the champion batter of the American Association as he rattled off a lengthy list of achievements. "He never spoke of himself, but in the third person," recalled the *Butte Miner* in 1908, "and his conversation which was of the braggadocio order, was always about baseball and the prowess of one Mr. Browning."[27]

Newspapers relished his legend and happily exaggerated certain aspects of it. The *Cincinnati Enquirer* wrote in 1891, "A great many newspaper men, knowing Pietro's weakness for newspaper notoriety, keep it up. Whenever they come into possession of a new story and are at a loss for someone to put it on, they almost invariably settle on [Pete]. It pleases Pietro and answers the purpose."[28] Over the years, newspapers went so far as to create a caricature of Pete. Quotes from him were written as a phonetic jumble of words, representative of the ballplayer's unique speech pattern, which was uncouth, grammatically reckless, and odd in its phraseology. When he could not find the right words to use, he simply invented his own. Most famous was his creation of the word "bingle" for a hit. In the early days of baseball it was used regularly but has fallen out of use. While this caricature of Pete was not wholly accurate, it was not wholly wrong either, and Pete did nothing to dissuade this notion of himself.

The *Louisville Courier-Journal* flatly declared, "When Pete Browning played with the Louisville Club he was recognized as the most eccentric man in baseball, and there is no question that Pete was entitled to this distinction, for he was a strange character, and he was one of the big drawing cards of those days."[29] For Pete, his worldview started and stopped with himself. One day when they were traveling, Pete's companion took him to the local telegraph office and explained the custom of the telegraph sounders giving the countdown to noon from the National Observatory in Washington, DC, so people could set their watches to the exact time. As noon approached, an annoyed Pete snapped his watch shut and announced, "Well, they're thirty-seven seconds slow."[30]

Pete became trapped in life and in death by the caricature created by sportswriters and the myth surrounding both the man and his career. It was easy for writers to cast Pete as a drunken, illiterate clown whose only redeeming quality was his ability to hit a baseball better than most. But the question has long lingered: who was the real Pete Browning? Was he a simple, uneducated man or a sharp thinker who was a few steps ahead of the game? Was he the major league's first batting superstar whose accomplishments have been overlooked or just an overrated, inept ballplayer? Was he one of the greatest right-handed hitters of all time or an obnoxious, hard-living drunk who simply bashed the ball all over the field with minimal skill? Pete was well known for going on multiday benders that might find him shirtless on a streetcar harassing other passengers or trying to fish in the gutter. Pete was famously misquoted as saying, "I can't hit the ball until I hit the bottle," but he often seemed to be living his life by that absurd credo. His fondness for liquor and brothels led to the epithet "Pietro Red Light Distillery Browning."[31]

Answering the questions about Pete's identity and his legacy as a ballplayer is not simple, as his life has been mythologized, romanticized, and stretched beyond recognition. Separating fact from myth is no easy task. For every story of drunken debauchery that seems too wild to be true, there is a sad tale of a lonely, broken man. About the unbelievable way Pete could hit a baseball, the *Courier-Journal* stated, "Although the matter has been a little over-drawn, many of these tales have the merit of being founded on fact."[32] Clouding the veracity of these stories is the fact that, like many folktales, they were passed around by word of mouth until they were actually written down and accepted as true. There was a slim line between fact and fiction, and Pete was always willing to talk about himself, sometimes telling the truth and sometimes not. Pete never let a good story or a chance to brag about his accomplishments be stifled by the truth. A little stretching of the facts was fine as long as he was expounding on his own growing but hazy legend.

Despite his individual accomplishments, Pete generally played on teams that were woeful underachievers and racked with dysfunction. Pete and those teams were a key part of baseball's early years and an important element of the history and development of baseball. Pete played most of his career in a rogue league that, like Pete himself, deviated from the norm and was often overlooked. That rogue league, also like Pete, experienced great success and great failure as it participated in the first full decade of professional baseball. There have been cursory examinations of Pete's life and career, but as one of the preeminent players in the early days of professional baseball, his role in the game deserves a deeper examination, including how he came to be overlooked and forgotten. This is his true story.

1

Childhood (1861–1876)

"Did you ever hear how old Pete Browning ran away from school to play ball?" asked a crank in 1891.[1] "Crank" was the nineteenth-century term for a baseball fan, and newspapers of the era commonly attempted to explain the outlandish, offbeat, and unconventional life of Pete Browning, the hard-hitting, hard-living slugger known as the Gladiator. The crank continued the tale: As a teenager, Pete displayed the skills on the baseball diamond that would define his life and make him one of the best players of his generation. At the time, he was an amateur ballplayer on one of the teams competing for the city championship in his hometown of Louisville, Kentucky. Game time was set for noon, which was problematic for the young phenom, as he was still in school. It was also problematic for the grown men on the team, who, despite Pete's age, had based their hopes of winning "upon his ability to paralyze opposing pitchers." As game time neared, Pete asked his teacher if he could be excused after recess so he could make the game. The teacher denied his request and instructed him to take the bell and summon his schoolmates back to class. According to the crank, everyone knew this was a mistake. "Pete took the bell, walked slowly to the door, then made a dash for liberty, not waiting to put his hat on. He ran up through the principal streets of the city, in his excitement ringing the bell as hard as he could. Out of breath, bareheaded, and still ringing the bell, he reached the ball-ground in time to take his position in the field." His presence lived up to the hopes of his teammates as he "swung his bat in a vigorous manner, batting in the winning run and from that time on he attracted the attention of the Louisville base-ball cranks."[2] After the game, Pete, who had always struggled mightily with his studies, dropped out and never returned to school. Later, he got his hat back from one of his former classmates, exchanging it for the bell he had run off with.

Pete was born Louis Rogers Browning on June 17, 1861, in Louisville, Kentucky, to Samuel (1814–1874) and Mary Jane Browning, née Sheppard (1826–1911). He acquired the nickname Pete during childhood and had a "trick of calling everybody 'Pete,' no matter whether his name [was] Tom, Dick, or Harry. . . . At last the name of Pete fell to him and will remain his for all time and as long as the grandfathers at their hearthstones will recount to their descendants the wonderful exploits of Pete when they themselves were boys."[3]

Pete was the youngest of seven children. He had three brothers, Charles (1850–1922), Henry (1853–1911), and Samuel (1857–1900), and three sisters, Florence (1851 or 1852–1935), Fannie (1859–1907), and Blanche (1854–1861), who died a few months after Pete was born. Among Pete's nieces and nephews was Tod Browning, the son of his oldest brother, Charles. Tod was a protégé of fellow Louisville resident and renowned filmmaker D. W. Griffith. Tod directed more than sixty movies between 1915 and 1939. He rose to prominence with his silent film collaborations with legendary actor Lon Chaney; gained acclaim for his 1931 horror classic *Dracula,* with Bela Lugosi; and became famous for creating one of the most unsettling films of all time, the cult classic *Freaks* (1932). *Freaks* is a dark tale of a gold-digging trapeze artist who plans to seduce one of her fellow circus performers (who is a dwarf), kill him, and steal his large inheritance. When the murder plot is discovered, the dwarf and his friends take vengeance, turning the trapeze artist into a deformed human-chicken hybrid. Even after several disturbing scenes were cut, the movie remained highly controversial. It was a commercial flop and effectively ended Tod's promising career. It is unknown what kind of influence, if any, Pete had on his nephew. Tod was born in 1880, just as Pete's professional baseball career was starting, and they lived two houses apart while Tod was growing up. On occasion, Tod may have acted as a batboy for his uncle's Louisville teams, although the role of batboy was not as well defined as it is today. It is hard to imagine that his famous uncle's swagger and boisterousness did not impact him. Much like Pete, Tod was a complex man full of eccentricities that branded him an outsider. At the very least, Tod was a lifelong, passionate baseball fan.

Pete's father, Samuel, was a well-known lumber merchant and grocer who was active in local politics, serving as a city delegate for both the Eighth and Eleventh Wards of Louisville. In 1874, when Pete was 13, Samuel was killed when a tornado blew through the city. His father's death was a traumatic event in Pete's life, but there is no evidence that it affected the family's financial situation, as they remained relatively wealthy. Pete never publicly commented on his father or his death. He grew especially close to his mother, Mary, who might have worked as a teacher at one time. Mary was an outspoken woman, a trait Pete inherited from her. She loomed large as an influence and was often involved in important decisions about Pete's career. He remained a bachelor his entire life, living in his childhood home at 1427 West Jefferson Street with Mary and his sister Fannie, who was two years older and never married. His closeness to his mother was likely a result of his being the youngest child in the family, as his three oldest siblings were moving out to start their own lives just as Pete was coming of age. The site of Pete's childhood home was demolished in the 1970s as part of an urban renewal project. A strip mall stands there now.

Pete was born at the outset of the Civil War in a divided state situated between the industrial North and the agricultural South. Kentucky was a nonsecessionist slave state whose families gave sons to both sides of the bloody conflict. Louisville was a divided city during the war. It was a stronghold of Union forces, but a large segment of the population was opposed to the Union, as economic interests and previous relationships often determined alliances. The post–Civil War Reconstruction years were a boon to Louisville. Its central location on the Ohio River and its importance as a train stop led to major growth in manufacturing. This swelled the city's population from less than 70,000 before the start of the war to more than 100,000 in 1870. This population boom continued throughout the remainder of the nineteenth century. Situated on the northern border of Kentucky, just south of Indiana, Louisville is influenced by both midwestern and southern culture and is often referred to as the northernmost southern city and the southernmost northern city in the United States. Louisville has long straddled these differences, resulting in a divided heart and soul. "In its heart, Louisville is a Southern city primarily because it desperately wants to be seen as Southern, meaning friendly, slow-paced, elegant. . . . But Louisville also . . . long identified with big-city aspirations associated with Northern culture, such as civil rights, cutting-edge arts, and sarcasm."[4]

For Pete, the truly defining aspect of his childhood that shaped who he became later in life was an ear infection that developed into mastoiditis, a bacterial infection of the mastoid, the prominent bone behind the ear. If the infection is untreated or treated poorly, the mastoid bone can deteriorate, resulting in hearing loss, blood clots, meningitis, and brain abscesses. Symptoms include nausea, vertigo, and debilitating headaches from the pressure buildup, which can persist if the condition is not treated. In Pete's case, the infection resulted in hearing loss and other symptoms that started in childhood and worsened throughout his life.

The first surgery to alleviate pressure buildup in the ear was performed in the sixteenth century, but it was attempted only sporadically in the years that followed. According to Professor Ricardo Ferreira Bento, chairman of the Department of Otolaryngology at the University of São Paulo School of Medicine, the dilemma doctors faced in the nineteenth century was "whether mastoidectomy was inherently risky or whether the real danger was the injuries that might occur in the inner ear before the removal of the purulent secretions."[5] In most cases, surgery was a last resort to save the lives of people suffering from complications. The surgery was performed more regularly in the latter half of the nineteenth century but did not become commonplace until the turn of the twentieth century. For Pete, this meant that he had no medical options to relieve the debilitating pain, so he drank heavily to numb it. It is not known at what age Pete developed the ear infection that led to mastoiditis, but it is most common in children aged two years and younger. At one time it was one of the leading causes of child mortality. It is now treated with antibiotics and is no longer the life-threatening condition it once was.

As a child, Pete was sickly and thin as a rail, but he grew to a sturdy six feet tall, 180 pounds. He was described as "long and ungainly, comical in gait and action . . . singularly tall and slender, slightly stooped."[6] Pete's unusual height (at the time, the average man stood five feet, five inches) led sportswriters to joke, "The fact that [he] is sixteen or eighteen inches taller than any other player . . . has enabled him to make several good 'grandstand' plays."[7] About his physical appearance it was said that he was "not blessed with a superabundance of personal beauty; in fact, if Pete was entered in a prize contest with this question as an issue against a hyena, the chances are that the animal would have the call in the pools."[8] Pete also possessed a pair of peculiar forward-pointing ears, and a bushy mustache grown as a teenager adorned his upper lip for the rest of life, enhancing his unique, imposing image.

For Pete, his mustache was tied to his ability to hit a baseball, and he obsessed over both his own and other players' "lip whiskers." In 1890 he advised Bill Joyce of the Brooklyn Ward's Wonders of the Players' League to shave off his thick, dark mustache, as it would improve his batting. When Joyce demurred and asked why Pete didn't remove his own mustache, he explained (referring to himself in the third person), "Pete is a blonde and you're a brunette Billy. A blonde mustache is good for the lamps [eyes] and a black mustache is not. Old Pete's mustache lights up his lamps and gives Pete a good eye. But a black mustache hurts the lamps, and you can't hit the ball so hard. If you had a mustache like old Pete's, you could knock the knots out of the center-field fence."[9] Joyce proved Pete's theory false. He retained his black mustache yet still managed to lead the National League in home runs in 1896 and finish second three other times. Pete was not alone in his belief that mustaches were good for hitters and their eyes. Catcher Albert "Doc" Bushong, who played from 1875 to 1890 with a number of teams and is credited as one of the pioneers of the catcher's mitt (to protect his hands for his other profession, dentistry), also sported a bushy mustache. He believed ballplayers should wear a mustache because being clean shaven "makes a man's eyes discharge water and weaken[s] the eyesight."[10]

Pete's eyesight was particularly important because, over the years, his hearing deteriorated due to the mastoiditis he suffered as a child. Pete developed an obsession with his eyes—or as he called them, "lamps." To help alleviate the pain and swelling around his eyes, he used a number of odd methods, such as dousing them with buttermilk, eating red peppers, or standing out in a storm with his face turned upward to let the rain wash his eyes out. He often smoked cigarettes on the way to games, exhaling the smoke through his nostrils so it would blow into his eyes. "It's good for the lamps," he said of his peculiar habits.[11]

By the time he was a teenager, Pete's hearing was already having an adverse effect on his social interactions. Being hard of hearing made learning extremely difficult and frustrating, which led to Pete skipping school and hiding his books under the porch of his good friend and fellow future ballplayer John Reccius. His excessive absences before eventually dropping out at age 15 left him functionally illiterate. *Sporting Life* wrote, "He neglected education and grew to manhood both homely and ignorant on every subject except base ball."[12] In 1886, when stories about his inability to write were circulating in the local newspapers, Pete attempted to refute this claim by sending his autograph to the baseball editor of the *Louisville Courier-Journal.* The scribbled, barely legible signature appeared in an article titled "Browning Can Write," but it may have done more harm than good, as both his first and last names seemed to be misspelled.[13] Years after his death, the newspaper summed up his lack of schooling: "Mr. Browning was not a gentleman overburdened with educational qualifications. All he knew was baseball, and with this knowledge he was satisfied, and never yearned to shine in the role of lawyer or doctor or some other profession."[14]

Pete's illiteracy, like much of his life, was overblown. According to the 1900 US census, he could read and write, and stories through the years would validate that he could do both at least minimally. In 1891 the *Cincinnati Enquirer* claimed, "Some people are under the impression that Lewis Roger [*sic*] Browning is a numb skull and that he cannot read or write. In this they are badly mistaken. The Gladiator is one of the closest newspaper readers in the profession. He buys every paper in the city in which he plays every day. Pete has an enormous scrap-book and keeps everything that is written about him good, bad, or indifferent."[15]

Pete spoke in a loud, sonorous voice, which is common among people with hearing issues. As a result, simple conversations became shouting matches as Pete's voice boomed and whoever he was talking to responded with equal volume in the hope the deaf ballplayer could hear them. His habit of calling everyone Pete was a defense mechanism to hide the fact that he was unable to hear people's names when introduced to them. Though he was often viewed as boisterous and confident, this may have been Pete's way of overcompensating for his lack of education and his inability to hear. Instead, he tried to exude confidence by dominating conversations with the one topic he was intimately familiar with: himself.

Some of the other side effects of Pete's malady were more consequential. He began to drink at an early age and remained a heavy drinker throughout his life. His excessive drinking and the negative behaviors related to it defined him almost as much as his unparalleled hitting ability. Throughout his career he regularly battled headaches and vertigo, and he found that whiskey eased the pain.

Even with his quirks, oddities, and eccentricities, Pete was popular among his friends, teammates, and rivals. Former player and manager Sam Trott, who spent the bulk of his career with the Baltimore Orioles, said, "Whenever there is a good-size collection of men, you will always find one who is of ways distinct from the others. Pete Browning of the Louisvilles, was the most eccentric person of my time. He had all sorts of odd habits and a disregard for convention. Everybody liked him though."[16]

Growing up, Pete led a comfortable life, as the Browning family was fairly well-off. They lived in the West End of Louisville, a working-class area stretching from downtown to the city limits around Twenty-Eighth Street between Main Street and Broadway. The neighborhood featured wood-frame houses, a railroad yard, several distilleries, and many saloons. The West End had a strong immigrant feel, with much of the population being of Irish or German descent. Pete developed a core group of lifelong friends both in the neighborhood and through baseball.

As a youth, Pete was interested in many athletic pursuits and loved the outdoor life, although, because of his ear problems, he couldn't take part in one of the most common pastimes for boys in Louisville: swimming in the nearby Ohio River. He was, however, a local legend in shooting marbles, winning so often that he returned the common or less interesting marbles to his opponents, keeping only the colorful agates, valued for their weight and density and used as shooters. His skill in the marble ring was so well known that he was eventually barred from many of the marble games in Louisville. Louisville baseball legend and Hall of Famer Harold "Pee Wee" Reese was also a champion marble shooter. He got his nickname in childhood, "peewee" being the name for a small marble. Pete was also recognized as a talented ice-skater. The *Courier-Journal* noted that he "could cut more funny figures and skate faster than any other boy of his acquaintance."[17] Even after he began playing professional baseball, he continued to ice-skate. In 1889, during the baseball off-season, the *Courier-Journal* reported, "He frequents the National Park skating rink and recently won a mile race on skates in a very credible time."[18] He was no slouch on roller skates either, winning a five-mile race in 1888 with ease.

But of all his athletic interests, it was baseball where he shone the brightest. Pete's love of and aptitude for the game were recognized early: "He showed a precocity with the bat, which predicted his future fame, and at thirteen was hitting the ball all over the commons."[19] A former teammate once said, "[Pete] has been playing ball since he was able to walk and without doubt will keep on playing until he is absolutely compelled to quit for want of physical strength."[20]

Pete first learned to play ball on the commons in the West End with childhood friends and future big leaguers Hub Collins, Fred Pfeffer, William "Chicken" Wolf, and the Reccius brothers, John, Phil, and Frank. Also part of that group was Zach Phelps, who would become one of the principal owners and president of the Louisville Eclipse/Colonels from 1884 to 1887, before being named president of the American Association baseball league. The boys often played under the watchful eye of the oldest Reccius brother, John William, better known as Bill.

Pete and Wolf remained close friends for life, and Pete bestowed the nickname "Chicken" on him. When the two were teenagers playing on the Eclipse, the local semiprofessional team, the manager instructed the players to eat a light meal before a game. Wolf ignored his manager's directions and indulged in a healthy serving of stewed chicken. Wolf played poorly, committing several errors, and Pete seized on the connection between the chicken dinner and Wolf's lackluster play and saddled him with the nickname "Chicken." According to another story, the origins of Wolf's unique moniker involved a chicken-eating contest with a Cincinnati sportswriter, with Wolf emerging as the clear winner. Either way, the nickname stuck among teammates, fans, and the local press. Wolf's true feelings about the nickname were never made clear, but halfway through his professional career he started going by "Jimmy," with no reason given for the change. Wolf's fondness for chicken continued throughout his career, though. In 1887 the *Courier-Journal* noted, "He will not eat any other kind of meat. He takes his fowl regularly three times. The Louisville players say that Wolf often eats as many as four chickens at a single lunch."[21] In fact, Wolf's weight was an issue throughout his 11-year career. Team pictures show a transformation from a thin young man to a husky one over the years. In 1886, while on a southern tour with the Louisville team, locals saddled him with the nickname "Balloon" because of his weight.[22] When contemplating a return to Louisville in 1892, Wolf assured the team's management that he now "weighs less than he has in years."[23]

All Pete's ballplaying friends went on to varying degrees of success in professional baseball. Other than Pete, Fred Pfeffer had the most success, playing 16 years in the National League as a second baseman, spending the bulk of his career with the Chicago White Stockings. He was recognized for his strong defensive abilities and was part of Chicago's famed "Stonewall Infield" of the 1880s, along with Cap Anson, Tommy Burns, and Ned Williamson.

John Reccius and Wolf both played on some of the first professional Louisville Eclipse teams, after being teammates for many years on the Eclipse's amateur and semipro versions. They were joined in 1884 by John's younger brother Phil and in 1886 by Hub Collins. Of those four, Wolf had the longest and most productive professional career, playing for 11 years, all but one of them with the hometown Louisville team. The fleet-footed Wolf won the 1890 American Association batting title and established himself as one of the most durable players of his time, twice leading the league in games played. John Reccius played only two professional seasons but was recognized as one of the best players on the semipro Eclipse team, which was a national powerhouse. His brother Phil played for eight solid years with Louisville. Collins played three years with Louisville before moving on to Brooklyn for another four seasons; he led the National League in runs scored in 1890 and was well regarded for his defensive skills in the outfield. Collins's promising career was cut short when he died of typhoid fever in 1892 at age 28. That core group was joined by Tom McLaughlin, another local boy who had played on the semipro Eclipse team before debuting in the majors in 1883. He led the American Association in games played in 1885 and was recognized over his five-year career for his standout defensive play.

Another of Pete's close childhood friends was future business and railway magnate Al Johnson, who owned several professional baseball teams. Johnson's father had been a colonel in the Confederate army during the Civil War and moved his family to Louisville after the war, settling in the same neighborhood where Pete and his friends lived. Louisville was a popular destination for Confederate veterans. So many of them became active and influential in local politics that it was often said Louisville joined the Confederacy after the war was over. Pete and Johnson went to school together (when Pete actually showed up), and they developed a close friendship. Pete once referred to Johnson as "the only friend he [had] in the world."[24]

Pete and his friends witnessed the growth and development of baseball not only in Louisville but also nationally. Organized baseball was in its infancy and was starting to grasp the nation's attention. The game Pete and his friends grew up watching and playing was vastly different from the modern one. Few fielders wore gloves, and those who did used simple leather models with the fingers cut off, allowing the same ball control one had barehanded, but with a little padding. Some early gloves were flesh colored, in the hope of disguising the fact that the player was wearing gloves. In the 1870s gloves were thought to be "unmanly," as cricket players didn't wear them.[25] Some players tried to protect their hands by catching the ball with their hats until it was outlawed in 1873.

Bats were originally whatever players could get their hands on—everything from axe handles to rake handles to wagon tongues. Players' bats came in all shapes and sizes; they were short, long, round, flat, fat, and everything in between. It was eventually discovered that rounded barrels worked best, although some players still used a flat-barreled bat when bunting. Generally, it was believed that the bigger the bat, the farther the ball would go.

Pitchers were required to deliver the ball from below the shoulder in either a sidearm or an underhand style, although some pushed the envelope and released the ball from above the shoulder. Those restrictions were removed in 1885, allowing an overhand delivery. Until 1887, a batter could request high or low balls from the pitcher. This advantage for the batter was balanced by the fact that the pitcher was positioned a mere 50 feet from home plate in a four- by six-foot pitching box, and until 1887, pitchers could take a short run before delivering the ball. Before 1884, a batter who was hit by a pitch was not awarded first base; he was given a moment to collect himself and rub the spot where he had been struck. This made hitting a dangerous and daunting endeavor, as pitchers regularly threw at batters to move them off the plate. Batters faced pitchers without the protection of modern batting helmets, wearing only simple cloth hats. Even something as basic as the number of balls constituting a walk was still being figured out in the early days of the game. At the end of the 1870s, it took nine balls for a walk to be issued; this was changed to eight in 1880, seven in 1882, six in 1884, back to seven in 1886, five in 1887, and finally four in 1889, all in an effort to speed up the game.

Rules at the time did not allow substitutions, and teams were permitted to change players only in the case of an injury so severe that the player could not continue. Teams set their lineups for an entire game. There was no assembly line of relief pitchers coming in to pitch to one batter. If a pitcher was struggling, the only remedy was to swap positions with another player in the field.

Baseball was becoming very popular in Louisville and beyond. The *Courier-Journal* addressed this popularity in an 1866 article praising the game and attempting to drum up interest in it, noting, "Louisville is large enough, and our young men have plenty of leisure time at their disposal to afford at least one thousand clubs." The article provided a detailed explanation of how the game was played for the uninitiated:

> In playing the game one fellow takes the club, or bat, and stands on a line. In front of him stands another fellow, who shies the ball at him. Club fellow hits the ball, drops the club, and "takes out," like a chap of our acquaintance once did at the battle of Chickamauga. A chap on picket gets hold of the ball, throws it at another chap, when club fellow quits running. Another fellow takes the club, and the same moves are gone through, which are repeated ad-libitum, until one side goes out, when the other side comes in. When everybody goes out it is called, "innings." A great deal depends on the legs in this game. When you are "in," you are "out," and when you are "out" you score "innings." It is a delightful game for young ladies, but they have to play it in the dark, in consequence of having to divest themselves of all portions of their apparel that will interfere with their running. It is a splendid game for keeping one warm, hence it is always played in the summertime. By all means, boys, give us some more base ball.[26]

The Louisville Base Ball Club (LBBC), the first of its kind in the city, was organized in 1858, three years before Pete was born. A few months later, another club, called the Phoenix, was started as competition for the LBBC. Over the years, other clubs and pickup games popped up across the city. Clubs were originally intended to provide exercise and camaraderie, with games being played between teams made up of the club's own members. Eventually, clubs challenged one another, with each putting forth its best nine players. These challenges evolved into regularly scheduled games, with clubs competing for supremacy and eventually vying for the city championship.

Games between teams from various groups and workplaces were also held regularly throughout Louisville. In 1859 the city hosted a game between married and unmarried men of the Eclipse Club, with the married men proving victorious and winning by a dozen runs. In the wake of the bachelors' defeat, someone commented, "It is absolutely disreputable for [the unmarried men] to allow a parcel of old fogies to beat them in this manner."[27] On another occasion, the LBBC offered to compete against anyone who showed up, and it ended up defeating a pickup team of 14 players by a score of 55–14.

The Civil War contributed to the growth of the game both nationally and in Louisville. Young soldiers who played baseball for recreation while in the army returned home and created many new clubs across the country. In Louisville, which already had an established baseball community prior to the war, returning soldiers fostered a boom in the development of teams in the postwar years. After the war, the Washington Nationals, one of the most prominent teams of the era, organized a series of tours around the country. Where the team stopped was largely determined by the developing railway system, and the Nationals became one of the first eastern teams to travel west of the Allegheny Mountains. At each stop they played the best local teams. The tour came to Louisville on July 17, 1867, and the streetcars heading to the game were bursting with fans packed "inside, on top, and hanging out both ends."[28] The visiting Nationals were not welcomed warmly by the local fans, however. With the city's large population of ex-Confederate soldiers and supporters, the crowd treated the visitors like "invading yankees." The unruly fans showered the Nationals with boos and insults, behavior that "was not at all in accordance with the reputation for chivalric sentiments which Southern cities have hitherto claimed." Newspapers singled out female fans for their unwelcoming attitudes: "The Nationals . . . though from the shores of the Potomac, had too much of the North about them apparently to merit the favor of the Southern women."[29]

Despite the fans' bad behavior on that occasion, baseball was extremely popular in Louisville. The *Courier-Journal* hailed the growth and renewal of the game after the war:

> We note with pleasure the revived interest manifested by the young men of the city in the splendid game of baseball. One club was established but a short time since and has already its full complement of members. Another is in the process of organization, and will, we learn, begin playing during the coming week. Far from being to the detriment of each,

> the existence of several clubs, by exciting a generous rivalry between them, continues the interest, increases the pride of each member in his own club, and this tends to the perpetuation of all. We could wish for the spirit to grow among our young men, that other clubs would be founded.[30]

Two years before the Nationals came to town, "the first game of ball ever played in [Louisville] that attracted any attention" was contested on July 19, 1865, between the local Louisville Eagles and the visiting Nashville Cumberlands. Both of them had already whipped all the other local teams and longed for new nines to conquer, so a formal challenge was issued. The two sides met on a large vacant lot at Nineteenth and Duncan Streets, near the current location of Boone Square Park. A massive crowd gathered, no doubt made larger by the lack of an admission fee, as there was no fence around the field to hold back the crowd. It is believed Louisville won 20–5, but there is no verified box score or newspaper account to confirm this. In his unpublished manuscript titled "History of Baseball in Louisville," longtime Louisville sportswriter A. H. Tarvin claims the score was 22–5, as recorded by Mrs. John Dickens, the Cumberlands' official scorer, wife of the team's captain and shortstop, and "the first of her sex, anywhere, to have any connection whatsoever with baseball." As the game was still new to many of the hometown fans, they were unaware their team had won until Mrs. Dickens climbed on a table and announced the score.

At the start of the 1866 season, the *Courier-Journal* tried to entice newcomers to play the sport: "Pitch in, young gentleman. The exercise will strengthen both the muscular and intellectual man."[31] Later in the year, when yet another club was formed in Louisville, the paper proudly declared, "Baseball seems to be all the rage."[32] Over the next decade, the game grew at a rapid pace in the city. A look at the scores of the weekly games reveals a multitude of teams representing neighborhoods, places of business, and even someone who had recently died. Every week there seemed to be an announcement of another club forming. It was common for players to play with several clubs throughout the season.

Despite the popularity of the game, not everyone in Louisville was fond of the fast-growing sport. In a lengthy editorial in the *Courier-Journal* in 1865, the writer argued that, given the "widespread mania" of baseball, the old adage "too much of a good thing, is an admitted fact," and even "the most laudable pursuits are rendered value-less by being overdone." The counterargument was also made: "Young men, especially in our cities, are a set of flat-breasted, thin-armed, spindle-shanked fellows, whose muscular development has been hitherto sadly neglected," and physical exercise is beneficial.[33] Another issue was that, while most ball clubs were initially satisfied with playing a game or two a week with their own members, many had ambitions beyond that and wanted to play against other clubs in the city. An editorialist who supported those ambitions declared that resolutions should be drawn up "demanding that employees shall be allowed eight hours each day in which to practice the manly and intellectual sport of baseball."[34] Many feared baseball's seemingly inevitable evolution from a simple way for men to exercise into something else entirely: "It cannot fail to have been noticed that some of these associations devote three, four, or five days at a time to their games; that they are not satisfied with playing on their own grounds for their own benefit and amusement, but that they thirst for popular applause, and are rapidly transforming their members into professional athletes."[35]

Those fears about the transition from amateur clubs to professional athletic teams were realized in 1876 when Louisville became a charter member of the National League. This eight-team professional baseball league consisted of the Chicago White Stockings, Philadelphia Athletics, Boston Red Stockings, Hartford Dark Blues, Mutual of New York, St. Louis Brown Stockings, Cincinnati Red Stockings, and Louisville Grays. It created the model for professional sports in America and established the world's oldest professional sports league, which is still in existence today.

Louisville was about to join the ranks of professional baseball, and Pete and his friends would play a huge role in the city's fortunes over the next two decades.

2

Amateur Days (1877–1881)

"The Eclipse Club, a leading organization in the West End, will try conclusions with the professionals on the Louisville grounds this afternoon," wrote the *Louisville Courier-Journal* on April 13, 1877. The city's professional team, the Grays, was set to open its National League (NL) season in a month against Cincinnati. The preseason exhibition against the semipro Eclipse was a chance to get rid of the off-season rust and prepare for the regular season, about which the Grays had high expectations. For the Eclipse, which had been making a name for itself on the amateur circuit, it was a chance for the players to test their mettle against the professional Grays. The *Courier-Journal* continued, "It is not expected that the game will be close or that the professionals will be defeated, but the Eclipse boys will try to make things interesting and endeavor to keep the score of their opponents down to respectable figures."[1]

Unfortunately, the Eclipse boys lost 22–1 to the talented Grays, which many had picked to win the NL title that year. The game was unremarkable, for the most part, other than an Eclipse player taking a foul ball to the mouth, which loosened several teeth. The powerful Grays dominated the game, holding the Eclipse scoreless until the ninth inning, when a pair of errors—a missed fly ball by center fielder Flip Lafferty, followed by a throwing error from shortstop Bill Craver—allowed a run to score. The newspaper noted this lack of offense, stating, "The West End boys proved rather weak at the bat." Still, there were glimpses of the talent that made the Eclipse one of the premier amateur teams in the city. "They atoned for [their weak hitting] with some very fine work in the field . . . and in the face of the heavy batting done by the professionals, the showing is an extraordinarily good one."[2]

The most remarkable aspect of the game is that it was the debut of 15-year-old Pete Browning. He was the youngest member of the team, still two months shy of his sixteenth birthday. For someone so steeped in myth, rumor, and lore, it is appropriate that Pete made his debut against the Grays on Friday the thirteenth. He played third base, even though the game preview listed him as playing first base, and went an uninspiring 0 for 4 at bat. Years later, in 1891, the *Courier-Journal* disputed the date of Pete's debut, claiming he first appeared in 1872, playing third base for the local Olympics team. This seems unlikely, as he would have been only 11 years old at the time. A player named Browning (no first name given) made a handful of appearances for the Olympics between 1874 and 1876, and this might have been Pete. The Olympics (which changed its name to the Riversides in 1876) was a prominent club in Pete's West End neighborhood, and for years it was one of the top clubs in the city. A 13-year-old Pete, who was tall for his age, might have been good enough to play against grown men in 1874. The Browning who took the field with the Olympics between 1874 and 1876 played in the outfield and batted near the bottom of the lineup, mostly against lesser competition (brand-new clubs, junior or amateur teams, and intrasquad games), so perhaps the club was giving its young, talented player a chance to prove himself. It is also possible that the Browning mentioned was Pete's older brother Henry, who also played ball, but nowhere near as well as his younger brother. The two brothers played together September 25, 1877, versus the Amateurs. Pete hit 4 for 6, with a double and two runs scored, while Henry managed only a single hit. Following Pete's death, a story in the *Courier-Journal* noted that his career had begun at age 14. However, Pete made his *confirmed* debut a year later against the professional Grays.

A few months after the loss to the Grays, the Eclipse players had a chance to redeem themselves in another exhibition game on July 28. The day before the game, assuming the same outcome as the first meeting between the two teams, the *Courier-Journal* made this prediction: "The Grays play the Eclipse. It will be pudding for somebody."[3] It was, but this time, with Pete pitching, "the Grays were thrashed by the Eclipse nine," 4–0.[4] It was a mighty effort against the seasoned professionals, who were in a three-way tie for first place in the National League heading into the game. The 16-year-old phenom, using a looping, slow curve, struck out the side to end the game. Pete's poise and skill on the diamond made people take notice of the teenager, who played third base, second base, and pitcher and found success against older and more experienced players. As Pete gained more attention from the baseball cranks in Louisville, so did the Eclipse.

The Eclipse was one of the oldest clubs in Louisville, playing its first game July 14, 1859. The club derived its name from the legendary eighteenth-century racehorse and sire Eclipse—a name that resonated strongly in Louisville, which was considered the country's horse-racing hub. The Eclipse became one of the leading clubs in the region, along with the Louisville Base Ball Club. By 1865, the *Courier-Journal* was already reminiscing about "the truly Homeric battles between the Louisville and Eclipse Ball Clubs in the days before war."[5] The rivalries extended off the field, as fights were common among fans, and local bars often banned talk of baseball. The Eclipse operated through the 1860s but then folded and ceased to exist. In 1874 the club was revived by Bill Reccius, the older brother of John and Phil, Pete's childhood friends and later teammates. At that point, the club built an enclosed ballpark at the corner of Twenty-Eighth and Elliott Streets. The Eclipse was semiprofessional and functioned like a co-op, with the players splitting whatever admission fees were collected from spectators. In 1881 the club began to pay salaries to the players when it appeared that it was going to become part of the American Association, a new professional baseball league. It was claimed that Pete's first contract, which he negotiated himself, was for the simple sum of "as much ice-cream as he might want to eat daily."[6] Years later, his salary for that season was placed at the more realistic figure of $50 a month.

As Pete matured as a player, he developed a unique defensive posture. He stood perched on one leg with the other extended in front of him, pointed toward the oncoming base runners, to function as a deterrent and protection against contact with them. "Pete was afraid of players coming in on the bases," said teammate John Reccius. "He had a habit of standing on one foot and extending the other knee if he saw a fielder approaching him. He always declared that if the man ran into the bone (his knee), he would be put out of business and 'Old Pete' would escape injury."[7] Throughout his career, he was referred to as Old Pete and the Old War Horse, even though he was never the oldest man on any team he played for.

Given his hearing problems, it is understandable that Pete feared being unable to hear an approaching base runner barreling toward him and took steps to protect himself. But his unconventional style often overshadowed his accomplishments as a fielder. Many viewed his fielding as a liability, even though statistics generally prove otherwise. While he was no Willie Mays, Brooks Robinson, or Ozzie Smith, he was not quite the defensive burden the press made him out to be.

Sportswriters often portrayed Pete as bumbling and inept in the field. This made for good copy and furthered the narrative of Pete as a one-dimensional player whose only value was in swinging the bat. One story illustrates the popular view of Pete's defensive skills, or the lack thereof: One night when Pete was out to dinner, he found a fly in his soup and called the waiter over. The waiter responded to his predicament by saying, "Don't worry Pete. There is no danger in you catching it."[8] And in 1891 the *Pittsburgh Dispatch* claimed that a Michigan man owned a mouse that could catch flies and suggested that the mouse be signed to replace Pete. This reputation became part of his ballplaying identity but was never entirely accurate. Pete, however, did little to dissuade this opinion. He delighted in talking about his skill with the bat but rarely boasted about his fielding, mentioning it only to remind his audience that he was vastly more important to the team as a hitter. This narrative took hold and became part of his ingrained identity. Invariably, modern articles rely on this assumption about his fielding skills without providing evidence either way.

Although Pete was never ranked among the top fielders of his generation, his career statistics show that he was not one of the worst either. Twice in his career (1884 and 1887) he was in the top four for putouts by an outfielder, and twice (1887 and 1888) he was in the top three for double plays turned by an outfielder. Throughout his career, his fielding percentage was generally right around the league average. Often, his defensive skills are judged incorrectly when his stats are viewed through the prism of the modern game. Pete played in an era when fielders didn't wear gloves and errors were common. With the advent and improvement of gloves, errors have decreased, and fielding percentages have gone up drastically since the nineteenth century. At first inspection, Pete's career average of 31 errors a season seems like an astronomical number, especially compared to the average of 10 errors per season between 2010 and 2019. But when Pete was playing, the league average was 51 errors. Pete exceeded the league average for errors only twice, and both of those seasons (1882 and 1884) were early in his career, when he was playing primarily in the infield. Up until the 1883 season, he played exclusively in the infield, splitting his time among second base, third base, and shortstop. But after being run over a number of times due to his inability to hear the oncoming base runner, he was moved to the outfield. During the 1883 season he played about half his games in the outfield and played most of the rest at shortstop. The following season he again split his time between the outfield and the infield, starting most often at third base. By 1885, he had made the transition to the outfield and played there almost exclusively, except for a couple of games at first base toward the end of his career. This raises the question, if his defensive skills were so lousy, why continue to play him at positions that required more skill instead of just sticking him at first base? The answer is that his move to the outfield was due not to a lack of defensive skills but to his inability to hear base runners barreling toward him. A move to first would not have solved this issue. His hearing continued to deteriorate throughout his career, so a move to the outfield was the only safe option. It should also be noted that most of his defensive troubles were self-inflicted, having less to do with his ability and more to do with his lack of effort.

The 1886 and 1887 seasons helped define the perception of Pete as a horrendous fielder. He led the league in errors by an outfielder in both years and finished in the top four in 1888 and 1890. But his reputation as a defensive liability was largely due to his peculiar habits in the field. He did not like contact with runners and went out of his way to avoid it. Even when he was moved to the outfield, he continued to stand in an odd manner. Similarly, his reluctance to chase down balls and waste energy he thought was better saved for batting led sportswriters to joke that he wore a deep hole in the outfield where he stood. In 1888 his lack of effort in the field caused the *Courier-Journal* to sarcastically report that the city's General Council had allotted money for a monument to be erected but, after attending a game, decided that "Pete Browning who was like a statue in center field, would be just the thing."[9] His reluctance to move in the field was also attributable to his hearing issues. He was unable to hear the other fielders calling for the ball or approaching him, so on fly balls and pop-ups, he routinely deferred to his teammates. He was once questioned about his refusal to change his position based on a batter's tendencies, despite being instructed to do so by Cleveland Infants teammate Jimmy McAleer in 1890. The batter sent a long fly over Pete's head, resulting in an inside-the-park home run. McAleer scolded him, "If you had been back by the fence you could have caught that ball." Pete replied, "Yes, and I could have took it in if he had hit where I was standing. Don't forget that."[10]

Pete's defensive skills are best summed up as a mixture of exceptional skill, wasted talent, and laziness. He routinely made plays that caused both fans and sportswriters to gush, yet he could just as easily give up on a fly ball because he simply lost interest. The *Courier-Journal* went so far as to call him "one of the best infielders who ever played in Louisville," but then noted that "he lost his nerve after being run over and spiked by players on several occasions and was shifted to the outfield, where he always played after that time."[11]

Over the years, his laziness in the field became more of an issue. Pete believed he was indispensable to the team as a hitter and should waste as little energy defensively as possible. Instead, he thought the younger players on the team "ought to do the running," as he had been hired to hit the ball "and not run his breath out chasing three-baggers." He believed it was beneath his dignity to pursue the ball. "Youse kin git fellers ter run after does hits," he said, "but what good is dey outside of dat? Can dey walk up to de plate wit tree on bases an line 'em out, bling, blang, de way old Pete does?"[12] This single-minded devotion to hitting was duly recognized by the *Washington Post:* "Pete was a little off in his roof garden and had only one idea in his head, day or night. Anything that concerned his precious batting average was meat and drink to him. It made no difference how many fly balls he dropped or let get by him as long as he landed two or three safe ones during a game."[13]

Pete also refused to slide for fear of hurting himself, claiming, "If I should attempt to slide into a base my legs would drop off."[14] The *Courier-Journal* agreed: "Pete cannot slide. He is too large, and one or two attempts would lame him for life."[15] Later in his career he proclaimed, "Old Pete is too good a hitter to slide to a base. If Old Pete can't hit them far enough for him to get there without sliding, he will have to stay on home plate. Pete will get there, but he will get there running and not skating on his stomach like ordinary players. If he wants a three-sacker he will hit it far enough to get there safe and sound, and on his feet, or he won't get there."[16] John Reccius was also known for his reluctance to plow up the dirt.

Because of Pete's refusal to slide, he was an easy out at times. "Pete was clever enough to get a long start on the pitcher," said noted manager, player, and innovator Arthur Irwin, "but instead of hitting the ground for a slide, he ran over the bases, and was a soft mark for the base men. Pete was afraid of twisting an ankle or springing a charley horse."[17] Patsy Tebeau, who managed the Cleveland Infants when Pete played for the team in 1890, recalled him saying, "What? Old Pete slide! Supposing Old Pete would take a crimp in his shaft and be laid out of the game for a month or two, what would the club do without Pete and his bat? If I say it myself, Old Pete wins as many games with his stick. . . . Pete will never slide. He's too plentiful with his bat."[18] Avoiding an injury was not Pete's only concern when it came to sliding. "There is no use soiling your clothes and increasing your laundry bills when you don't have to," he said.[19]

Several ideas were tried to encourage Pete to slide. John Dyler, captain of the Eclipse, threatened to fine him 50¢ if he didn't slide. After being fined, Pete told Bill Reccius, "Dyler fined 'Old Pete' fifty cents. 'Old Pete' can't slide, no use talkin. Don't care if he fines me a dollar and a half, ain't going to slide. See if I do."[20] Tebeau, well known for his confrontational style and rough and rowdy ways, tried a completely different approach and taught Pete to "throw a jolt into the ribs of the baseman as he crossed the base" to get him to drop the ball.[21] The first and only time Pete tried the technique was against Pittsburgh in 1890. After getting a shot in the ribs, Pittsburgh second baseman Yank Robinson responded by decking Pete with an uppercut to the jaw.

Despite his aversion to sliding, Pete proved to be an effective base runner. The *Washington Post* noted, "He would have equaled Harry Stovey if he had plowed up the dirt with his shape by sliding into bases."[22] Stovey was one of the best base stealers of the era, leading the league in steals multiple times and ending his career with 509. The *Cincinnati Enquirer* agreed with the *Post:* "If Pete would go in feet or head first, he would be one of the best base runners in America."[23] Pete finished with a respectable 258 career thefts (in seven seasons).

Stolen bases were not an official statistic for the first part of Pete's career. Prior to the 1886 season, *Sporting Life* wrote about adding stolen bases as an official statistic: "It would be one of the most interesting studies in base ball to compare a player's base hit percentage with his base running percentage."[24] Steals were first tracked in 1886, when they appeared in the game summary but were not recorded as an official statistic. The following year, the steal was given a column in the game's box score. That year, a steal was officially defined as: "Every base made after first base has been reached by a base runner, except for those made by reason of or with the aid of a battery error (wild pitch or passed ball), or by batting, balks or by being forced off. In short, [it] shall include all bases made by a clean steal, or through a wild throw or muff of the ball by a fielder who is directly trying to put the base runner out while attempting to steal." This lengthy definition evolved over time, eventually being reduced to the modern version: "The baserunner advances a base unaided by a base hit, a put out, [or] a fielding or batter error."[25] In the premodern era, stolen base numbers far exceeded those in the modern era. In 1887, the first year steals were recorded as an official statistic, six players surpassed 100 steals, led by Hugh Nicol with 138 thefts; Pete had 103 that year. Since 1887, as the definition of a steal was clarified, there have been only 15 instances of players surpassing the 100-steal mark, accomplished by eight men (Hall of Famer "Sliding" Billy Hamilton, who played from 1888 to 1901, exceeded 100 steals four times, while Rickey Henderson and Vince Coleman each did it three times).

Amateur baseball had long enjoyed a passionate following in Louisville, but the arrival of the Grays in 1876 redirected public and press attention to the new professional team. Crowds flocked to Louisville Baseball Park for Grays games, and sportswriters devoted their column space to the professional team. That would soon change.

In 1877 the Grays seemed poised to capture the NL pennant. After a slow start, the team caught fire, winning 15 of 18 from July 3 to August 13 and going 3½ games up in the standings. Then the wheels came off thanks to a seemingly endless string of costly errors. The Grays went winless over the next nine games, with eight losses and a tie. As this slump was unfolding, team president Charles E. Chase received an anonymous telegram with the ominous warning "Watch your men," the implication being that the team's poor play was due to some of the players taking bribes to lose games.[26] Reporter John Haldeman, son of Grays owner and *Courier-Journal* publisher Walter Haldeman, was intimately familiar with the inner workings of the team, having covered the Grays all season and even participated in a game on July 3 when shortstop Bill Craver was unable to play. Grays manager Jack Chapman moved regular second baseman Joe

Gerhardt over to shortstop and put Haldeman in at second. Haldeman was not a complete novice; he played locally with the Eagle Juniors club and often worked out with the Grays. In what is credited as his only major league appearance and the only time in major league history a reporter filled in for an injured player, Haldeman went 0 for 4 in the Grays' 6–3 win over Cincinnati.[27]

Haldeman then went back to reporting on the team. As the season started falling apart during the nine-game winless streak, Haldeman aimed his pen at the Grays, questioning the players' motives on the field. He wrote, "I had followed the club so closely during the season, and was so well acquainted with its inner workings, what it could and what it could not accomplish, that I knew that 'funny business' had been going on during its last Eastern trip."[28] Over the next month, he wrote a series of articles exposing players' involvement with gamblers. Eventually, it came to light that four players—Bill Craver, Jimmy Devlin, George Hall, and Al Nichols—had taken money to throw games. The four men were expelled from the club, and the National League banned them from professional baseball for life.[29]

The scandal rocked the National League, which had hoped to break away from the gamblers and shady business plaguing its predecessor, the National Association of Professional Base Ball Players. The NL eventually recovered and put the scandal behind it. But professional baseball in Louisville would not do the same. The following March, as the season was gearing up to start, a headline in the *Courier-Journal* blared, "No Base Ball in Louisville This Season." The stockholders and directors of the Louisville Base Ball Club had decided that, after "full and free consideration of the situation, it was unanimously resolved to resign the club's membership in the League." The newspaper reported, "The disgust in this community by the development of the rascality in last year's players . . . were the causes that prompted the action of the Louisville club in declining to put a nine in the field this season."[30] It recommended that strong amateur clubs be formed and all proper aid and encouragement be given to their success. Professional Major League Baseball would not return to Louisville until 1882, and its teams would not rejoin the National League until 1892.

With the absence of the Grays, the Eclipse positioned itself as the premier team in Louisville. After its rebirth in 1874, the Eclipse regained a place of prominence. It became the city's powerhouse amateur team and displaced the Olympics not only from its ranking as the strongest team in

Louisville but also from its park. Located on a plot of land extending from Twenty-Eighth to Twenty-Ninth Streets and between Elliott Avenue and Magazine Street (the current site of Elliott Park), Olympic Park—renamed Eclipse Park—became the second enclosed ballpark in Louisville when a nine-foot-high fence was erected around the field. Inside the fence, a grandstand and a clubhouse were built in the right-field corner. The stands would eventually be expanded to accommodate 800 fans. Renovations would increase the capacity to 5,000 in 1884. Eclipse Park would remain the team's home until 1892, when it was destroyed by fire.

Throughout 1876 the Eclipse piled up lopsided wins among the local teams, and by 1877, it was considered one of the top teams in Louisville. As the Eclipse's profile was being raised, so was Pete's. Despite his quirks, he was developing into one of the top players in Louisville and garnering national attention for his work at the plate, all at the tender age of 17. In 1878 the Eclipse had a record of 23–11–1, losing only four games to in-state opponents. The following year, against a schedule packed with national opponents, the team went 22–11, outscoring its opponents 238–137, with 18-year-old Pete leading the way with a .335 batting average. Pete's success made it clear to him that he had a future as a ballplayer. Even though the Eclipse was just a semipro team that played the vast majority of its games on Saturdays, Pete listed his occupation in the 1879 Louisville City Directory as "Base-Ballist."

By 1880, the Eclipse was firmly ensconced as the city's elite team and one of the best non-NL teams in the country. The Eclipse was often referred to as the best home team in baseball, as its players were all local; it did not recruit out-of-state players. Many other non-NL teams, such as rival Akron, Ohio, paid their players and were considered professional independent clubs. The Eclipse finished the 1880 season 26–3, going undefeated over the last three months of the season and battering its opponents 360–56. The team was so dominant that, following a 28–0 win over visiting Evansville (in which Pete slugged four hits and scored five runs), the Eclipse's pitcher and catcher played those positions for the visitors in the next day's rematch to make the game more competitive.

Despite his success in 1880, 19-year-old Pete was already struggling with severe health issues. That summer he was described as being "thin as a knife and as yellow as a sand dollar."[31] Even with his poor health (and likely increased drinking), he continued to produce on the field and again led the team in batting with a .382 average.

That same season, the Eclipse played a memorable game against its local rival, the Louisville Base Ball Club, on May 29 at the baseball grounds on Fourth Street. The two teams were remembered for their passionate rivalry, which was "just as spirited and intense as now exists among the teams in the various towns of the many organized league circuits."[32] Thanks to two hits and two runs from Pete and a four-hit shutout from pitcher John Reccius, the Eclipse whitewashed the LBBC, managed by sportswriter Haldeman, 20–0. The win cemented the Eclipse's place as the city's elite team. Haldeman blamed the loss on Reccius's "illegal" style of delivery, claiming he pitched with a "regular shoulder throw of the ball" rather than the below-the-shoulder style required at the time.[33] For the Louisville Base Ball Club, Fred Pfeffer, Pete's pal from the commons, struggled at the plate, going 0 for 5, and committed six errors in the field. The following season Pfeffer joined the Eclipse full time at second base, allowing Pete to move to third. The addition of Pfeffer strengthened a team already referred to as "invincible" by the *New York Clipper.*[34]

With the 1881 season, the Eclipse became a major force beyond Louisville and Kentucky. Regional rivalries with the Chicago and Cincinnati teams were mostly lopsided, with the Eclipse dominating. One exasperated Cincinnati sportswriter asked, "Can't Cincinnati get together a club that can defeat the Eclipse of Louisville?"[35] Chicagoans shared that sentiment and organized a team consisting of the best players from a number of clubs, its sole purpose being to defeat the "invincible" Eclipse. It did not. The *Courier-Journal* mocked that team with this headline: "The Last Grand Effort of Chicago to Wipe out the Eclipse Proves Mournfully Fruitless."[36] Later that season, the Eclipse whipped the Brooklyn Atlantics, one of the first true powers in professional baseball, winning three out of four games and cementing its national credentials.

Even with all its success in 1881, the Eclipse still struggled against the team from Akron, Ohio. Unlike Louisville, Akron actively recruited players and paid them regular salaries, whereas the Eclipse relied exclusively on local players and did not pay them at the same level. Akron was so strong that the National League built open dates into its schedule so that when teams visited Cleveland, they could play exhibitions against the nearby Akron team. Akron was so talented that 14 of the 19 players who spent all or part of the 1881 season with the team were playing in the major leagues the following season.

During the 1881 season the Eclipse lost only ten games, but eight of those losses were against Akron, including the worst defeat of the season, a 14–2 drubbing at the beginning of September. The Louisville team defeated Akron only once that season, though their most memorable game was one in which neither side was victorious.

On June 26, 1881, Akron was in Louisville for a four-game series. Though not billed as a contest to determine the independent championship of the United States, the series was generally regarded as such. The teams featured a staggering array of talent. Of the 18 men who played in the game on June 26, 16 would later play at least one game in the major leagues. They included a future Hall of Famer, Akron second baseman Bid McPhee; two batting champions, Pete and Akron's Ed Swartwood; a 284-game winner in Tony Mullane; and Pfeffer, one of the nineteenth century's greatest second basemen.

Akron had taken two of the first three games and seemed poised to continue its dominance in the series finale. The Eclipse's regular pitcher, John Reccius, was in the box, while Akron countered with Mullane. It had been reported a few days earlier that Pete had all but given up on the idea of playing any more games this season on the advice of his physician. But despite his poor health, Pete played. The Eclipse got on the scoreboard first with an RBI triple by Pfeffer in the second inning. Akron tied it up in the sixth inning on a throwing error and then took the lead the next inning on a pair of errors. The Eclipse tied the game in the eighth when "Pete Browning—reliable Pete—still sick, but ambitious came to the bat to do or die. He called for a high ball, and after biding his time, a swift out curve came squarely over the plate. Pete swung the willow viciously, and once more he saved the honors of the day. The sphere went whizzing between third and short, on a deadline for the left field."[37] The ball bounded to the fence, and Pete had a stand-up RBI double. "That sick man, Browning, is an artist when he gets his liver pad properly adjusted," raved the *Courier-Journal.*[38] (A liver pad was a quack medical treatment consisting of a pad or plaster worn on the skin over the liver.) This was the second time in a month a visibly ailing Pete had delivered a big hit in a crucial situation. On May 22, "pale as a ghost and trembling like a leaf," Pete had come through with a two-run double to put the Eclipse ahead for good in a 12–9 win over Chicago.[39] This time, his clutch hit evened the score, which remained tied after the conclusion of nine innings. Play continued until the game was finally called in the nineteenth inning due to darkness. Second baseman Pfeffer, who played a marvelous defensive game with six putouts and 12 assists, declared years later, "This battle really put us on the map."[40] The following day the two sides replayed the game to settle the draw, with Akron prevailing 14–5.

One of the Eclipse's many wins in 1881 was not without controversy. On August 21 the team sponsored by the White Sewing Machine Company of Cleveland visited Louisville. The Cleveland team was well regarded, and a crowd estimated at between 2,000 and 3,000 gathered for the contest. The trouble had started the night before when Cleveland's African American catcher, Moses Fleetwood Walker, was refused accommodations at the St. Cloud Hotel in downtown Louisville. Walker was a talented ballplayer who was making a name for himself in the various minor leagues and semipro leagues scattered across the Midwest. Racial bigotry was common in the United States at the time, and the baseball diamond was no exception. The racism Walker had experienced the previous night resumed the next day when he took the field. During warm-ups, members of the Eclipse objected to his presence on "account of his color." The *Courier-Journal* speculated that the Eclipse players did not want Walker in the game because they feared his "reputation of being the best amateur catcher in the Union." This was unlikely, as they had faced many talented players throughout the season without complaint. Cleveland protested, but to no avail, and as the game started, Walker was on the bench. In the second inning, Cleveland's replacement catcher complained of badly bruised hands and said he couldn't play anymore. The large crowd cheered for Walker to take the field, and he reluctantly acquiesced. In response, "Johnnie Reccius and Fritz [Fred] Pfeffer . . . walked off the field and went to the club house, while other players objected to the playing of the quadroon." Instead of forcing the game to end, Walker decided not to play, and the protesting Eclipse players returned to the field and finished the game, which they won 6–3. The local paper sided with the visiting team, explaining, "No rules provide for the rejection of players on account of race, color, or previous condition of servitude."[41]

Ironically, Walker made his major league debut in Louisville on opening day of the season three years later, playing for Toledo against Pete and his Eclipse teammates. He was the second African American to play at the major league level, the first being William Edward White, who played one game for Providence in 1879. Unlike White, who passed as a white man, Walker was open about his heritage and faced racial bigotry and hostility. Walker struggled in his debut on May 1, 1884, going 0 for 3 at the plate and committing four errors in the field. His team lost 5–1. Walker's lackluster play was noted in the newspaper account of the game: "Walker the colored catcher, who has been spoken of as something of a wonder, appeared to be badly rattled and managed to make all the errors himself. His throwing to bases was very poor."[42] The outspoken Pete had no public comment.

Throughout the 1884 season, Walker felt the stress of racial hostility from fans and opposing teams. It was worse when that hostility came from teammates. Pitcher Mullane, an open segregationist, was awed by Walker's skills, calling him "the best catcher I ever worked with." But he also made it clear that he didn't respect Walker because of his race. "Whenever I had to pitch to him," Mullane recalled, "I used to pitch anything I wanted without looking at his signals." Early in the season, after Mullane threw a fastball when Walker had called for a curveball, Walker headed to the pitching box to have a chat. "Mr. Mullane," he said, "I'll catch you without signals, but I won't catch you if you are going to cross me when I give a signal."[43] For the rest of the season, Walker caught Mullane without knowing what kind of pitch was coming.

Walker's younger brother, Weldy, also made his major league debut in 1884 for Toledo, but he lasted only five games. Following his poor start against the Eclipse, Walker's play improved, but a rib injury and a .263 batting average hindered his chances; he played in only 42 games for Toledo during the 1884 season before being released on September 22. He never played in the majors again, but it was not his middling batting average or injury that kept him out of the majors. Despite his rough debut against the Eclipse, Walker was still recognized for his standout defensive skills and probably would have continued to play in the majors if not for a "gentlemen's agreement" between the two leagues blackballing African American players. That agreement held firm for 63 years, and Walker was the last African American to appear in a major league game until Jackie Robinson broke the color barrier with the Brooklyn Dodgers in 1947. The exclusion of Walker and so many other talented African American players prohibited Major League Baseball from featuring some of the best players in the country, as many never got the opportunity to play in the majors or did so only at the end of their careers when they were past their prime.

The Eclipse closed out the 1881 season on October 2 with a 7–2 win over the Cincinnati Ravens, ending the year with a 36–10–1 record. Pete finished second on the team in hitting with a .333 average, behind Joe Sommer's .350. Despite ongoing health issues, Pete played in 40 of the team's 47 regular season games.

The 1881 season also saw the start of Pete's fraught relationship with the press. On July 2 newly inaugurated president James A. Garfield was shot at the Baltimore & Potomac Railroad Station in Washington, DC, by Charles Guiteau, a disgruntled office seeker. Guiteau felt his contribution to Garfield's election victory had been sufficient to justify the position of consul in Paris, even though he spoke no French or any other foreign language. Garfield lingered for months before finally dying on September 19. As Pete strolled down the street the day after Garfield's death, the newsboys cried out the headline. "Who's that you say is assassinated?" asked Pete. "Garfield," the boy shouted into the deaf player's ear. Pete's response: "What league did he play with?"[44]

Over the years, numerous stories highlighted Pete's perceived ignorance of everything but baseball. After he retired, he supposedly overheard friends talking about the USS *Brooklyn* being hit 30 times in the Battle of Santiago de Cuba during the Spanish-American War. Pete seemed to have no idea that the United States and Spain were at war. What attracted his attention was that Brooklyn had been hit 30 times. Without missing a beat, he asked, "Who pitched for Brooklyn? I'd like to have got me lamps on him for five singles in five times up! Old Pete can kill those bum pitchers."[45] Pete's seeming ignorance grew with his legend and was used to discredit his intelligence, but those who knew Pete best said he was fully aware of how he was perceived. "[He] really had a bit of cunning," explained a friend, "and many times got credit for saying funny things by accident when in reality he knew the humor of them."[46] Sportswriter Harry Weldon, a friend of Pete's, confirmed this: "Pete is not stupid . . . as his talk would seem to suggest, and, with an eye to the main chance, he has turned these stories to his own advantage. He is fond of seeing his name in print, and treasures every article that appears about him, no matter whether good, bad, or indifferent. He thinks they are a good advertisement, and Pete is a great believer in advertising."[47]

Following the final game of the 1881 season, much of the team remained intact for a southern exhibition tour through St. Louis and Memphis, followed by a four-game series in New Orleans in early November.

The Crescent City had high praise for the team and the display it put on. "The Eclipse team, during its stay here, has added to the laurels it already possessed and has proved itself a team of first-class ball players," declared the *New Orleans Democrat*. "One after another the local teams have been beaten, and each time the Eclipse boys seemed to play a better game than they had before."[48] The Eclipse went 10–2–1 on the road trip and returned home on November 22 to a grand celebration.

At the wild, boozy party held to commemorate the team's homecoming, many speeches and toasts were shared throughout the night, but the best came from a drunken, blushing Pete, who was roused to address his teammates. He got to his feet and, in his own peculiar speaking style, delivered this eloquent gem: "See here, you guys; you shut up."[49] Amid wild applause, he returned to his seat.

Everyone was enjoying the success of the 1881 season, as the Eclipse finished the year with the second-best record among non-NL teams, trailing only the New York Metropolitans. Everyone was also looking forward to the next season and the new professional league the Eclipse would be joining. "Up to the present date no players have been engaged for the next season, and it is not known of what material the club for that season will be made," reported the *Courier-Journal*. "It is about time for the [American] Association to find out. Players must be obtained as early as possible or the club will be left out. It is remarkably true up to this date no players, not even the local giants, have signed for 1882."[50]

Nearby rival Cincinnati was also set to join the new professional league and was an early favorite to win the pennant. To be competitive, the Eclipse not only had to keep its best players from leaving for bigger paydays elsewhere but also needed to look beyond Louisville to entice talented players to sign with the club. "Louisville don't want to be supporting the rear in the finish of the season," stated the *Courier-Journal* in its end-of-season wrap-up. "And that this may be prevented it is necessary the Eclipse shall gather together a nine, not of amateurs, but of first class ballplayers."[51]

It was clear that no matter who Louisville signed, young Pete Browning would be the centerpiece of the team going forward.

3

First Pro Season (1882)

"There is a movement on foot in the East to establish another league at 25¢ [admission] to games, to be composed of Albany, New York, Philadelphia, Washington, and Pittsburgh in the East, and Cincinnati, Louisville, and St. Louis in the West," Horace Phillips, manager of the Philadelphia Athletics of the Eastern Championship Association, informed Bill Reccius, manager of the Louisville Eclipse, in August 1881.[1] Phillips sent the same letter to other influential baseball men in the aforementioned cities, inviting them to a meeting in Philadelphia on October 10 to discuss forming a new league.

This planned gathering begs the question: why did Phillips and others feel the need to create another professional baseball league only five years after the National League was established in 1876? The NL model turned baseball into a true national, professional game by centralizing the power structure, encouraging a professional atmosphere both on and off the field, and legitimizing baseball as a real business.

The National Association of Base Ball Players was the sport's first formal governing body. It established a professional category in 1869 when some teams began to pay their players. Several teams in the association, led by the Cincinnati Red Stockings, made it clear that they intended to become fully professional, leading to the formation of the National Association of Professional Base Ball Players, known simply as the National Association (NA), in 1871. The NA was a loose confederation of professional teams; there was no central authority governing the league. Any team that paid its players could join the NA simply by paying dues. Each team created its own schedule and played against whatever other teams it pleased, regardless of league affiliation. The only requirement was that teams play a specified number of games against other teams in the NA. But the lack of a central governing body meant there was little incentive to follow the rules, as the only penalty for failing to do so was forfeiture of the team's dues—a minor inconvenience. The league's larger and richer teams raided the rosters of weaker teams throughout the season. Teams dropped out midway through the year as they lost players and games. This led to unsupervised scheduling, unstable membership, and dominance by one team, the Boston Red Stockings, which won four titles from 1872 to 1875. Gambling also plagued the NA, as there was little oversight of outside influences. This model proved to be unsustainable. In 1876 William Hulbert, the no-nonsense owner of the Chicago White Stockings, set out to revive the reputation of professional baseball, which he believed had been tarnished by the NA and the influence of gambling. He wanted to create a league with a strong central authority and more stringent guidelines for teams, so he helped found the National League.

The eight teams in the National League kicked off their inaugural season on April 22, 1876, with a game between the Philadelphia Athletics and the Boston Red Stockings. The league featured six strong teams from the old NA—Chicago White Stockings, Philadelphia Athletics, Boston Red Stockings, Hartford Dark Blues, Mutual of New York, and St. Louis Brown Stockings—and added two new clubs—Cincinnati Red Stockings and Louisville Grays. Although the NL provided a stable governing authority and brought a sense of respectability and professionalism to baseball, it was beset by problems over the first six years of its existence. Clubs challenged various league rules and were expelled for failure to follow them. The NL's membership fluctuated between six and eight teams, and in six years, it never played a season with the same teams.

During those years, several other leagues were playing across the country, but they were generally less organized and more regionally based than the NL; they were more of a forerunner to the modern minor leagues rather than actual challengers to the NL. In 1877 the International Association (IA) was established, with teams in both the United States and Canada. The IA hoped to rival the NL and implemented several rule changes with the sole purpose of challenging the NL's supremacy. Because the IA lacked a set schedule, teams played in multiple leagues, creating a chaotic season. Like the NA, the IA was a loose confederation of teams that lacked a true central authority. It struggled through three seasons, with teams coming and going each year. In 1879 the Buffalo Bisons and Syracuse Stars both left the IA for the NL, which contributed to the IA's demise the following season. The issues that led to the end of the upstart league were common among other leagues. The *Cincinnati Enquirer* wrote, "Since the death of the International Association in 1879, various efforts have been made to revive opposition to the [National] League by starting similar organizations. All have so far proved signal failures. The chief cause of this has been in the fact that they were poorly managed and lacked strong backing."[2]

Cognizant of the issues that had plagued the NL and ended other leagues, Phillips set out to gauge interest in forming a new league. He hoped to include cities that had been excluded from the NL to give them an incentive to back the endeavor. Therefore, before the proposed meeting in Philadelphia, two independent teams, the Brooklyn Atlantics and the Philadelphia Athletics, headed west to play against potential members of the new league—Cincinnati, Louisville, Pittsburgh, and St. Louis. Much like the Eclipse, the Atlantics had already achieved some notoriety for its strong play against national competition. Phillips's proposed league hoped to rectify the mistakes of the past by including successful preexisting teams that had strong financial backing and were well managed.

Upon returning to Philadelphia after the successful trip west, Phillips declared, "The movement [for a new league] was meeting with great favor in St. Louis, Pittsburg, Louisville, and Cincinnati."[3] The *Courier-Journal* reported, "A couple of well-known ball men from St. Louis will be here to consult with the Eclipse management this week as to the feasibility of establishing a new league between the East and the West." The men from St. Louis then traveled to the East Coast to meet with representatives in Boston, New York, and Philadelphia. "The new league seems just now to be a certainty," declared the *Courier-Journal*.[4]

At the October 10 meeting in Philadelphia, only one of the invitees, O. P. Caylor from Cincinnati, showed up. His hometown team had been dropped from the NL when it refused to ban alcohol in league parks and prohibited clubs from renting out their parks on Sundays. Undeterred by the lack of other attendees, Phillips and Caylor discussed the possibilities of a new league and concluded that it could be successful. After the meeting they sent telegrams to the no-shows insinuating that theirs was the only city not represented at the gathering and inviting them to another meeting on November 2 in Cincinnati.

It is unclear why no other teams sent representatives to Philadelphia. There seems to have been confusion about the nature of this meeting. The *New York Clipper* referred to it simply as an "informal meeting."[5] Louisville did not even elect delegates to represent the club until October 7, so they were clearly not intent on attending the October 10 meeting. Instead, they focused on a convention addressing the formation of a new league to be held in St. Louis on October 20. The October 20 meeting made more sense for the Louisville representatives, as the team was scheduled to be in town for a series of exhibition games that weekend.

Eventually, all the representatives from the different cities came together on November 2 at the Gibson House in Cincinnati. Clubs in six sizable cities—Brooklyn, Cincinnati, Louisville, Philadelphia, Pittsburgh, and St. Louis—were proposed to form the new league. Among this group, the teams from Cincinnati, Louisville, Pittsburgh, and St. Louis were in locations disparagingly called "river cities," the implication being that they had lower morals or social standards. Brooklyn soon dropped out and was replaced by Baltimore. Members of the new league thought it would be strong, as the population in their six cities outnumbered the population in the NL's eight by approximately half a million.

Representatives at the November 2 meeting agreed to call the new league the American Association of Base Ball Clubs, or simply the American Association (AA). They believed "it would be well . . . not to have the word 'League' appear in the name of the new organization, as other words are just as expressive, and that one has already been appropriated."[6] In addition to the name, they decided on rules for the upcoming season beginning in the spring of 1882. They adopted most of the same playing rules used by the NL, with a few differences.

The new league expressed its desire to be viewed as an equal and peer of the NL, not an affiliate or subsidiary. In a show of independence, the AA refused to request membership in the League Alliance (LA), baseball's first minor league. It had been established in 1877 and was affiliated with the NL. The LA protected the contracts of independent clubs, enabled NL clubs to play potentially profitable games on off days, and assessed clubs and their players for possible recruitment into the NL. One of the most contentious and long-standing issues arising from the AA's refusal to join the LA was the NL's refusal to recognize the contracts of players and clubs in the AA. NL president and White Stockings owner Hulbert flatly said, "The League does not recognize the existence of any association excepting itself and the League Alliance."[7]

Both leagues tinkered with their rules every season. Some rules were initially implemented by one league and then adopted by the other. Over the years, creating a uniform set of rules became more of a necessity as the two leagues played more and more games against each other. Finally, in November 1886, a joint committee with representatives from each league set out to draft one set of common rules to be used in 1887. Initially, the two leagues differed on many of the game's operational rules. For instance, the AA allowed the home team to choose the umpire for a game, and that team was required to pay him, whereas in the NL, the visitors picked up the tab. Individual teams in the AA controlled their own affairs, having greater freedom in the operation of their clubs and stadiums than the NL allowed. AA teams set their own ticket prices, usually 25¢, half the price of the NL's. AA teams could play games on Sundays, and because several of them received financial backing from breweries, AA teams could sell alcohol at games, which was banned by the NL.

The AA decided its championship would be determined by the percentage of games won, not the total number of wins, which deviated from the NL's system. This was a point of contention among many of the early professional sporting leagues. The National Football League (NFL), for example, had disputed champions in four of its first six seasons, with the league's executive committee making the final determination. The NFL, like the AA, used winning percentage to decide the champion, the difference being that all the AA teams played the same number of games, whereas early NFL teams played anywhere from 6 to 20 games against various competition. In the 1883 season the NL adopted the AA's method of awarding its championship.

The AA started life with a chip on its shoulder in response to the way the NL looked down on it. The AA wanted to distinguish itself from the puritanical NL, which was perceived (not always accurately) as more of a gentlemen's league: it didn't play games on Sundays, gambling was barred, and the 50¢ ticket price ensured a more mild-mannered, middle-class audience. In contrast, the AA's 25¢ tickets, Sunday games, and alcohol sales drew rowdier working-class fans to the games. The addition of Sunday games was an innovation. The standard workweek was six days, so working people now had the ability to take in a ballgame on their day off and have a beer while doing so. The AA became the world's first professional sports league designed to beat its competition by accommodating blue-collar tendencies and attitudes toward spectator sports. With the number of legendary boozers who populated the AA's rosters and the fact that many of the teams' owners were involved in the liquor business, the league truly earned its nickname: the Beer & Whiskey League.

This was the heyday of the first generation of baseball as play improved, competition increased, and a still developing rule book attempted to streamline the game and make it more watchable. In addition to cheap tickets, games on Sundays, and selling alcohol, the AA implemented the novel idea of allowing women at games. Observers noted that "ball players like to have ladies attend games, but ladies do not like to mingle in a crowd where men are drinking and puffing cigar smoke."[8] Yet clubs did little to deter what was viewed by some as poor or immoral behavior. Even when there were complaints of drunken behavior in the presence of the ladies in attendance, teams made only a halfhearted effort to deal with the offending patrons.

The AA's mass appeal expanded baseball's initial fan base, and attendance skyrocketed. Teams built brand-new modern stadiums to keep up with the demand. With its revolutionary concepts and forward-thinking approach, the AA burned bright as a comet when it exploded across the sporting world in the 1880s. The AA excited fans and delivered some of the best baseball of the decade, at times equaling or even bettering the NL.

Louisville joined the rest of the league in charging only 25¢ for tickets, but it was slow to allow the sale of alcohol. Some in the community claimed, "When drunken hoodlums get on the grounds it is always a signal for decent lovers of the sport to stay away."[9] Originally, the team refused to pay the $500 for beer concessions, and a beer stand was set up outside the gate. The Eclipse eventually joined the rest of the league in selling alcohol at its games, with no concern about the presence of drunken hoodlums. Even with the addition of a beer stand in the stadium, some Louisville fans, whether for financial reasons or because they preferred the vantage point, watched games from the trees lining the edge of Eclipse Park on the corner of Twenty-Eighth and Elliott Streets. Because they still wanted to enjoy their beer during games, these tree-sitting fans formed "beer pools."[10] Stationed at the bottom of the tree was a young boy whose job it was to run to Kelly's Bar across the street and get growlers (nickel pails full of beer). He would then hustle back to the tree and attach the growler to a long rope so the thirsty fans could hoist it up.

Pete's feelings about the new league are unknown, but given his oft-stated desire to run his own bar, he probably approved of the sale of alcohol at games. And he was no doubt pleased that he could play professional baseball without leaving the comforts of his hometown. His limited education meant that he left nothing in the way of a diary that might have revealed his inner thoughts. Later in his career, the press was more than willing to print anything he said, but in 1881, despite being considered one of the best young talents in the country, he was not most sportswriters' go-to person for a quote. That would change over time as his stature both on and off the field grew.

As the National League prepared for the upcoming season, it held its annual meeting in Chicago on December 7, 1881, where several new rules and proposals were discussed. One of the new rules adopted for the 1882 season was a policy stating that players would wear shirt and hat colors based on their position, not their team affiliation. This radical idea came from sporting goods entrepreneur Albert Spalding, who was on his way to becoming one of the most important figures in the first generation of baseball. He began selling baseball equipment from a single storefront near Chicago's ballpark in 1876. He soon secured a contract to be the NL's sole provider of baseballs, uniforms, and other gear. Spalding was recognized for his influential work in modernizing the game and was inducted into the Baseball Hall of Fame in 1939. His Hall of Fame plaque calls him an "organizational genius of baseball's pioneer days." Spalding had many innovative ideas over the years. Some proved to be massively influential and helped the game evolve into the modern version we recognize today; others, like the new uniforms, not so much.

For their inaugural 1882 season, some of the AA teams followed the NL's new uniform policy. All the players would wear white pants, hats, and belts, with their positions distinguished by the color of their shirts: catchers wore scarlet, pitchers light blue, first basemen scarlet and white, second basemen orange and black, third basemen gray and white, shortstops maroon, right fielders gray, center fielders red and black, left fielders white, and substitutes green and brown. The problem with this color scheme was that fans could tell the teams apart only by looking at the players' stockings, as each team wore uniquely colored socks. The new look received a glowing review from the *St. Louis Globe Democrat,* however: "These [uniforms] are the neatest ever seen on the ball grounds in St. Louis, and are odd from the fact that no two players are dressed alike.

. . . This mingling of colors gives the team a bright and handsome look and makes it an easy matter to distinguish the man at bat."[11] Despite its enthusiasm for the new uniforms, the *Globe Democrat* admitted, "The League 'costumes' look pretty, [but] will prove impracticable owing to the confusion they will cause on the field."[12]

The novelty of the new uniforms quickly wore off, as the wild color schemes perplexed both players and fans. In retrospect, the idea of using colors to identify positions seemed silly, as the first baseman was obviously the guy standing by first base, and the pitcher was the player hurling the ball toward the batter. Confusion ensued in a number of games when, in the heat of the moment, a player threw the ball to someone he thought was his teammate, only to find that he had thrown it to the base runner. Hall of Famer Jim O'Rourke, player-manager for the NL's Buffalo Bisons at the time, said, "It is an insult to all of us to make a professional baseball player dress like a clown. If we are unfortunate enough to play near a lunatic asylum, we are likely to wind up inside looking out."[13]

A few weeks after complimenting the uniforms, the *Globe Democrat* retreated from its previous praise: "It is very probable that the present uniforms of the League players will be changed next year. The various colors, instead of helping to distinguish the players, has the opposite effect of confusing the eye. When grouped upon the field the uniforms do not have a picturesque effect."[14] The experiment proved to be a complete disaster and was abandoned in June. The only winner in the uniform fiasco was Spalding, who was tasked with reoutfitting the teams, resulting in a financial windfall for the sporting goods magnate.

Pete and his teammates from Louisville prospered and experienced some of their greatest professional seasons while in the AA. Initially, Bill Reccius, longtime manager of the Eclipse, was expected to stay on in that capacity if the team joined the new league, but at a meeting of club stockholders at the end of the season, Reccius was surprisingly dropped. He was replaced as manager by Denny Mack, who would also play shortstop.[15] The Eclipse then began to assemble its roster for the upcoming year and the debut of the AA. Heading into the off-season, the most pressing question involved salary and what Louisville was willing to offer compared with other teams. Some of the team's better players were attracting attention from the NL, with Pete, Joe Crotty, Fred Pfeffer, and Joe Sommer getting offers from Brooklyn and Pittsburgh. The *Courier-Journal* observed, "To keep these most excellent players here it is necessary for the management to offer some extra inducement."[16]

Even with the salary issue, the team was expected to remain mostly intact. The exception was Sommer, who left to join the new AA team in Cincinnati, now known as the Red Stockings. His departure was not a surprise, however, as he had played for the Cincinnati Stars during the 1880 season and had joined Louisville only after the Stars were dropped from the NL. In addition, second baseman Pfeffer shocked the hometown fans when he signed with the Troy Trojans of the NL, having been insulted by Louisville's low salary offer. His move was the start of a 16-year major league career that saw him become one of the best second basemen of the premodern era. He spent all but one season in the NL, leaving for one year in 1890 to join the upstart Players' League. Even with the loss of Sommer and Pfeffer, Louisville assembled a strong lineup that included a number of players from the previous year's team. Pete, Crotty, John Reccius, and Wolf all agreed to play for the Eclipse in the new league. Added to that core were outfielder Leech Maskrey and outfielder-catcher Dan Sullivan from Akron and Denny Mack from Indianapolis.

Louisville strengthened its roster at the end of the 1881 season when it signed Irish-born, ambidextrous pitcher Tony Mullane, who had tormented the Eclipse as a member of the Akron team. Mullane was familiar with the Eclipse, having played against the team ten times during the 1881 season, including pitching in the epic 19-inning draw. Rumors of Mullane's move to Louisville had started as early as June 1881, but he signed with the NL's Detroit club instead and made five starts, going 1–4. He signed with the Eclipse near the end of the season and made his debut in a four-game series at the end of October in St. Louis. Akron later made unsubstantiated claims that the Eclipse had "stolen" Maskrey, Mullane, and Sullivan by paying them large sums of money.

Mullane proved to be a generational talent, posting five straight 30-win seasons while compiling 284 wins over his 13-year career. That impressive record and his ability to throw with either hand led to his being described as "the twirling craftsman of the Association, the two-handed palmer of the pigskin globe."[17] His dashing good looks earned him other nicknames, including Count Antonio, Count Macaroni, and the Apollo of the Box. Opposing teams took notice and promoted the days he pitched as "Ladies' Day," encouraging female fans to attend. Mullane was also known for being extremely cheap, wearing his clothes until they were tattered rags. *Sporting News* reported, "Tony Mullane has the reputation of being the closest man in the profession. No one ever saw him spend a cent . . . he wore a ten dollar suit until the seat of his pants had entirely disappeared, and he would not have invested in a new suit even then had not the city authorities interfered."[18] Still, he was a vain man who cared about his matinee idol good looks, and he was known to wax the ends of his mustache before a game. While Mullane was pitching for Cincinnati against Kansas City, Jumbo Davis hit a line drive back up the middle that looked "like it was shot from a rifle." The crowd saw Davis swing his bat and then watched as Mullane fell limp to the ground. When the spectators saw blood, some assumed he had been shot from the stands. But the ball had hit him squarely in the face, breaking his "Grecian nose." The first question the narcissistic Mullane asked the doctor when he regained consciousness was, "Will it spoil my good looks?"[19]

Mullane was also an unrepentant wife beater. His first wife petitioned for divorce, claiming that "he got angry, struck her in the face with a pepper box, chased her to the pantry, cut her with a knife on the head and hand, struck her on the head with a water pitcher and threatened to cut her throat with a razor," all because "she chided him about his bad play on the professional base ball field."[20] Mullane left his wife destitute, telling her that if she needed money she would have to earn it. She later claimed he had threatened to kill her. During his playing days, Mullane was generally disliked by most of his teammates because they felt he was not a team player. One said, "He is for Tony Mullane first, Tony Mullane second and Tony Mullane third. He has certainly proved to the satisfaction of ninety-nine out of every hundred that he don't care a rap for the club."[21] *Sporting News* called him a "man of the most sordid nature."[22] Mullane's sordid nature was even more surprising given that he was a teetotaler amidst a league of drunks.

The new lineup for the Eclipse was put to the test December 11, 1881, when the team traveled to New Orleans to play the Western League champions from Chicago. This was "the first time in the history of baseball that two professional clubs were pitted against each other in the Crescent City."[23] In front of 1,500 people, Pete had a miserable day, going 0 for 4 and committing two errors. The Eclipse lost 4–1.

By mid-February 1882, Louisville's lineup for the upcoming season was nearly complete, and despite the loss in New Orleans, the Eclipse was prepared to compete for the inaugural AA championship. In a letter published in the *New York Clipper*, Eclipse president J. H. Pank expressed his optimism for the upcoming season: "We consider this a strong team and hope to come out first in the league."[24] Following two early season exhibition losses against Detroit of the NL, it was clear that, despite the optimism, the Eclipse roster still needed help. The club signed two players, Canadian Jimmy Knowles from Lowell, Massachusetts, and Guy Hecker from Oil City, Pennsylvania, to solidify and strengthen the starting nine.

The addition of second baseman Knowles was intended to allow Pete to move back to third base, where he had played the previous year. Knowles was described as a "strong, active young man, with the principal weight about the shoulders and looks like he might knock the cover off the ball."[25] Despite the team's high hopes, Knowles, who joined the Eclipse on April 20, was injured from the start, experiencing arm and finger problems. He missed the next two exhibition games before suiting up for two games against the Cincinnati Buckeyes, going 2 for 8 and playing miserably in the field. He was released the following day. Knowles's inglorious stint with the Eclipse lasted only 11 days; he did not even make it to the start of the season. He would not return to the major leagues until 1884.

On May 1 Louisville signed George Pierce from the Cincinnati Buckeyes to replace Knowles. He met the team in St. Louis for its opening series versus the Browns. It was a sign of things to come when the *Courier-Journal* misspelled his name Pearce. He lasted only nine games before being released at the end of May. He signed in June with the Baltimore Orioles. The departure of Pierce meant Pete had to move back to second, while Bill Schenk took over at third. Pete played the bulk of the season at second base but also spent some time at both third and shortstop.

While the signing of Knowles and the subsequent addition of Pierce proved to be flops, the signing of Guy Hecker, known as the "Blonde Guy," was anything but. Mullane had played with him at Oil City and suggested that the Eclipse obtain the hard-hitting, husky Hecker as a first baseman and backup pitcher.

Hecker started playing baseball as a young boy in Oil City, Pennsylvania. He said, "I always had a hankering after the ball and bat, and sometimes it got me into trouble that was not very easy to get out of." He explained that while he was playing ball with a local team, he decided he wanted to join up with a nearby semipro team in Springfield, Ohio. "At that time," he said, "I was quite a healthy young kid, but probably not old enough to know what was good for me." Late at night, he snuck out of his parents' house and left town. A short time later, during the third inning of a game, Hecker's father, who had tracked him down, stormed out onto the field and pulled him off. "When he got me alone, he walloped me to his heart's content, and I never left home after that until I began to play professionally," remembered Hecker.[26]

Like Pete, Hecker was physically imposing. He was as tall as the lanky slugger but carried more weight in the midsection. Hecker was a solid, all-around player and is often considered the best combination pitcher-hitter of the nineteenth century. He was the Shohei Ohtani of his day, as he captured the AA's triple crown of pitching (wins, earned run average, and strikeouts) in 1884 and won the AA batting title in 1886, edging out teammate Pete by a single percentage point. He played in Louisville for all but one season of his nine-year career. Unlike Mullane, Hecker was universally loved by his teammates and was remembered for his easygoing nature and "gentlemanliness."[27] In addition, his sharp baseball mind and leadership skills were compared to those of Hall of Famer John Montgomery Ward. "Hecker studied the game from every angle, he talked incessantly about it," wrote the *Courier-Journal,* "he dreamed about it and was hurt to the quick when his teammates failed to enthuse over it as much as he. . . . He was immaculate in his habits, his dress, and in his bearing, and his playing was an art imparting to the game a touch that was superbly colorful."[28] Hecker addressed his professional approach to baseball in a booklet he wrote in 1885 entitled *Hecker's Guide to the Art of Pitching.* In it, he explained, "To play ball merely as a pastime or for recreation one cannot devote such practice and study to the many theories advanced pro and con, as to derive a benefit therefrom. . . . To become a professional and successful 'ball tosser' however is quite another thing and requires an attentive study of the points and rules of the game and a continuous regular training in order to fully develope [*sic*] the physical powers." Hecker had a steadying, calming influence on Pete, as the two were good friends and regularly roomed together on the road.

Heading into the 1882 season, Louisville was the youngest team in the AA, led by 21-year-old Pete, 20-year-old Wolf, and 22-year-old John Reccius. Pete was already recognized as an elite player. "He can play second base, shortstop, or third with the best in the Country, and is powerful with the stick," wrote the *Courier-Journal.*[29] With this recognition came rumors that Pete was leaving Louisville for a chance to play in the National League. These rumors persisted throughout the spring, with the strongest being a potential swap between Detroit and Louisville: second baseman Joe Gerhardt for Pete. Gerhardt was looking to return to Louisville, where he had played with the Grays in 1876 and 1877. The *Detroit Free Press* reported, "Gerhardt is anxious to play in Louisville and Pete to enter the League. It would be the most sensible move in the world to make an exchange. Louisville would be pleased, Detroit would be pleased, and everybody would be happy and satisfied."[30] A few days later, the *Courier-Journal* countered the *Free Press*'s claim: "Gerhardt, it seems, does not want to enter the profession now, and Browning would prefer remaining here. Browning has grown up playing ball on the commons and has many admirers who would hate to see him go."[31] The trade never happen, and Pete stayed in Louisville. Gerhardt, however, got his wish and served as the Eclipse's player-manager for one season.

The AA began the season after holding what was described as "one of the most successful meetings ever held by a base-ball organization in this country." The new league hoped it would portend success for the season, as it would be taking on the established and powerful NL. The *Cincinnati Enquirer* reported, "The results [of the meeting] show that [the] Association will succeed beyond the most extravagant expectations of all the founders of the body. The clubs are all in splendid financial condition, have good teams, and the season looks very promising."[32]

The 1882 season did not start out well for Pete, who had suffered from a long, unexplained illness in the off-season. Pete claimed he lost 40 pounds, though this was likely a typical Pete exaggeration, as it was later reported that he lost only 14 pounds while sick. After recovering, Pete insisted that he was "ready to hit anything in the shape of a ball."[33] But as the season neared and the team prepared to leave for a trio of exhibition games in St. Louis, Pete was taken with an "indisposition" at the last minute, and no amount of coaxing could get him to travel with the team. He claimed he had caught a cold "and had a little stiffening in the neck." The *Courier-Journal* was unconvinced: "There is no doubt he is unwell, but he has played a good game of base ball in worse condition. . . . Pete is a fine player, and that fact is known outside this city, and there is a suspicion that he himself is aware of his reputation." The paper wrote, "It was thought he could play if he wanted to." Pete seemed to back up the accusation, claiming "he had been a fool."[34] It is not clear why he refused to leave with the team. He showed up at the train station to see his teammates off, and they tried to persuade him to go, although there was fear that this effort might create bad feelings between Pete and the club. Whatever Pete's reason for not wanting to travel, everyone hoped it would be smoothed over without causing friction between the Eclipse and its temperamental star.

One possible reason for Pete's reluctance to travel with the team was reported in the *Cincinnati Commercial* on May 12. At the beginning of April, Jim O'Rourke, manager of the NL's Buffalo Bisons, had written to Pete and tried to convince him to desert his club and come to Buffalo. Perhaps Pete was considering it. Recognizing the deviousness of his request, O'Rourke had asked Pete to keep "mum." He enticed Pete with the promise of advance money, but as the *Commercial* asserted, "[O'Rourke] probably didn't know that Browning's mother could buy him and the whole Buffalo Club without hurting her bank account." This was confirmed by the *Buffalo Commercial* a few months later: "Unfortunately for the Buffalos Pete is the son of wealthy parents and plays for fun. He is contended [*sic*] to remain in his home city."[35] As the war of words between the two leagues started to heat up, the Buffalo paper observed, "It is about time that such men as Soden of Boston, O'Rourke of Buffalo, and Banesoff of Detroit, were shown up as the kind of men they are. The Association Club players get their money regularly, and that's more than League players can say."[36]

Regardless of the reason for Pete's reluctance, the following day management ordered him to travel to St. Louis and join the team. He arrived at the train station with his bag in hand, favorite bat slung over his shoulder, and (in a clear reference to showing up drunk) "something to rub his neck. They say it was 13-years old. He left in good spirits."[37]

He arrived in St. Louis in time to participate in a 15–3 win, a game in which his play in the field was hailed as "especially brilliant."[38] The *St. Louis Republican* went even further, calling Pete "Louisville's 'Brag' man." "He performed wonders," gushed the *Republican,* "and it is doubtful if such fielding has ever been surpassed in St. Louis. At all points of play his work was brilliant."[39] This ability to play well, even when hampered by alcohol, gave Pete little incentive to curtail his drinking. Two losses to St. Louis followed, after which the Eclipse headed home for three exhibition games against the Cincinnati Buckeyes before kicking off the regular season back in St. Louis on May 2. Pete shrugged off the losses and the team's poor play. "I am saving my hits for tomorrow's game," he declared in his cocksure manner. "I'll promise them a picnic too."[40]

That would not prove to be the case. In the opening game of the season, a 9–7 loss to St. Louis, the "great and mighty" Pete went a miserable 0 for 4 as he sawed air.[41] Two more losses in St. Louis behind so-so play from Pete tempered the Eclipse's high hopes for the season.

Following the 0–3 start, Pete caught fire. In the return series at home versus St. Louis, he scorched a "hot, low fly just over the center-fielder's head" for a double, and the Eclipse posted a 2–1 win.[42] He then hit .375, with two homers and a double, in Philadelphia, but the Eclipse lost three of the four games. He hit another memorable four-bagger in an exhibition game in Atlantic City, bombing the longest hit ever seen on the grounds—a frozen-rope liner over the center-field fence.

Despite his heroics with the bat, Pete's performance received mixed reviews from local sportswriters. He was criticized for not "knocking more grounders," although fans admittedly liked the long ball, and "Pete gets them . . . frequently."[43] It is often misstated that Pete was single-mindedly concerned with big, awe-inducing hits. That criticism, like many of the negative comments about him, is overblown. A player does not end his career as a .341 hitter, win three batting titles, and finish in the top three in batting average nine times in ten years by simply swinging blindly for the fences. Pete proved to have a good eye and patience at the plate, generally striking out well below the league average. Conversely, despite his good eye at the plate, he generally walked below the league average, but this is harder to quantify, as the number of balls required for a walk was in constant flux early in his career. Pete did express a dislike for walks, preferring to swing at the ball every chance he got.

Notwithstanding the criticism from sportswriters, Pete was fast becoming a fan favorite for his herculean power at the plate as he drilled the ball all over the park. At home games, his older brothers were often in the stands leading the cheers for their little brother. When Pete had a bad day with the bat, which was rare in 1882, his brothers permitted a certain amount of booing, but when the critics became too harsh and their comments too personal, the brothers were known to chastise their fellow fans.

Pete stayed hot for the rest of the season. A month after the games in Philadelphia, he went 3 for 4 in Baltimore and hit another monster shot that would have been a clean home run anywhere else, but he had to settle for a double. In the same game he proved his worth as a base runner. Pete was caught in a rundown between second and third, and with some fancy footwork he evaded the tag and regained his base. After the game he boasted, "It takes a whole nine to put me out between bases."[44] By July 8, Pete was hitting .414 and was far and away the leading hitter in both leagues, besting the NL's Cap Anson's .397. Anson, a future Hall of Famer, was one of the game's first superstars.

As Pete was establishing himself as a player with no peer, the Cincinnati Red Stockings were doing the same as a team. Cincinnati caught fire at the end of May and moved into first place on June 13. The team would not relinquish the top spot in the standings for the remainder of the season, finishing 12½ games ahead of second-place Philadelphia.

It was not all smooth sailing in the AA's inaugural season, though. Throughout the first half of the season, there were regular complaints about the AA's decision to allow the home team to select the umpire for a game. These troubles culminated on June 29 when Louisville walked off the field over a disputed call in the fifth inning, after which the umpire awarded the win to St. Louis. Even though the *Cincinnati Enquirer* wrote that Louisville had acted "babyishly" in walking off the field, it was becoming clear that allowing the home team to choose an often biased umpire was a mistake.[45] A few weeks later, the AA changed the rules. The AA chose three umpires who had no affiliation with any of the teams; these three would travel with the away teams, ensuring a neutral presence. In addition, home teams would no longer pay the umpires; their salaries and travel expenses would be covered jointly by the AA and the teams, creating a professional umpiring class. The NL would eventually follow the AA's lead.

Even with his hot bat, Pete occasionally struggled in the field. On June 9 versus visiting Philadelphia, Pete played a miserable game at second base. His poor fielding and three errors "surprised the audience. They were the most feeble-minded, imbecile ones ever witnessed on a ball field." The *Courier-Journal* claimed that while Pete still "clings to his cunning at the bat," his "second base play has grown faulty here lately."[46] To avoid being trampled by advancing runners, Pete had taken to standing out of the base path and refused to move. Still, despite his defensive shortcomings, Pete was absolutely on fire at the plate.

Pete was not the only member of the Eclipse to excel in the 1882 season. Pitcher Mullane was on his way to the first of five consecutive 30-win seasons (minus 1885, when he was suspended for the entire year for breaking his contract) and recorded a couple of historic firsts. On July

18, after falling behind 7–1 against the last-place team from Baltimore, the right-handed Mullane began pitching with his left hand in the fourth inning, becoming the first ambidextrous pitcher in the major leagues. Mullane had taught himself to throw left-handed after being injured in a long-distance throwing contest a few years prior. Mullane threw the Baltimore batters off balance with his switching back and forth. The Eclipse rallied to tie the score 8–8 in the eighth inning on a homer by Hecker but eventually lost in the ninth when Baltimore's weak-hitting Charlie Householder hit a home run. Despite the valiant effort by Mullane, the *Courier-Journal* laid the defeat squarely at his feet: "He pitched a game against which any nine boys could have won. He was brought to task for his pitching and claimed that his arm was sore, but this is a very lame excuse. He ought to have been in shape after fifty hours' rest. A great many people here claim that he was trying to see how pretty a ball he could put over the plate for the home boys to hit."[47]

Later that season, Mullane achieved another milestone when he tossed the first no-hitter in AA history against Cincinnati on September 11. Eight days later, teammate Hecker equaled the feat when he pitched a no-hitter against Pittsburgh. This was an impressive accomplishment for the new league, as the NL had witnessed only five no-hitters over the first six seasons of its existence, while the AA's Louisville team had tossed two of them eight days apart. Hecker's no-hitter also marked several other firsts: the first time the losing team scored a run in a no-hitter, the first time a team recorded a second no-hitter for a franchise, and the first time a team threw two no-hitters in a single season. The significance of these achievements was not fully recognized until later, when the difficulty and rarity of no-hitters were better understood. At the time, neither fans nor sportswriters viewed a no-hitter as anything special; it was just another ball game, not worthy of the highlight reel. Neither Mullane's nor Hecker's no-hitters got much press coverage. Mullane's feat was summed up in a single sentence: "Cincinnati played a fair fielding game, but never made a hit." However, his remarkable pitching was included in a long list of highlights for the Eclipse that day.[48] Hecker received even less praise. The *Pittsburgh Times* simply noted at the end of the article: "The home nine failed to get a base hit off Hecker during the entire game."[49]

During Mullane's no-hitter, Pete was involved in another unusual and unlikely-to-be-repeated occurrence. At the time, AA teams could use substitute runners for injured players if each team agreed to do so before the game. Louisville was using Hecker as a substitute runner for Pete, who was nursing a pulled leg muscle. Every time Pete came to bat, Hecker was stationed behind the catcher, ready to run if Pete got a hit. Pete struggled at the plate, going hitless through seven innings. In the eighth, Pete finally hit a hard shot into right field and, in his excitement, took off for first. A confused Hecker stopped running. Pete reached first base safely but was ruled out when Dan Stearns tagged the bag. The umpire rightly determined that Hecker was the legal base runner and had failed to run. Pete received the dubious distinction of being the only player to reach base safely but not be credited with the hit because he was called out for being an illegal base runner.

With Pete's hitting, Mullane's and Hecker's no-hitters, and the league-leading play of Cincinnati, the AA was producing some of the most exciting baseball of the summer of 1882. Perhaps buoyed by the return of Major League Baseball and the first-place Red Stockings, the *Cincinnati Enquirer* went so far as to claim that "every club in the American Association has received a larger patronage this season than any of the [National] League clubs, with the possible exception of the Chicagos."[50]

As the summer wore on, Pete continued at a blistering pace, leading the league in hitting by a large margin. Up to that point, Pete's drinking had never noticeably impacted his game on the field. That changed on August 12, a relatively cool summer day, at home against Philadelphia. "Twelve hundred people attended and saw with deep regret their too much pampered pet, Pete Browning lose the game for the home team by his miserable work at second," scolded the *Philadelphia Times*. In the 4–3 loss, Pete, who was visibly drunk, made three errors. Embarrassingly, he was called out for walking back to his base after a foul ball by Hecker (the rule stated that a player had to run back). The Philadelphia fans laughed and jeered at Pete's humiliating performance. The *Times* concluded by noting, "Louisville would have won but for Browning's clumsiness."[51] For the *Courier-Journal*, Pete's performance in the field capped a disastrous season at second base, and it called for the team to make changes. "Browning as a second baseman is a failure, a fact that all lovers of the sport discovered long ago, but which the managers of the Eclipse club seem yet oblivious. They may possibly discover it by the end of the season, after he has lost them more games than they can afford to lose, and when too late to remedy the evil. He knows how to bat but should be placed in the outfield and put under severe training in base-running."[52]

The day after Pete's drunken display against Philadelphia, the *Courier-Journal*'s criticism was even more pointed: "Browning made his appearance on the ball field most palpably under the influence of liquor," adding that "his playing and conduct on the field was maudlin to the extreme, and excited the laughter and derision of the crowd." The newspaper then denounced the team's lax handling of Pete and his excessive drinking: "Management permitted him to enter the game. There is not another player in the nine who, under the same conditions, would have been allowed to come on to the field." It heaped much of the blame on team president Pank, who sat on the players' bench during the game and seemed oblivious to Pete's drunkenness. "Mr. Pank could not possibly have been blind to Browning's actions," it wrote, "and why he remained silent is only explained by the fact that Browning has always been permitted to do as he pleased." The *Courier-Journal*'s frustration was evident as it concluded:

> Browning since the opening of the season, has become too big for this city and has been a very unharmonious element in the club. The present management of the nine has not shown the ability to hold the young man down and it had better release him. He is a valuable man if properly handled, but as long as he stays here, he is likely to do as he pleases. He is injuring himself, as all of his many friends see it, and they would not be sorry to see him play elsewhere. The management, however, cannot afford to let this last offense go by unnoticed. It calls for some summary and stringent action; in fact, the young man should be squarely sat upon.[53]

None of those things happened. In fact, Pete re-signed for the 1883 season at a salary of $200 a month. Even more frustrating, he continued to play well. He had led the AA in hitting for much of the season, and that did not change. A 19-game hitting streak through the month of August lengthened his lead. By September 8, he was hitting .392, besting second-place Hick Carpenter by nearly 50 percentage points. He was also outpacing NL leader Dan Brouthers. Hall of Famer Connie Mack, who briefly played with Pete in 1891, recalled that Pete attributed much of his success at the plate during the 1882 season to chewing gum. Many players were known to place a piece of gum on their hats for good luck, but Pete, who always did things his own way, "plastered it in his eyebrows."[54]

Pete did not slow down in the final month of the season. On September 12, in a 10–4 win over eventual league champion Cincinnati, the ball seemed to leap off his bat. He went 3 for 5 with a triple and two homers, one of them a grand slam. He kept up this torrid pace until September 21, when he declared he was too sick to play in a game against Pittsburgh. No further details were given, but he missed the last ten games of the season. It made no difference. Pete ended the year batting .378 and led both the AA and the NL in hitting. The *Buffalo Commercial* tried to minimize Pete's achievements by pointing out the assumed talent gap between the NL and the AA: "To be sure he leads Brouthers in batting slightly, but this is nothing to his credit when one considers the difference in the pitchers of the [National] League and American Association."[55] This was a point of contention throughout the existence of the two leagues and a major factor in evaluating Pete's legacy.

Pete firmly established himself as a major talent with one of the most overlooked, unheralded, yet statistically dominant rookie campaigns ever. It was only the third time in the short history of professional baseball that a rookie led the league in batting. More than a century later, it still ranks as one of only five times this has happened—Ross Barnes in 1876, Abner Dalrymple in 1878, Tony Oliva in 1964, and Ichiro Suzuki in 2001 being the others. (It should be mentioned that Barnes was not a true rookie, as he had played for five years in the NA, but 1876 was his first year in the NL.) Pete's batting title also made him one of the youngest batting champions of all time, joining Ty Cobb (1907), Al Kaline (1955), Alex Rodriguez (1996), and Juan Soto (2020) as the only champions aged 21 or younger. In addition to leading both the AA and the NL in batting average, Pete led the AA in on-base percentage (OBP; .430), slugging (.510), on-base percentage plus slugging (OPS; .940), and wins above replacement (WAR—the number of wins a player added to the team above what a replacement player would have added; 4.5). He did not just lead the league in those statistical categories; he lapped the rest of the field. His batting average led the league by more than 30 points, his OBP by 59, his slugging by 19, and his OPS by 79. Although batting average is generally the statistic that gets the attention of fans, as it is easy to understand, an even better measure of a hitter's value is OPS. A high OPS can identify which player helped his team win the most games throughout the season. Pete's adjusted OPS (OPS+, which attempts to normalize OPS across the entire league by accounting for external factors such as a home ballpark's dimensions) was 223—the highest ever by a player aged 21 or younger and the highest by a true rookie.

There is an old baseball adage: You are either scoring runs or driving them in. The other stuff is just fluff. There was very little fluff in Pete's 1882 season. His OBP and OPS were miles ahead of the rest of the league, so he was clearly driving in and scoring runs in abundance. Runs batted in (RBIs) were not an official statistic in the AA in 1882, so it is hard to gauge how many runs Pete drove in, but based on his other numbers, it was quite a few. He finished fourth in the league in runs scored, attributable largely to the lack of hitting taking place behind him in the Eclipse's lineup. He also finished second in the league in home runs and fourth in total bases.

In the late 1970s famed baseball writer, historian, and statistician Bill James, one of the most influential minds in baseball analytics and statistics, developed the "runs created" metric, which measures how well a hitter performs one of the central aspects of his job: creating runs. According to James, "With regard to an offensive player, the first key question is how many runs have resulted from what he has done with the bat and on the basepaths . . . but [a player's] job was not to hit doubles, nor to hit singles, nor to hit triples, nor to draw walks or even hit home runs, but rather to put runs on the scoreboard. How many runs resulted from all of these things?"[56] In simple terms, runs created estimates a player's offensive contribution in terms of total runs. It combines a player's ability to get on base with his ability to hit for extra bases, then divides these two measures by the player's total opportunities. Runs created shows that there is a predictable relationship between batting and runs. In Pete's case, he was extraordinarily valuable, leading the league in runs created in 1882 and again in 1885, as well as finishing in the top five for six straight years from 1882 to 1887.

But Pete's season was not only about batting; it was also about fielding. Shattering the perception that he was weak defensively, and despite playing only 42 games at second base (which placed him outside the top five for games played at second), he finished the year fifth in putouts, assists, and double plays turned by a second baseman. It was truly a monstrous rookie season.

The 1882 season proved to be a triumph not only for Pete but also for the new AA. The *New York Times* reported, "The season has proven a very successful one in a financial view and the clubs who form the Association are not the least disposed to sever their connection with it. The majority of the clubs are strengthening themselves by engaging league players for the next season and are paying larger salaries than the League nines."[57] The AA's sound financial footing gave it confidence heading into the next season, as it increased the schedule to 98 games and added two new teams in Columbus and New York. The success and growth of the AA were perfect for homebody Pete, who, despite much speculation and many public comments, never really pursued the idea of leaving his hometown of Louisville. The outlaw slugger and the outlaw league would have a symbiotic relation during their run together, with Pete's swagger helping to define the rebel circuit.

As Pete was establishing himself as a first-rate major leaguer, he was also establishing a major-league drinking problem. Pete's drinking, combined with a heightened sense of isolation as his hearing continued to decline, foreshadowed darker days ahead. Despite the massive success of his rookie year, the seeds of trouble were sown at the end of the year as he missed games for various unspecified ailments and self-inflicted troubles.

Pete drank to numb the pain from his mastoid condition and claimed he could stop drinking if he wanted to. Yet this did not seem to be the case, as he regularly exhibited troubling behavior related to his drinking. It would have been easy for Louisville to dismiss a lesser player, but Pete was one of the best not only on the team but also in the country. Like many athletes, he was saved by his talent. He was suspended and fined but never suffered any major consequences. He may have damaged his reputation, but he continued to play ball, and his immediate needs were met. He had money and legions of followers who propped him up and supported him, no matter what. But ultimately, the constant second chances and the overlooking of his real problem with alcohol did more harm than good.

The *Courier-Journal* ran a story about drinking issues in the league and subtly referenced hometown boy Pete's drunken antics at the end of the year. "The Association next year should adopt some more stringent regulations concerning the habits of its players. There are several members of the Eclipse Club, and one in particular, who should be limited in his privileges. Everyone knows to whom this refers, and it is not necessary to give the player's name."[58] The Louisville papers initially approached the team's drinking and behavior problems with tact, choosing to write in vague terms and generalities. This would change over time. The Cincinnati papers ran the same story but did not show the same restraint, throwing a jab at their nearby rival by closing with these words: "Poor Pete Browning."[59]

4

Battles with the Bottle (1883)

Legend says Pete first developed a taste for alcohol while playing baseball. During amateur games, a keg of beer was routinely placed at third base to reward batters who made it that far. Those who reached the foaming fountain were entitled to a glass. Pete hit so many three-baggers and home runs that there was little beer left for anyone else.

In 1888 the *Louisville Commercial* suggested a different origin of his drinking, although it still involved baseball. The newspaper claimed that a 16-year-old Pete was playing in a pickup game with some older men and dominating the game with his pitching. The opposing team began to ply him with beer, and soon Pete, a nondrinker at the time, was rendered useless as both a pitcher and a hitter.

Pete provided a slightly different explanation for why he drank. As usual, it all came down to his ability to hit a baseball. In 1895, while visiting with ex-teammate Tom Brown, who was in town with the Washington Senators, Pete told him:

> Old Pete was brought up on these yere grounds and right yere old Pete trained his lamps to take the starch out of Mattie Kilroy's sizzlers and iron out Bobby Caruthers curves. I'll tell you how Old Pete did it. Do you see that distillery outside the left field fence? Well, every time [Pete] flash his lamps on that distillery and imagines that he is going to get a flash on the best red eye in the place if he can get a hit. Then Old Pete gets kind of thirsty, and when Pete needs tonsil varnish, he can turn any kind of trick. Pete's mind is fixed on the high balls over the

> distillery, and his lamps is on any low ball that comes up to the plate, and then something is going to come off. Bing! Away goes the ball and Pete has plunked out his hit. A man's got to have his noodle and his lamps with him in this game, and Old Pete never leaves his at home.[1]

However Pete discovered alcohol, he developed an immediate taste for it. It served a number of purposes for him. It helped ease the lingering pain from his childhood bout of mastoiditis and gave him liquid confidence in public, where his poor hearing and lack of education left him feeling inadequate.

Over the years, Pete would prove that his immense skills on the field were rivaled only by his troublesome alcohol-related exploits off it. The tales of his drinking adventures were both comical and sad. In the early years, his heavy drinking was dismissed as simply the recklessness of youth, a time of life when one's irresponsible behavior and overindulgences are more easily overlooked. No one recognized it as the lifelong problem it would become. Further impacting people's perception of Pete was the lack of understanding of alcoholism in the late nineteenth century. Among participants in the growing temperance movement, the concept of habitual drunkenness as a potentially treatable disease was gaining ground, although the modern understanding of alcoholism as both a physical and an emotional dependence on alcohol was not yet recognized. Pete's heavy drinking would become his dominant personality trait both during his lifetime and after it, clouding the public's understanding of who Pete actually was.

Despite his drinking, there was plenty of optimism surrounding Pete and the Eclipse heading into the 1883 season. Pete was coming off a hugely successful rookie year in which he had led the American Association in almost every offensive category. His drinking tended to decrease during the off-season, and any alcohol-related issues or indiscretions from the previous season were forgotten. To prepare for the upcoming season, Pete regularly traveled to the nearby hot springs resorts and stayed for an extended time, apparently making an attempt to remain at least somewhat sober. How successful he was is unclear. Based on the mythologized narrative, he drank only during baseball season, but there is ample evidence that this was false.

Louisville hoped to improve on its third-place finish in the 1882 season and challenge the defending champion Cincinnati and the strong rosters of Philadelphia and St. Louis for the pennant. Added to the core of Pete, Guy Hecker, Leech Maskrey, Dan Sullivan, and Chicken Wolf were veterans Joe Gerhardt, Jack Gleason, and George Latham. Besides playing second base, Gerhardt would serve as manager. It was also hoped that thirty-year-old first baseman Latham would provide leadership to a team that had been the youngest in the AA the year before. Latham was known for his extensive and inelegant vocabulary and was a perfect fit for the unruly Louisville team. He also sported two of the greatest nicknames ever: Jumbo, for his stocky build, and Juice, for the huge wads of tobacco he shoved in his mouth during games. Finally, Louisville signed local Tom McLaughlin, who had played with Pete on the semipro Eclipse team and was finally getting an opportunity to play major league ball.

In preparation for the 1883 season, Pete stayed in good physical and financial shape by playing in a series of exhibition games with the Eclipse in New Orleans versus the local Remy Clarkes. He was sharp and focused, as reported by the press: "Pete Browning has never played better here: his work at short and at the bat was first class."[2]

Following the successful trip to New Orleans, Pete's season got off to another hot start, as he smoked two home runs over the first six games.[3] He started the year with a 19-game hitting streak stretching from May 1 to June 5 (although he missed three games during that time due to illness). Memories of his drunken escapades at the end of the previous season faded as his strong performance at the plate once again put him among the top AA hitters. However, a late-June slump, a leg injury in July, and his apparent indifference to team rules refocused attention on how much of a distraction he could be.

Ahead of a four-game home stand against Cincinnati in July, renowned sportswriter O. P. Caylor wrote in the *Cincinnati Commercial Gazette,* "Pete Browning has been soaking his royal hide in Kentucky sour-mash lately, and the Louisville papers have been reading temperance lectures to him for a week. So far as Cincinnatians are concerned, Pete may get stone-blind drunk this week and remain so till Saturday night. For Pete Browning sober is considerable of an ingredient of any ball game he interests himself in."[4] Heading into the series, Louisville was second in the standings behind the Philadelphia Athletics, which the Eclipse had just played, dropping two of three games. Even with the two losses, Louisville was on fire, winning 13 of 18 games over the previous month. Pete was off to another blistering start and second in the league in batting behind

Pittsburgh's Ed Swartwood. Then he stumbled. In the third game against Philadelphia he went 0 for 5, and his fielding, along with that of teammate Jack Leary, was harshly criticized. The following day, in a rain-delayed game called in the fourth inning, he went 0 for 1 before being hit in the leg by a pitch and leaving the game. (Despite claims that Pete was not hit by a pitch until 1890, this was actually the first time.)

It would have been easy to dismiss a few bad games as the team having an off day or a player experiencing a slump, both of which are natural over the course of a long baseball season. But there were rumblings in the local press about the behavior of many of the Eclipse players. In May, after a handful of drunken incidents, Gerhardt held a meeting to remind the players about the rules, singling out Leary for his off-field actions. Gerhardt's opposition to alcohol was purely related to its adverse effect on performance. When he initially refused to sign with Louisville at the beginning of the year, the club sweetened the deal by offering him one-third of the stadium's bar receipts for each game. To increase sales, Gerhardt was known to head to the bar and sling a few drinks to thirsty fans while waiting for his turn at bat.

A few days after the team meeting, the *Courier-Journal* wrote, "A nine cannot play ball if over one-half the players are full of beer and the rest have to do all the playing."[5] Complaints about the team's bad behavior continued for the next month, and things came to a head in June, when Gerhardt resigned as manager. He made it clear to the team's directors that he just wanted to play ball and not have to deal with the managerial aspects of the job. The veteran player had grown tired of the daily headaches that came with babysitting the out-of-control players. The team's directors talked him out of resigning, and he resumed his managerial duties a few days later. This was followed by a vague statement published in the *Courier-Journal* on July 8: "If a player does not even attempt to do his duty, the management should take very decided action in the case."[6] The paper did not mention names, but given the team's behavior over the past month, local sports reporters knew trouble was brewing. A few days later, the *Courier-Journal* called Pete out by name: "It is a matter not to be disguised that Browning's conduct lately off the ball field has been by no means exemplary. A man who will persist in drinking continually and getting drunk cannot expect to do good work and a stop should be put to it."[7] Pete's heavy drinking had become the worst-kept secret in Louisville. Coverage of Pete's drinking adventures grew into a competition among the local papers, with the stories becoming more and more outlandish. And many of the seemingly hard-to-believe stories were true, or at least based in truth.

Pete's leg injury and slumping play stoked public criticism of his drinking habits, forcing a reevaluation of whether both the injury and the slump were caused by his frequent drunkenness. The local papers believed that this was the case and regularly said so in their coverage. There had long been rumors of Pete's excesses, but this was the first real sign of things to come. His antics near the end of the 1882 season, though heavily covered in the papers, had been long forgotten. The negative criticism literally and figuratively fell on deaf ears. The club's lax handling of the situation did not help, as it was reluctant to punish the team's best player. Pete had occasionally been fined, but up to that point, he had not been benched or suspended.

Whenever Pete missed a game, it was fair to ask whether it was due to an actual injury or his excessive drinking. In July, however, he seemed to be genuinely hurt, as he missed eight consecutive games. Pete's injury was the start of a horrendous month for the Eclipse, and the team's hopes of a promising season began to fade away. While Pete was out, the Eclipse did not just play poorly; the team fell apart. The *Courier-Journal* went so far as to call the 9–3 loss to Cincinnati on July 14 "an alleged game of baseball." The Eclipse had arrived in Cincinnati riding a three-game losing streak and with a roster full of injuries. In addition to Pete's injury, Gerhardt "was very lame," and George Latham and center fielder Henry Luff "were both suffering from lame arms." Shortstop Leary, who had been receiving harsh criticism for his heavy drinking and weak hitting, was called out for an "overwhelming attack of laziness."[8] He was released from the team a few days later. Catcher Dan Sullivan, whom Caylor described as a "keg of beer [who] will catch," was battling a leg injury that kept him out of the starting lineup for a few weeks.[9] Things only got worse. In the series against Cincinnati, pitcher Guy Hecker missed the train and had to charter a locomotive to get him to the game on time. The *Courier-Journal* reported the following day that the 127-mile run "was made in two hours and fifty-three minutes including five stops." Of course, the paper couldn't resist taking a jab at the husky, slow-footed Hecker, adding, "If Mr. Hecker could round bases at the speed which he averaged on this hair-raising trip, home-runs would be a common thing with him."[10]

The Eclipse's struggles and injuries continued. During a four-game series against St. Louis, one writer, with tongue firmly in cheek, reported that an ambulance rolled into Sportsman's Park as confused fans looked on, and from "its door issued a stream of crippled and invalids in various stages of capacity and incapacity. At last they were recognized as the Louisville team who were about to play the St. Louis nine."[11]

The actual condition of the team was no joke. The injuries were piling up, and "they went onto the field under the most depressing circumstances."[12] Pitcher Sam Weaver had been struck in the midsection with a hard-hit ball and was still suffering. Sullivan was so lame he was unable to bend his right knee. The stocky Latham was under the weather—or, more accurately, under the sun—as the thermometer approached 100 degrees in the summer months. Pete was still limping around the field. The newspaper reported, "The Eclipse Invalid Corps of former ball-players were defeated yesterday. . . . The Mayor will be requested to issue permits to the hospital for the club on its return."[13]

Pete returned to the lineup on July 19 after missing eight games. He made his presence felt immediately, banging out three hits in an 8–3 win over Columbus. The paper took note of his impactful return, proclaiming, "Browning has not forgotten how to bat since he was laid off."[14] Still, Pete was not fully healed, and another player had to run for him when he got a hit (a legal substitution in 1883). Despite the win, things never got back on track. The following day, Latham was fined $50 for drunkenness, and Luff was suspended for the same offense. A few days later, after another all-night bender, Luff had a run-in with a hotel night clerk and was charged with resisting arrest. He was reinstated a few weeks later and played in a couple more games before being suspended for the remainder of the season for insubordination. He never played in the major leagues again. Luff was replaced by Walter Prince, formerly with the Woonsocket Camels. Prince was not an upgrade, lasting only four games and hitting a meager .182 before being released.

The wheels were coming off the season, and it seemed that most of the team was too drunk to care. The Eclipse management took steps to discipline the out-of-control players who showed little regard for the rules. "They have tried to influence the players more by kindness than authority heretofore, but finding that it would not work with some of them, they have resorted to other means. . . . In the future every player that disobeys the rules may expect to suffer for it," wrote the *Courier-Journal*.[15] Despite the new discipline policy, the tailspin continued. The Eclipse suffered another three-game losing streak and won only four of nine games through the end of July, dropping from second to third in the league standings.

Meanwhile, Cincinnati, Philadelphia, and St. Louis were separating themselves from the rest of the league as they engaged in a three-way fight for first. In Louisville, frustration boiled over following a 14–4 loss to St. Louis. "The club should pension its cripples and put its other members on the retired list," wrote the *Courier-Journal.*[16] In a series of articles, the newspaper attacked both individual players and the team as a whole. It mocked Latham for suddenly coming down with a "sickness" after being fined for repeated drunkenness, and it chided the rest of the team for a lack of effort. According to the *Courier-Journal,* the team's only success was in helping St. Louis and Cincinnati try to wrest the lead from Philadelphia. Surprisingly, it made no mention of Pete. Either he had curtailed his drinking (not likely) or the local press was willing to overlook his personal shortcomings as long as he continued to produce on the field.

The Eclipse's season continued its downward spiral. On July 26, while sitting in front of the St. James Hotel in St. Louis, Gerhardt suddenly doubled over and vomited in a manner "quite startling" to those with him. He was "prostrated by a partial stroke of paralysis" affecting the left side of his body from his shoulder to his knee.[17] He had been complaining of pain in his left arm for a while, but it was attributed to "rheumatism" and given little thought. Gerhardt also had epilepsy and had suffered similar attacks before. The exact cause of Gerhardt's stroke could not be determined, but Maskrey believed he knew. On May 24 the team had a game at Sportsman's Park in St. Louis, and it was Ladies' Day due to the presence of former Eclipse pitcher Tony Mullane, who had joined St. Louis at the start of the 1883 season. During the first inning, Gerhardt was struck by one of hard-throwing Mullane's pitches, after which he "uttered a groan, and dropped as if shot, and stiffened out like a dead man."[18] Maskrey angrily declared, "You can just bet your life that I believe that ball, and nothing else, is the cause of his being paralyzed."[19]

There was bad blood between Mullane and the Eclipse following his one season with the club, and some believed he had thrown at Gerhardt intentionally. The hot-headed Mullane spewed a number of comments about Eclipse players, referring to Hecker as a "regular pudding" he could strike out whenever he wanted.[20] The bad blood carried over to the 1884 season, when Mullane plunked both Hecker and Wolf with pitches in the opening game. The feud between Mullane and his ex-teammates lasted for the rest of their careers. During their brief time as teammates in Louisville, Pete and Mullane were remembered as "pretty near chums," but after Mullane left Louisville, their relationship deteriorated.[21] Over the years, they traded insults in the newspapers and battled on the field. Mullane tried to rattle Pete by throwing at him whenever he was at bat. For Mullane, throwing at batters was part of his repertoire. He regularly brushed back hitters who crowded the plate, defiantly saying, "Watch me polish his buttons."[22] His penchant for hitting batters was one of the reasons for the AA's rule change in 1884, awarding the batter first base after being hit by a pitch. Mullane and Pete's frosty relationship continued when they reunited as teammates in Cincinnati in 1891. "They still prefer to remain comparative strangers," wrote the *Pittsburgh Press.* "It makes Pete mad every time he thinks of [Mullane], and Tony avoids all references to old times."[23]

Gerhardt's debilitating condition further weakened a team already decimated by injuries. "We have been bad enough, everybody knows, since Sullivan and Browning were hurt, and now my sickness will take the heart out of the boys," said Gerhardt.[24] A few days later, Sullivan was declared out for the rest of the season. As a result of these losses, the team was forced to reevaluate the lineup daily and shuffle players around the diamond. Pete ended up at shortstop—one of the most important defensive positions—to shore up the middle of the infield. This move belies his supposed lack of skill in the field.

By August 1, Pete's leg was fully healed, although others had not yet recovered from their various ailments. Louisville had dropped seven games back of first-place Philadelphia. "The managers of the Eclipse Club should have hired two ambulances to convey their nine to the ball grounds yesterday," lambasted the *Cincinnati Enquirer*, "as most of the members of the aggregation were in far better form for a ward in a hospital than they were to participate in an exhibition of the national game."[25] All these injuries finally laid the team out on August 8, in a game against Cincinnati. Catcher Ed Whiting sustained a serious ankle injury when a runner slid into him while he was protecting home plate. Whiting was helped to the bench, and it was determined that he was unable to finish the game. Whiting's injury was the final straw. A dejected Gerhardt (who was able to continue managing the team after his stroke) informed the umpire that with Whiting's injury, combined with Weaver's cold, Latham's eye injury, and Pete's cramps, the Eclipse had only eight able-bodied men, and he asked that the game be terminated. Cincinnati agreed, and the game was halted in the eighth inning.

Even after his leg healed, Pete had some health issues going forward. He missed a game with a severe case of cholera morbus (diarrhea), but he was now hitting the ball like he had the year before. By early August, he was fourth in the league in batting. His confidence was fully intact, and he promised he would be leading the AA in hitting by the close of the season. By September 10, he was doing just that. But Pete's strong hitting was not enough to carry the rest of the club, which was now mired in fifth place, trailing Philadelphia, St. Louis, Cincinnati, and a resurgent New York, which had gone 26–14–1 over the previous two months. It was a disappointing showing for Louisville after being within one game of first place on July 4. The injury-plagued month of July dropped the Eclipse like a rock in the standings, and even as players began to get healthy again, the team never returned to its earlier form.

While acknowledging the devastating injuries the team had suffered throughout the summer, local sportswriters took a bigger view of the problems plaguing the Eclipse. The real culprits, they said, were "management and the public," as both are "to blame to a certain extent. The former in not paying sufficiently high salaries to engage good players and the latter in not patronizing the club sufficiently to enable it to do so readily."[26] Management's approach to signing new players was heavily criticized for failing to recognize potential talent when recruiting players to Louisville and offering contracts. Low salaries and an inability to attract top-level talent were the same complaints voiced by the *Courier-Journal* prior to the 1882 season. The paper compared the lowly, cellar-dwelling Baltimore team, which finished last in the AA in both 1882 and 1883 but regularly packed the stands, and the Eclipse, which struggled to fill its own stands throughout the season despite having the ability to contend with the best in the AA. "In Baltimore, the people turn out by the thousands no matter how poor their club is. If they had a good club there at the first of the season as the Eclipse, the grounds would not hold them," stated the *Courier-Journal.*[27] Despite the lack of support from the fans, the team's play was not impacted by the sparse attendance at home games. During the 1880s, Louisville posted a .572 winning percentage at home and a .352 winning percentage on the road. The 220-point difference was one of the largest by any team in that decade.

Team president J. H. Pank countered the accusations about the players' low pay. "The talk about the Eclipse club being low salaried is all a mistake," he said. "There is not a man in the nine that is not getting as much money as he asked for, and the salaries of a couple of them have been raised a hundred percent by the directors without solicitation on their part." He also took aim at the lack of support from the fans, noting, "While the club is on excellent financial footing, the public have not shown the degree of interest which would warrant an expenditure of money at a dead loss to the management."[28] None of the players refuted what Pank said, but none of them defended it either.

The Eclipse found its groove again over the last month of the season, winning 10 of the final 15 games, including taking three of four from eventual AA champion Philadelphia to close out the season. The lone loss to Philadelphia was a gift from Hecker, who put the winning run on second via a wild pitch in the tenth inning, allowing Philadelphia to win the pennant by one game over St. Louis. Pete was no help that day either, as he was unable to get the ball out of the infield, going 0 for 5 at the plate.

The Eclipse's late-season surge proved too little too late. The team finished in fifth place, 13½ games out, with a 52–45 record. The *Courier-Journal* speculated, "Had the home nine played through the season with the same vim they are now playing they would have been the leaders, with no other clubs within reach."[29] The disappointing season brought nothing but questions about what could have been. What if injuries hadn't ruined the month of July? What if the team didn't collapse at the most inopportune times? What if management held players accountable for their disruptive actions?

Although many of Louisville's struggles could be blamed on the players' out-of-control drinking, the Eclipse was not the only team in the AA whose roster was populated with overindulgent lushes. It was common for players to show up to games bleary-eyed and hungover. Some players handled their liquor better than others, but every team was affected in some way by professional baseball players' heavy-drinking lifestyle. Editorials in papers across the country criticized their hometown teams' off-field choices and questioned players' flippant attitudes and failure to appreciate the opportunity to play baseball for a living, as opposed to actually working. The *Pittsburgh Commercial Gazette*'s complaints could have been about any team in the AA:

> A ball player's path in summertime is on beds of flowery ease. He gets a big salary, travels all over the country, stops at good hotels, and has the best of everything. He is paid by the public to furnish one hour and [a] half of amusement each afternoon, and he certainly should be able to keep clear of whiskey during the season, especially as he has the winter to get even. The great trouble with some men . . . is that they look on base ball as merely a pretext to open their pores and enable them to sweat out the whiskey they drank the night before.[30]

Over the last month of the season, while the team was winning and playing some of its best ball of the year, Pete's bat cooled. He hit a pedestrian .250 and went multiple games without getting a hit, although he finished strong, going 2 for 5 with a triple in the final game of the year—a win over Philadelphia. The strong finish reminded everyone what the Eclipse was capable of. Several players, including Hecker and Pete, re-signed with the team a few weeks after the season ended, providing hope for next year.

Pete's late-season slump cost him the batting title, but he finished second with a .338 average. Originally, St. Louis's Tom Mansell was announced as the AA batting champion, but after much justified complaining from the media and fans (Mansell had played in only 27 games), Pittsburgh's Ed Swartwood was named the league's leading hitter, with a .357 average. This confusion about the standards for determining league leaders was something both the AA and the NL struggled with during the game's formative years. The criteria eventually became standardized, but in the early years of baseball there was no consensus on the number of games or at-bats needed to qualify as a league leader. David Nemec, who has written several books on nineteenth-century baseball, states, "The best that can be said is that in every season the winner was at least a reasonable choice (if not always a correct one)."[31]

Despite finishing second in his sophomore season, Pete was still in rarefied company. Since 1876, only five rookies have won a league batting title. Of those five, only two finished second or better in their sophomore season: Hall of Famer Tony Oliva, who won back-to-back titles in 1964 and 1965, and Pete, with his first-place title in 1882 and second-place finish in 1883. The Eclipse recognized his accomplishments and presented him with an elegant rosewood bat, mounted in silver and appropriately engraved, to honor his standout work at the plate.

Once the season ended, Pete's injury and his struggles off the field seemed to be forgotten. But Pete was one drunken night or one boozy bender away from showing up too inebriated to play. His 1883 season proved that as long as he could hit the ball better than most men in the league—which he could—his shortcomings on the field and drunken indiscretions off it would be overlooked.

5

The Louisville Slugger (1884)

It is hard to separate truth from fiction, and as the saying goes, truth can be stranger than fiction. But in the case of Pete Browning, fiction has become truth. Over the years, the myth surrounding him grew larger than the truth, and the line between the two blurred almost to the point of nonexistence. Stories of his greatness on the field and his shortcomings off it have been readily shared, and the facts have been stretched beyond recognition over time. The most famous legend involves Pete's link to Louisville-based Hillerich & Bradsby, best known for its famous Louisville Slugger baseball bat. He is considered not only the namesake of the bat but also the reason behind the company's creation. The Hilleriches produced the first-ever custom-made bat for Pete, long before they got into the bat-making business. Like much of Pete's life story, this one contains mystery, speculation, hyperbole, and even some truth.

According to the legend, Pete was suffering through the first extended slump of his career in 1884. (Up to that point, he had never gone more than two consecutive games without a hit.) After another miserable game in which he broke his favorite bat, Pete was approached by 17-year-old John "Bud" Hillerich, son of John Frederick (J. F.) Hillerich, who owned a woodworking shop in downtown Louisville. Bud offered to make Pete a new bat, and late one night the two of them covertly entered the J. F. Hillerich Carpentry Shop at 118 First Street. J. F. was opposed to using his lathes to make baseball bats; he thought the company's future lay in producing stair railings, porch columns, and swinging butter churns. He also preferred not to be connected to baseball, which had a bad reputation due to the scandals, gambling, and drinking associated with it. This was especially true in Louisville, where the Grays' game-fixing scandal of 1877 was still fresh in everyone's minds. Pete and Bud picked out the perfect piece of ash and set out to create the ideal bat.[1] As wood shavings gathered at their feet and a woody smell lingered in the air, Pete hovered over Bud's shoulder as he worked, eyeing every detail. He stopped Bud occasionally so he could swing the bat and make sure it possessed the heft and feel he wanted, and together they created the perfect slugger, incorporating the round barrel shape used today. The next day Pete broke out of his slump with three hits (some claim he got four), and the legend of the Louisville Slugger was born.

After that, the Hilleriches began to produce bats for the Louisville team, based on Pete's recommendation. At first, they produced a standard set of bats that players could choose from, but they soon realized that, like Pete, players wanted custom-made bats to meet their individual needs. The flat sticks and crude bats of yore were abandoned. The bat-making side of the Hillerich business grew slowly, but J. F. eventually recognized the potential and relented. When an injury ended Bud's baseball career, he was able to devote more time to the bat-making side of the business. In 1914 the *Louisville Herald* wrote, "Young Hillerich saw the possibilities of a big bat business and his father was so pleased with the enthusiasm that Bud displayed in the idea that he gave his consent to the project, and they lost no time in forming the foundation for the Louisville Slugger success."[2]

In 1894 the Hillerich company registered the trademark "Louisville Slugger," which clearly referenced a player, not the city. As his hometown's iconic batting champion, Pete was hailed as the "Louisville Slugger" by a headline in the *Louisville Post* on June 17, 1891. The Louisville Slugger name eventually became synonymous with the bats produced by the Hillerich company, and once it made the commitment to bat production, business exploded. By 1896, Hillerich & Son was thriving, as it received orders for more than 75,000 bats.

The Hilleriches gained national exposure in 1905 when future Hall of Famer Honus Wagner signed a deal with the company, becoming the first player to endorse a bat and one of the first American athletes to endorse sports equipment. He also became the first player to have his autograph on a bat. At the time, Wagner, who began his career with the Louisville Colonels in 1897, was in the midst of capturing eight batting titles in eleven years. Eventually the Hilleriches partnered with salesman Frank Bradsby, who was known for his marketing expertise, and the Hillerich & Bradsby Company was formed in 1916.

Pete's involvement in the birth of the Louisville Slugger has been questioned. There is no mention in newspapers of the meeting between Bud and Pete and no mention of it in Pete's obituary, and that omission has often been used to discredit the story. But why would there be coverage of it in 1884? A player was simply having a bat made to replace one he had broken. It would have been impossible to foresee what would develop from that encounter. Skeptics cite this lack of documentation as evidence that the bat making did not happen, but they miss an important point. Why would Pete give credit or claim a connection to a company that did not start to make bats professionally until at least six years after that first encounter and did not gain national recognition until long after he retired?

Over the years, there have been slight variations in the facts, adding to the confusion. For example, the basics of the story remain the same, but the dates differ. Usually 1884 is cited as the year of the fabled bat-making event, but one version claims it happened in 1889 and that Pete's breakout game was an August contest against the Philadelphia Athletics and pitcher Sadie McMahon. Louisville did face McMahon twice in the month of August that year, with Pete going 1 for 4 in a 7–0 win in Philadelphia and 0 for 4 in a home loss. Neither was the multihit slump-ending game mentioned. In addition, Bud's age is usually given as 17 when the bat making occurred—his actual age in 1884. And his disregard for his father's wishes seems more like the act of an impetuous teenager than that of a 22-year-old man intimately involved in the family business, as he was in 1889. Also casting doubt on this version is that in 1890 the Hillerich company signed an agreement with the Simmons Hardware Company of St. Louis to sell its bats, called Falls City Sluggers at the time, to nonprofessional players. It seems improbable that Pete's first custom-made bat was turned in August 1889 and less than a year later the business had blossomed to such an extent that it was reaching out to nonprofessional players and expanding to other cities.

A story published in 1944 detailing how Hillerich & Bradsby helped the war effort by producing stocks for guns, which "the soldiers and marines adore," also covered the company's history. The article mentioned the meeting between Pete and Bud and the bat Bud made. It claimed that replicas were later produced and stamped "Pete Browning model, July 15, 1887." No explanation was given for the date, and 1887 is not mentioned in any other stories.[3] For Pete, that day was fairly insignificant. He went 1 for 4 with a double (his first non-multihit game in a week) and sat out the next two games with a charley horse. When he returned, he got multiple hits in three of the next four contests.

Bud's son gave an interview to the *Tampa Tribune* in 1968 and further muddied the water. He claimed his father started making bats for the Cincinnati Red Stockings in 1884 and that the meeting between Bud and Pete did not happen until 1890, when Pete walked by the shop one night, saw Bud working on a batch of new bats, and stopped in and asked Bud to make him a couple of bigger-barreled bats.[4] This story has two major problems: first, Pete played the 1890 season in Cleveland, and second, why would Bud make bats for his hometown team's biggest rival?

J. F. Hillerich's obituary in the *Louisville Times* on January 17, 1924, corroborated the version that had Pete wandering down the street and going into the store to inquire about having a new bat made. Although the obituary confirmed that Pete's was the first custom-made bat the Hilleriches produced, it claimed Pete asked J. F. himself to make the new bat, which he did. After finding success with it, Pete returned to the store to have more made, claiming, "That bat is a slugger."

Pete's slump and the breaking of his bat are remembered as taking place anywhere from early in the season to late spring to midsummer. Also in dispute is exactly what he did during the first game with the new bat. Some stories claim the new bat was turned in April, during the team's preseason. Pete was in a slump that month, hitting only .250, but there was no breakout game. He started the regular season slowly, and his improvement seemed to coincide with surgery on his mastoid (discussed later). Louisville played only eight games at home in June, and Pete got three hits in two of those games, but they did not follow any noteworthy slump (although one followed an 0-for-4 day). During the month of July he logged three three-hit games at home, though one was a less-than-impressive 3-for-7 outing in a 15-inning, 5–4 win over Baltimore. The other two could have been the alleged breakout game, but again, they did not follow any particularly noteworthy slump (although one came after an 0-for-5 day). Through August and September Pete had no three-hit games. He had no four-hit games at all during the season, but he did have two five-hit games, only one of which took place at home (and none of the versions mentions five hits). These discrepancies do not mean the meeting between Bud and Pete never took place. It is more likely that the details have been confused and exaggerated over time to fit the narrative.

Pete's practice of using custom-made bats was established in an 1891 article in the *Pittsburgh Press:* "Of the many thousands of ball cranks in this city yesterday there was not one half as happy as Peter Browning," it wrote. "Three hits on Friday, one of them a home run, and a notification from the express office that a package was waiting for him. When the charges were paid it proved to be a small crate of ash bats, thoroughly smoke dried, and almost black in color. Pete almost hugged the crate and tears stood in his eyes. They were tears of joy, as he contemplated the elegant proportions of the home runs, triples, doubles and singles they represented in the future."[5] A few weeks after the shipment arrived, and after Pete had hit two home runs in three days, the newspaper reported, "Those smoke-colored bats of Pete Browning are very much in demand."[6] Throughout his career there were various mentions of Pete's hometown-made bats, but they were nothing more than brief asides. An article in the *St. Louis Republic* in 1901 discussing the evolution of baseball bats made a stronger, more direct connection: "There's a firm in Louisville that has turned out standard bats for many years—they made the sticks Pete Browning used to do so much execution with."[7] A 1909 article by Boston sportswriter Bill Spargo titled "Baseball Bats of Great Players" appeared in papers across the country. Though light on details, it is important for several reasons. It appeared four years after Pete's death and seven years before the company changed its name to Hillerich & Bradsby. Spargo lays out the basic facts of the story, with some slight differences. He names J. F. as the original bat maker, writing, "Nearly a quarter century ago a wood turner named Hillerich made three bats for his son, and one of these fell into the hands of a ball player who, when that bat was disabled, ordered more of the same model. This was the start of the ball bat business for J. F. Hillerich & Son, who for years past have turned out many thousands of bats each year."[8] The article does not name the ballplayer, but given Pete's penchant for acquiring bats he fancied, he cannot be ruled out. The Eclipse played any number of exhibition games during the 1884 season that Bud might have been involved in. Bud himself seemed to validate this version in an interview he gave to the *Philadelphia Inquirer* in 1940. He said Pete noticed Bud's bat and, after breaking his own, asked, "How about turning out a war-club like yours? If I had a bat that felt right, I'd murder these pitchers."[9]

However, an interview Bud gave to the *Louisville Herald* in 1914 just added more fuel to the speculative fire. Bud claimed he did not actually make a new bat for Pete but merely used a lathe to scratch a circle around one of his existing bats, telling the superstitious and slumping Pete that he was putting a home run in the bat for him. According to Bud, Pete got the promised homer that afternoon. In 1884 Pete hit only two homers at home: on May 10 against Indianapolis and on August 24 against Toledo and former teammate Tony Mullane. The May 10 homer is a strong possibility. It followed an 0-for-4 game the day before, with a struggling Pete hitting a mediocre .250 over the first eight games of the season. Although Pete went only 2 for 4 (not the three hits usually mentioned), it was a breakout game for him, including the home run described as "the longest line hit ever made on the grounds." Pete came to bat in the seventh inning "with blood in his eye, and hit a terrific liner, which struck the centerfield fence near the farthest corner."[10] As he returned to the bench after circling the bases, Pete, who had been instructed to bunt, cut off manager Mike Walsh and said, "Boss, I know you are going to raise hell, but Larry McKeon put her where I like 'em and I had to plug her in the nose." Years later, in an article reminiscing about the glory days of Pete, John Reccius, Guy Hecker, and the Eclipse, the writer described the home run as "going high over the junction of the center and leftfield fences" before "dropping in a basket of clothes which a negro woman was removing from the line."[11] The specifics of the events recounted in this article must be taken with a grain of salt, as it also claimed the homer happened in Indianapolis—a place where Pete never hit a home run. This simple confusion of facts shines a light on how easily fiction can turn to myth. A change of one simple fact allows the myth to grow wild like a weed, forever altering and confusing the truth.

Two prominent New York sportswriters weighed in with their own stylized retelling of the story. Fred Leib, sports editor of the *New York Telegram,* told his version in February 1923 as part of a series of articles on baseball's history written for the Elias Sports Bureau. Leib's version claimed that Pete approached the Hillerich company in the hopes that someone (not Bud or J. F., but some unnamed employee) would be able to replace his broken bat. According to Leib, Pete responded with four, not three, hits the following day. The following year, Bozeman Bulger, sports editor of the *New York World,* added his own spin to the tale. His version placed J. F. Hillerich squarely in the middle. According to Bulger,

J. F. "never tired of telling the story of Browning's night visit to the then small factory." J. F. offered to make Pete a new bat the next day, but a distraught Pete insisted that he needed it right away. "Listen, I don't care what it costs," pleaded Pete. "I'll buy supper for the gang. You fellows stay here and then get the man on the lathe. I want that bat turned just right. But I've got to have it tonight."[12] Like in Leib's version, Bulger claimed Pete stung four hits the next day. It is easy to discount these stories for their misstatement of facts, as Pete had zero four-hit games in 1884, but they are likely based on the information available at the time, combined with a touch of fanciful storytelling.

Other versions also omit the name of the person who made the bat, referring to him as one lone "turner" who was an "ardent fan" working late in the shop who was convinced to help Pete. A 1924 article in the *Courier-Journal* titled "Where Famous Sluggers Get Perfect Clubs" claimed Pete and an unnamed worker inspected all the wood in the shop and found a piece of timber "free from blemish. . . . The turner's magic [then] produced an exact duplicate of the broken slugger, and Pete, without waiting for the final polishing, hurried to bed."[13] The next day, he had his three-hit game.

Several people have challenged the assertion that Pete's was the first custom-made bat produced by the Hilleriches. One was Gus Weyhing, who played with Bud on a local team and then had a solid 14-year major league career. In this version, either Bud made a bat for himself or his father made Bud a bat. Weyhing used Bud's bat in a game and liked it so much that it ended up in his possession. Other players soon discovered its appeal and were beating a path to the Hilleriches' door. This does not necessarily exclude Pete's involvement. He was friendly with Weyhing and could have first discovered the beauty of Hillerich bats from Weyhing's stick and then approached one of the Hilleriches to have his own made.

The loudest of the challenges came from Arlie Latham, a carefree jokester recognized as one of the first clown princes of baseball. Known as "The Freshest Man on Earth" (a popular song at the time) and remembered for his boisterous, cocky, ego-driven storytelling, he made the claim in an interview in *Baseball Magazine* in 1937. Latham said that after breaking his bat in a game in Louisville, he headed over to the Hillerich wood-turning shop, which was near his hotel, and asked to have a bat made. "Breaking a bat on the road in those days was like running out of gas in the wilderness," said Latham. "That night I happened to look out of my window and what do I see across the street? A sign, 'Hillerich & Son—Woodturners.' I made a beeline for the place."[14] According to Latham, he first encountered J. F., who told him they didn't waste time with that kind of foolishness, but then he met 17-year-old Bud, who agreed to make him a new bat. Latham was in Louisville with his St. Louis team for five games during August 1884 (the only time he played in the city that season), and he produced only three hits, so the new bat failed to improve his game to the point where it might have become part of baseball lore. It also seems unlikely that the cocky, vulgar, weak-hitting Latham and his .269 career average would have inspired Bud to disobey his father. Like Latham himself, this story contained more bravado than substance. But he spouted the tale for years, and many believed him simply because Pete wasn't around to say otherwise.

Pete and Latham were teammates in Cincinnati in 1891 and 1892, so it is likely that Latham knew about the Hilleriches through Pete, who was purchasing their custom-made bats for both himself and his teammates. Latham's tale is the same basic narrative as the one involving Pete, but with himself as the star. It appears there was tension between the two men during their time as teammates. Latham regularly dressed Pete down in public, including one occasion when he "roasted Browning unmercifully," even though "Pete was doing his best to help win the game," making every spectator Pete's friend and Latham's enemy.[15] It's purely speculation, but Latham's co-opting of Pete's story could have been born of a long-standing grudge, as he took one last jab at his long-dead rival.

Latham's version earned some credibility in 1942, when Bud wrote a letter "confirming" that Latham's bat was the first, but Bud had a good sense of humor and enjoyed keeping the mystery alive. His letter seems to be more of a wink and a nod to Latham rather than actual corroboration of his story. Back in 1940 Bud seemingly put the question to rest in an interview with the *Philadelphia Inquirer,* where he admitted that although he made a bat for Latham, Pete's was the first bat he ever turned, bolstering the belief that his letter was nothing more than humorous repartee with Latham. Louisville sportswriter A. H. Tarvin argued the same in *A Century of Baseball: 1839–1939,* in which he flatly stated that Latham had a bat made by Bud, but only after he had seen Pete's success with a Hillerich bat. Tarvin's claim should be taken seriously. Even though his account appeared almost 50 years after Pete played, Tarvin was a long-time sportswriter for the *Louisville Herald Post* and the *Louisville News Enquirer* and wrote extensively about the history of baseball in his regular columns "When Dad Was a Fan" and "Everything Baseball."

An advertisement appearing in the May 14, 1921, issue of the *Courier-Journal* also seemed to refute Latham's claim. It began: "From Browning to Babe Ruth, famous sluggers of the National Game, have hammered them over the fence with bats made in Louisville." This itself is not validation, but the ad continued: "Browning and his fellow players on the Louisville team were the first customers." The advertisement also adds to the confusion surrounding the legend, as it gave 1880 as the date of the first bat made by the Hilleriches (most likely careless editing). This mistake can be overlooked, as the ad, titled "Know Your City," was placed not by Hillerich & Bradsby but by Citizens Union National Bank. Another advertisement on August 15 tied Pete to the genesis of the company: "From the days of Pete Browning the most Famous Sluggers have depended on the Hillerich & Bradsby Co. factory for weapons that bring safe hits."

Clarifying Pete's role in the development of the Louisville Slugger is a 1922 *Courier-Journal* article detailing a visit to the Hillerich company by several well-known owners, managers, and players. The article highlighted Hillerich & Bradsby's ability to customize each bat to meet the specific needs of the player. According to the article, after cracking his favorite bat, Pete felt like he "had lost one of his best friends" and took his "damaged ash" to the "Hillerich Bat Factory" (note the refence to the company as the Bat Factory, which it was not at the time), demanding that they duplicate his broken bat in every detail. "It is said the new bat was a perfect duplication of the one that was broken," continued the article. "According to baseball historians, this was the first instance of a bat made to specifications."[16] This slight variation provides a sense of clarity and ties many of the slugger stories together. In 1884 the Hilleriches may have already been making some bats, to the extent that it was common knowledge around town and Pete knew where to go to have a new one made. Although his bat might not have been the first one the Hilleriches made, it was the first bat made for a professional player to his own specifications, making him the first player with a custom-made bat.

Hillerich & Bradsby seems convinced of Pete's role in its history, writing on the company's official website: "According to company legend, the first pro bat was created by 17-year-old Bud for Pete Browning in 1884. Browning was a megastar on Louisville's major league team, the Eclipse. One spring afternoon, Bud skipped out of work to watch the Eclipse play. He saw Browning break his bat and offered to make a new one at the woodworking shop. According to the story, in the next game Browning got three hits with the bat Bud made."[17] Of course, even that statement is qualified by referring to it as "company legend."

As Pete's stature grew, so did the Hillerich company's and the connection between the two. The shared story benefited both. For the Hilleriches, it linked their iconic brand with a local legend and one of the greatest players of the era. Pete's success on the field validated the company's unmatched skill at making bats. The Hillerich company revolutionized the bat-making industry as it developed a centering device for the lathe and automatic sanders. It also pioneered other innovations, experimenting with different woods, grips, and production techniques. The company's reputation was built on its willingness to customize bats to each player's specifications, and over the years, Pete has become a central figure in the Louisville Slugger brand, ingrained in its story and history. The legend of the first bat is told on every tour of the factory, and his image appears throughout the company's museum and on its website. Pete represents both the history and the potential of the Louisville Slugger. Hillerich & Bradsby believes that its bats help players make history.

The press's constant mythmaking and storytelling about Pete added to the legend but could not distract from the basic facts. Pete was one of the premier hitters not only in the AA but in the country. His first two professional seasons were a monstrous start to his baseball career. His 1882 season, which saw him leading the field in several offensive categories, ranks as one of the best seasons of all time, establishing his credentials as one of the top hitters of the 1880s along with Dan Brouthers, Ed Delahanty, and Cap Anson. Even with the assumed talent gap between the AA and the NL, Pete's accomplishments should not be minimized. He was not just slightly better than his contemporaries in the AA; he was vastly better.

Even before he met the Hilleriches, Pete was recognized for his bat mania. He took a deep interest in the tools of his trade and found value in all of them. For Pete, his arsenal of bats represented his power, his identity. In an age when players simply nailed the splintered pieces back together to repair broken bats, Pete's care went far beyond that of other players. He was remembered as being a great judge of bats, and he showed them off like a trainer proudly displaying his stable of racehorses. He would proudly declare, "Ah that is a fine two-year-old, and this one is four-year-old."[18] Pete's eye for bats was well known. "Pete . . . is an oracle on the subject of sticks," wrote the *Pittsburgh Press,* "and when he expressed his approval it must be a hardy man who would dissent."[19] Fellow players recognized Pete's expert eye and regularly "declared him to be the best judge of a bat in the country."[20] In 1892 slugger Tip O'Neill, while rummaging through the Cincinnati clubhouse in the preseason, came across a bat Pete had left there the season before. "That's a dang good piece of timber and it hangs well together," commented O'Neill, who then spent the rest of the day taking cuts with the "long forty-two-inch stick." According to the *Enquirer,* "After that it was impossible to separate the big left-fielder and the only relic of Pietro Browning."[21]

Pete amassed a large collection of bats over the years. At games, he was known to size up the opposing team's pile of bats, looking for any that struck his fancy. If he found one that did, he tried to work a trade, but he never traded one of his own bats—they were far too valuable to him. Instead, he just grabbed one from the team's supply of bats and traded that piece of lumber. Unlike other players, Pete never stole a bat, no matter how much he wanted it. He either traded for it or bought it. "Pietro buys all his bats, you can bet he does," clarified the slugger. Over the years, there was only one bat Pete coveted but was unable to obtain. "There is only one stick that I want," Pete said, and "Big Darby O'Brien has got it. If Pete could make a trade with him, he would lead the league in hitting, you can gamble on that."[22] Over his brief six-year career, O'Brien was never known for his strong hitting, yet Pete thought he owned the perfect bat.

Pete believed all bats possessed certain virtues and only needed the right player to bring them out. Despite his hoarding of bats, Pete was more than willing to share his collection with teammates. "I don't care how many people use my bats," he said, "there are plenty of liners in my sticks."[23] As teammates and friends found success with Pete's bats, it made sense for them to go to the source and have their own made. This supports the narrative that Pete spread the word about the Hillerich company, as his custom-made bats proved popular with teammates. The *Courier-Journal* wrote, "Many have followed in Pete's footsteps, not merely around the bases but to Louisville for the bats that get them on and drive them over."[24] The *Washington Post* agreed, writing, "Other players . . . in the hope of emulating Browning," started to use Hillerich bats, "and it is a common custom throughout the country."[25]

Pete brought a vast assortment of bats to games with him. He traveled with such a large collection that he was required to pay excess baggage fees on road trips. Unlike many other players, Pete believed that certain bats were better in certain situations. "Pete had an idea," explained the *Chicago Daily Tribune,* "which was a good one, and . . . he carried different bats to use against different pitchers. He used big light bats when hitting at speed, and shorter and more solid bats against slow ones, with long solid bats against the pitchers with fast curves and breaks."[26]

At the end of each season Pete began preparing for the next one by performing a meticulous care routine on his collection of bats. "Pete Browning was one of those old-time players who loved his bat first and the world second," stated the *Washington Post* in 1909. "He passed more time working over his big bludgeons than at any other vocation in his life. And he felt amply rewarded when, the next season, he found he had one or two that exactly suited him."[27] To prepare his bats, Pete soaked them in water for various lengths of time—some for a month, some for six weeks, some for longer—to add weight and heft to them. After they soaked for their predetermined time, he oiled them and rubbed them down with tobacco juice. Pete was remembered as "a great user of the weed, [and he] used to polish down his sticks in this way without any apparent reason until he commenced to believe that it made a difference with his hitting, and after that no wagon tongue of his ever escaped a coating of the obnoxious fluid." According to George Van Haltren, who started his professional career in 1887 and went on to work as a manager, umpire, and scout, Pete was the first player to do this. Van Haltren said Pete's goal was "to roughen the surface of the stick and prevent so many fouls slipping off one side or the other."[28] Rubbing tobacco juice on bats became common practice, as players believed it hardened the grain of the wood or "set the seams" and made them last longer. Hall of Famer Ty Cobb, who also used a Louisville Slugger, subscribed to this belief. He rubbed tobacco juice on his bats with a hollowed-out steer bone and even used specific brands to achieve a better effect. "My own favorite prescription was a chewing tobacco called Navy Nerve-Cut, the juiciest kind I ever discovered," recalled Cobb. "Using the steer bone, I rubbed in Navy by the hour."[29]

Pete's obsession with his bats extended to naming them after biblical figures. He was superstitious and believed that each bat had a predetermined supply of hits. When his hitting cooled off with one bat he retired it to his mother's home (where he also lived), tagging each one with a card detailing its accomplishments. At one point, Pete claimed he had 205 bats lining the walls of his basement. He turned some of his treasured bats into balusters for stair railings.

In addition to the new bat he got from the Hilleriches, Pete prepared a number of other bats for use in the 1884 season. With his ever-expanding arsenal, Pete hoped to follow up the previous season's runner-up finish with a return to the top of the league in batting.

Pete was not the only one preparing for the new season. The Eclipse started the year by making several changes. The board of directors changed the team name to the Louisvilles, and the junior team became known as the Eclipse. The following season the team name was changed again to the Colonels, which remained the name for the rest of the club's existence. Improvements to the stadium were also planned, including tearing down the existing stands and erecting new ones capable of seating 5,000 fans. The team announced a tougher approach to player misbehavior following the embarrassments of the previous season, and the *Louisville Commercial* reported the details:

> There is to be no further encouragement of the petty jealousies of players and no further engagement of lazy and drunken castaways. A system is to be established and strictly observed from the opening to the close of the season. If fines are imposed, they will not be remitted. If a player offends, he may depend that the heavy and impartial hand of an experienced and determined manager will be laid upon him. There are to be no more Learys and no more Luffs, and the name of Brown will be forever a dead and forgotten letter. Latham is to be kept within bounds, and Browning is to be no longer a petted gamboil good for one day and bad for another.[30]

The American Association was also making changes for the new season. Flush with confidence from its first two seasons and misguided by the belief that 1883 had been a financial success (in reality, many teams exaggerated their numbers), the AA moved ahead with expansion, adding the New York Metropolitans, Brooklyn Atlantics, Richmond Virginians, Indianapolis Hoosiers, Toledo Blue Stockings, and Washington Statesmen. In part, the expansion was in response to the formation of a new league, the Union Association (UA), which announced it would not follow the reserve rule followed by both the AA and the National League. Fearing that the upstart UA would sign the best players, the AA hoped to crush it before it got started by expanding into markets and regions the UA planned to play in. The competition for players between the AA and the UA lasted all season, with the UA getting the worst of it. After one trouble-plagued season highlighted by an inability to attract top-level talent, instability within the league (four teams were disbanded and replaced with teams from lower leagues), and scheduling issues, the UA folded at the end of 1884.

The newly christened Louisvilles started off strong, winning seven of the first nine games, including a season-opening three-game sweep over new AA member and 1883 champion of the Northwestern League Toledo. The first game of the year, a 5–1 win, featured the debut of African American Moses Fleetwood Walker, as well as some trouble from ex-teammate Tony Mullane, who was now with Toledo. Mullane hit Hecker with a pitch, and many in the crowd didn't think it was simply a case of a pitch getting away; they believed it was intentional and "loudly hissed" at Mullane.[31] Louisville extended the three-game sweep of Toledo to an 18–5 record over the first month of the season and took first place, one game ahead of the New York Metropolitans. "The Louisvilles have certainly one of the strongest clubs in the Association," gushed the local papers, "and they are a group of fine gentlemen."[32]

Meanwhile, Pete was recognized for his heroic actions off the field. On May 4, following a 5–4 win over Toledo, Pete saved a boy from being run over by a streetcar. The child, who was trying to cross the tracks, was struck by the mules pulling the streetcar and fell. Pete reached out and pulled the boy to safety moments before he was trampled underfoot. On the field, by most players' standards, Pete was off to a strong start, hitting .300 over the first nine games. But Pete was not most players. He was suffering from headaches and vertigo—the lingering effects of mastoiditis—and elected to have surgery to alleviate the pain and swelling behind his ears. He underwent surgery on May 12, while the team was in Toledo for a three-game series. The surgery was still in its infancy, and it was basically a crude attempt to relieve pressure in the ear by making an incision to drain the fluid. It was hoped that once the pressure was released, Pete's symptoms would improve or at least stabilize. He rejoined the team May 17 for a 7–0 win over Columbus after missing four games. The surgery was successful, and Pete was relatively pain free for the first time since adolescence. He went 2 for 4 with a double upon his return, and during the last two weeks of May Pete went on a tear, hitting over .400, including one stretch in which he hit triples in four out of five games.

Pete missed only three games for the remainder of the season, playing in 103 of the team's 110 games. The surgery that eased the pain in his head also led to a reduction in his drinking. It is unrealistic to think that he was completely sober, but over the years, Pete exhibited stretches of moderation and self-restraint, and this appears to be one of those times. With Pete's drinking under control, Louisville found greater success on the field with fewer distractions from its star player.

Near the midpoint of the season, Louisville was firing on all cylinders and in first place. On July 5 the *Courier-Journal* prematurely noted, "It now looks a certainty that Louisville will float the pennant."[33] Pete led the way, hitting a robust .387—good enough for fourth in the AA—with ten doubles, seven triples, and three homers. For the rest of the month, Louisville hung on to a slim lead—never more than one game. By the end of July, Louisville had slipped into second behind the red-hot New York Metropolitans, which won 14 of 15 games. Over the same span, Louisville's record was 9–6. The team ended the month of July by winning only two of its final six games, unable to keep up with the Metropolitans' torrid pace. After that, Louisville never seriously challenged for first, although the team had occasional moments of greatness. But this only added to the frustration, as it proved how talented the team was and how close it had come to winning the pennant in 1884. As temperatures cooled toward the end of the summer, so did the team's fortunes, as it fell seven games back of the streaking Metropolitans. The players' growing frustration culminated in a fight between Pete and Hecker on August 13 while on a train en route from St. Louis to Cincinnati. The two "locked horns in mortal combat." No reason was given for the altercation, but "there was lots of noise, [though] no broken bones."[34]

The sportswriters in Louisville heaped much of the blame on the team's management. They were especially critical of the team's handling of the relief pitchers for workhorse Hecker, citing in particular the poor play of Ren Deagle. Deagle signed with Louisville in June after being released by Cincinnati. He got off to a horrendous start, losing his first four games. "The managers of Louisville exhibited marvelous stupidity in their persistence in putting Deagle in the pitcher's box," complained the *Courier-Journal.* "He has proved his utter inefficiency as a ball player, and has already lost the club many more games than they could afford."[35]

Deagle finished the year 4–6. Louisville's pitching issues got so bad that Pete started a game on October 6 against Baltimore. It was disastrous. In only one-third of an inning, Pete walked three, gave up three runs on two hits, and threw a wild pitch, picking up the loss. Pete's poor performance showed that he had lost the pitching skills he had flashed as a youngster with the semipro Eclipse.

Immune from the sportswriters' criticism was Hecker, who was having a breakout season. In June he was hailed as "the best all-around player in the country."[36] He did nothing to disprove that notion throughout the season. He made 73 starts (plus two appearances in relief), ending the season with a 52–20 record while pitching 72 complete games and posting a 1.80 earned run average (ERA). He captured the triple crown of pitching: most wins, lowest ERA, and most strikeouts (385). He was no slouch at the plate either, hitting .297 and finishing in the top ten for slugging.

As the season started to slip away, Pete too became a target for the sportswriters' ire. His hitting remained above reproach, as he continued to be one of the AA's leading batters, but his play in the field became a regular object of criticism. On July 20, after several questionable games, the *Courier-Journal* reported that he had "lost his grip at third." A few days later, he was moved to first base. That move was not a permanent one, as he struggled at first as well. In early August he moved to second base to fill in for Joe Gerhardt, who had taken a leave of absence to tend to his terminally ill infant son, who died a short time later. Upon Gerhardt's return, Pete resumed his position at first, but he was eventually relocated to center field.

As a youth, Pete had played exclusively in the infield for the Eclipse, but his defensive shortcomings were becoming more pronounced. During the 1883 season Pete had played about half his games in the outfield, but with Louisville's roster changes preceding the 1884 season, a move back to the infield made sense. The move in August to center field was necessitated by a seemingly complete erosion of Pete's skills in the infield, or a complete loss of interest in the less glamorous defensive aspects of the game. It should also be noted that while Pete's surgery earlier in the year relieved some of his pain, it also worsened his hearing. As a result, even routine fly balls turned into comical adventures as Pete was unable to hear teammates who may or may not have been calling him off. He regularly surrendered all fly balls to his teammates, whether they wanted them or not.

The relocation to the outfield seemed to rejuvenate Pete's interest in defense, and he immediately started playing at a higher level. The *Courier-Journal* noted that he "covers as much ground in center field as any man in the country."[37] The local sportswriters spent the last two months of the season raving about Pete's performance in center field. They gushed about his defensive rebirth and recounted his heroics in the field, describing "a remarkable one-handed catch on the run,"[38] how he robbed "three drives in center field that seemed perfectly safe hits,"[39] and how he "covered himself in glory by making a marvelous running-catch of a fly which seemed surely out of his reach."[40] One headlined blared, "Browning's Brilliant Playing in Center Field,"[41] while another story boldly proclaimed, "Browning is playing the best game in center field of any man in the country."[42] Despite a defensive posture that had him perched on one leg like a deranged crane, at the end of the season he led the league in fielding percentage among all outfielders with at least 24 appearances. Even with such an impressive late-season showing, Pete's overall fielding percentage, which included the bulk of his season in the infield, was a pedestrian .902, coming in slightly above the league average of .898.

As usual, it was at the plate where Pete shone the brightest. Again, he was one of the leaders in hitting, finishing third with a .336 average, behind league leader Dave Orr's .354 and a mere fraction behind second-place John Reilly's .336. He finished among the top five in hits, doubles, and slugging percentage. Though not as dominant as his prior two seasons, 1884 was still a testament to Pete's skills with the bat, as he was the only player to finish in the top three in batting average in each of the AA's first three seasons.

A late-season surge saw the Louisvilles pull back into second place, only two games out. But they never got any closer, eventually finishing in third place, 7½ games behind the first-place Metropolitans, which won the AA title in only their second season in the league. It was Louisville's best finish yet in the AA.

The 1884 season featured the first World's Series between the AA's New York Metropolitans, led by batting champ Orr, and the NL champions, the Providence Grays.[43] These early series were disorganized affairs, with the terms arranged beforehand through negotiations between the owners. The number of games played ranged from as few as three in 1884 to as many as 15 in 1887. In 1884 Providence swept New York in a best-of-three series behind future Hall of Fame pitcher Charles "Old Hoss" Radbourn, who hurled three complete games.

Pete probably paid little attention to the World Series. He was not a participant, so it held little interest for him. He spent the off-season as he normally did, preparing his bats for next year and trying to stay out of the public eye.

A Hitter of the Old Style (1885)

For the most part, Pete had a quiet off-season. *Sporting Life* reported that he was arrested in December 1884 for public drunkenness, but he denied it. It also reported that Pete had pledged to quit drinking, but there is no evidence he planned to give up booze. This became a familiar pattern: Pete would experience some sort of alcohol-related trouble, and the local papers would report his promise to abstain from drinking. Whether Pete actually said those words or it was just wishful thinking by the papers is unclear, but either way, Pete had no intention of going on the wagon. Most of Pete's troubles with liquor surfaced with the arrival of the new season. During the off-season, when he was out of the public eye, his indiscretions tended to fly under the radar. His drinking also lessened in the off-season. Physical activity and the heat of the baseball season exacerbated the symptoms of his mastoiditis, driving him to drink more to relieve the pain. The off-season meant less physical activity, less pain, and therefore less drinking. A rumor also circulated in the local papers that Pete was engaged to be married, but nothing ever came of it.

Pete caused a minor controversy when he initially declined to join the team for a series of exhibition games in the South in March. He eventually relented and agreed to make the trip. However, he misheard where they were departing from and went to the Main Street depot instead of the Maple Street depot. By the time he realized his mistake, he had missed the train and was forced to travel separately from the rest of the team.

Otherwise, Pete spent the off-season as he usually did: meticulously preparing his large collection of bats for the upcoming season. This was not Pete's only obsessive quirk; he also spent an inordinate amount of time caring for his eyes, or as he called them, "lamps." He relied on a never-ending stream of odd home remedies to alleviate the pain and swelling around his eyes caused by mastoiditis. In an era of questionable medical practices, and given Pete's limited education, it is not surprising that he turned to a host of peculiar treatments to care for his all-important lamps. "You can't line one out unless you have got good peepers, Old Pete knows that and he takes good care of 'em," he explained. "He never washes 'em with soap and water. It won't do. It will ruin the best lamps in the world. Pete closes 'em up when he is washing, then waits until about 10 o'clock when he goes out in the streets and looks right up in the sun two or three times. That opens 'em good, and then he can line 'em out."[1]

Buttermilk was an integral part of his eye-care routine, and he had some delivered every morning during the season. He drank two glasses at bedtime, asserting, "It [is] a great nerve steadier."[2] He also bathed his eyes in buttermilk first thing every morning, insisting it was necessary "to make [me] see properly."[3] Although bathing his eyes in buttermilk probably provided some immediate, soothing relief, this practice actually put Pete at risk for a bacterial infection. His consumption of buttermilk was probably most beneficial for his eyes, as buttermilk contains lutein, which is known as the "eye vitamin." It is a strong antioxidant and helps protect and improve eye function.

On rainy days, Pete stood with his head turned skyward to let the rain rinse his eyes out. In pursuit of the perfect eye care, he was also known to drink two tablespoons of Worcestershire sauce at dinnertime, gulp down Tabasco sauce mixed with mustard and ginger, and hang his head out the train window as it chugged along, hoping to catch ashes or cinders in his eyes. "Clinkers are good for the peepers," explained Pete. "Let a big one blow in your lamptenies and it will clean 'em out so you can drive a phony pitcher to drink."[4]

Pete was adamant that smoking cigarettes improved his eyesight. "There is nothing like the smoke of a cigarette to put the eyes in trim to solve a twisting, sizzling curve." To illustrate the power of cigarette smoke, Pete told the story of hard-hitting "Long" John Reilly. One day, Pete was in the dressing room, taking a few puffs on a cigarette before heading out to bat. Reilly was "pained" to see his friend partaking in the "pernicious habit" and asked Pete why he was smoking that "vile thing." Pete explained it helped with his hitting, and then promptly cracked a three-bagger. Upon seeing Pete's success at the plate, Reilly tried "to borrow, beg, or buy a cigarette." He found one, took a couple of good puffs, and stroked a line shot of his own. Reilly was soon smoking regularly, but he saw no improvement in his hitting. He tried all brands of cigarettes before finally giving up the habit. Pete, of course, knew the reason for Reilly's struggles. "It was because he didn't have the confidence in the smoke," he said.[5]

The fact that a player of Reilly's stature was willing to try Pete's unconventional approach showed Pete's influence on other players and what they thought of him. Despite never being named team captain or taking on any kind of official leadership role, Pete's influence loomed large. Players emulated his quirks in the hopes of being able to hit like him. At meals, Pete would tell the rookies and youngsters on the team to order the most "absurd and hideous compound . . . [like] pancakes with onion dressing and sugar on top and tripe with maple syrup," claiming it would help their batting. There is no evidence that Pete actually indulged in these insane concoctions himself, but given his success, it was hard for the rookies to ignore him. "The juveniles would accept whatever Pete said," explained former player Bill Everitt, "and would order the same stuff until Pete's ingenuity was exhausted of devising new cruelties for them."[6]

Pete was not above adopting the strange habits of other successful players in the hopes of improving his game. For example, he always touched third base with his left foot as he came on or off the field, even if it meant going out of his way and crossing the diamond to do so. When asked about it, Pete explained that on one occasion, as he was leaving the field, he happened to touch third base and stung a triple in his next at-bat. The next inning, Pete did not touch third and failed to get a hit. That settled it for Pete. From then on, he made sure to touch the bag. He later offered conflicting stories as to the origin of this long-standing habit, claiming he picked it up from Hall of Famer Sam Thompson after observing him do the same. One day, Pittsburgh's George "Doggie" Miller decided to have a little fun with Pete and actually carried third base off the field at the end of the inning. Pete ran around in a frenzy looking for the bag. When he spied Miller with it, he chased him around the park until Miller finally relented and replaced the base. Pete was also known to avoid walking through puddles, so his trek off the field at the end of each inning could turn into a zigzagging odyssey to dodge the puddles that often formed on the poorly manicured fields as he headed toward third to touch the bag before making his way to the bench.

For Pete, every day was full of routines, habits, and superstitions that had to be followed. Socks had to be picked up in the right order, sand had to be rubbed on his bats in the morning before a game, certain foods had to be eaten, and he always had to have a chew of fine-cut tobacco. Failure to adhere to these routines, Pete believed, meant that he would not get any hits that day. Of course, Pete's routines and superstitions were apt to change based on how he performed on any particular day. Once he forgot his shoes and borrowed a pair from Chicken Wolf. He stung four hits while wearing the borrowed shoes, and of course he believed that Wolf's shoes were the key to his success.[7]

Pete liked his sleep and hated to be disturbed, regardless of the situation. In 1892, while Pete was playing with Cincinnati, the team was returning home from St. Louis when its train was hit by a freight train. Two sleeper cars were knocked off the tracks and slid down a steep incline. Longtime baseball manager and executive Frank Bancroft, who was Cincinnati's business manager at the time, recalled the scene: "Somehow, some way we scrambled out in pajamas or without them, and took census of our numbers," he said. "Bid McPhee had a smashed nose, Frank Dwyer had a skinned elbow, and there were a few minor injuries, but nobody was killed or crippled. And then to our utter horror, we found Charley Comiskey and Pete Browning were missing." The two men were eventually located—still asleep in one of the cars. As the other players rejoiced in finding their teammates alive and well amongst the wreckage, Pete had only one thing on his mind. "Wotinell do you mean, anyhow," Pete bellowed, as he took a swing at the man nearest him. "How often have I told you guys I had to have me sleep or there'd be trouble?"[8]

Despite Pete's numerous quirks and superstitions and his belief that they powered his hitting, pitcher Gus Weyhing credited his success to something much simpler. Weyhing, who had known Pete for years, said, "I always attributed Pete's natural hitting abilities to his mania for batting continually during practice." He went on to explain: "Every morning in our practice on the home grounds Pete would be found at the home plate, bat in hand, tossing and hitting the ball. He never cared about ramming puny grounders to the infielders but pushed all his muscle against the ball and sent it to the deep outfield. On the trip Pete would sneak off to the grounds of the visiting clubs early of mornings and practice with the players of the opposing teams."[9] All his oddities, quirks, superstitions, and endless practice came together for Pete in 1885.

The 1885 season featured a seismic change in pitching. The prior season the National League had allowed pitchers to throw the ball overhand for the first time, removing the requirement that they release the ball below the shoulder line. This was a revolutionary change in the role of the pitcher; rather than simply delivering a "fair ball" that the hitter could put into play, the pitcher gained more control over the game. The impact was staggering. The NL batting average plummeted from .262 to .247, and runs per game fell from 5.78 to 5.51 as pitchers saw their strikeout and shutout numbers increase drastically. Fans, who were accustomed to witnessing their star batters lace hits all over the field, creating a contest between hitter and fielder, now saw pitchers dominating batters who were unable to put the ball in play.

The American Association started the 1885 season clinging to the below-the-shoulder delivery rule, but umpires were struggling to enforce it. Finally the AA owners relented, calling an emergency meeting at which they abolished the below-the-shoulder rule on June 8.

Shortly after the rule change, Pete was perusing the *Cincinnati Commercial Gazette* with Guy Hecker. After carefully studying the picture on the front page, Pete turned to Hecker and confidently said, "This is an excellent illustration of it."

"Of what?" asked Hecker.

"Why, of the unrestricted style of pitching. It looks exactly the way Caruthers and Henderson does it," answered Pete.

"Why you big jay," laughed Hecker, "that ain't a pitcher. That's Bartholdi's Statue of Liberty."

"Shoo," replied a surprised Pete. "I thought it was the unrestricted style."[10]

Pete would be unfazed by the change in delivery style, as he would put together one of his best statistical campaigns in 1885, leading the league in numerous categories, achieving a career high in home runs, and producing a nearly 30-point jump in his batting average from the season before.

Louisville headed into the 1885 season with an upgraded stadium that included a new area for ladies and their escorts, improvements to the stands, an extension of the outfield by moving the left-field fence back 40 feet, and modern amenities such as luxury boxes, or what was described as "a special room . . . for invited guests and officers of the club."[11] The club also refuted the rumor that it was dropping out of the AA after the season and being replaced by Cleveland, calling it "ridiculous to the extreme."[12]

Louisville still had five players from the original 1882 roster—Pete, Guy Hecker, Joe Crotty, Leech Maskrey, and Chicken Wolf—as well as two homegrown players in third baseman Phil Reccius and second baseman Tom McLaughlin, who joined the team in 1883. Rounding out the lineup were first baseman John Kerins, who had played with Indianapolis the year before, and shortstop Joe Miller, who came over from Toledo. As usual, the local papers were over the top in their preseason praise and predicted the new lineup would "give the people of Louisville honest base ball and . . . win the championship if they can."[13] The *Louisville Commercial* observed, "That the team is much stronger than last year cannot be denied, as the new players are largely men of experience, tried and not found wanting. The taking of Reccius from third base and playing him in the pitcher's position only insures Hecker a sure and valuable assistant."[14] More importantly, given the team's issues over the past few seasons, it was happily reported that none of the men were drinkers. But that was quickly proved false.

Despite the belief that the team was much stronger, Louisville limped out of the gate, starting the year 2–6 before winning 14 of the next 20. This hot streak only moved Louisville into fourth place, six games behind the red-hot St. Louis Browns, at the end of May. This was followed by 11 losses in the next 15 games and set the trend for the rest of the season—moments of inspired greatness followed by moments of mediocrity. Unfortunately for Louisville, the mediocrity overshadowed the greatness. And at times, the mediocre drifted into the abysmal, such as the 19–2 loss to Philadelphia on June 13. One headline screamed, "Were They Drunk?" and the local paper called it the "worst fielding game ever known in the American Association," as the team committed 17 errors. In fact, the players "made errors with such rapidity that it was difficult to score them." Surprisingly, Pete committed only one error while going 2 for 4 at the plate. The *Courier-Journal* tried to find a silver lining in the disaster, reasoning that "Louisville will win Monday's game, because the Athletics are exhausted from running around the bases."[15]

Much of the team's poor play was attributed to the same old issues: the players' drinking and off-field behavior. A month into the season, Louisville was sitting in fifth place, seemingly headed for a repeat of 1883. The *Courier-Journal* warned, "If any members of the club are drinking or gambling Manager [Jim] Hart should see that it is at once stopped. The disastrous experience of 1883 resulted from too much liquor."[16]

Local sportswriters were blaming the players' unsavory off-field habits for their poor performance:

> It is reported upon good authority that several members of the local club have been playing poker and drinking whiskey lately from sunrise to sunset. This sort of thing ought to be stopped at once. Ball players are hired to play base ball and not poker, and there are strong rules against intoxication which should be enforced. An inferior player who is sober and attentive is preferable to a superior player who goes into a game half dead from lack of sleep and intemperance. There is a way to stop excesses of this character and the management should let no grass grow in reading the riot act.[17]

Pete seemed to contradict this view, as even when half drunk he was twice as good as most other players. However, it does raise the question of how good he might have been if he had taken better care of himself.

The paper also cited a lack of on-field leadership and a possible feud among players, particularly between Hecker and relief pitcher Norm Baker. Jim Hart, in his first season as manager, was quick to refute these claims, denying any dissension and stating, "Each man is anxious to see the other succeed."[18] Hart's claim rang hollow when Baker was released soon after. Baker had pitched well early in the season but had cooled off recently. When he left Louisville, his record was 13–12, but it seems his play on the field was not the only reason for his release. "Baker was not at all popular with the other players," reported the *Courier-Journal.*[19]

Heading into the season, Pete was his usual confident self and declared that he was going to "lead the American Association batsmen this season."[20] But Pete's early season was marked by streaky play. After a 14–4 loss to Brooklyn in which he blasted a home run and a triple, Pete was roundly criticized for his fielding when he "calmy allowed two easy flies to drop at his feet."[21] Hart defended his best player, who was being accused of falling back into old habits, by stating that Pete drank nothing but ginger ale. But there is no proof that Pete's beverage of choice had changed.

Pete's performance in the loss to Brooklyn was representative of the up-and-down nature of his play. His highs were matched by just as many lows. After a game in which Pete had three hits but also struck out twice, the *Courier-Journal* stated, "Browning does not do things by halves."[22] The press may have overstated Pete's streakiness, as during the first six weeks of the season he went hitless in only three games and logged a 29-game hitting streak from May 9 to June 20, clubbing six doubles, five triples, and four home runs.

Even with Pete's hot hitting, the team continued to struggle both on and off the field. On May 27 catcher Dan Sullivan, whose play had been described as "rotten" and whose batting average had fallen below .200, assaulted William Osborne, sports editor of the *Louisville Commercial,* in the team's dressing room. Before the game started, Sullivan approached Osborne, who was with two lady friends, and said he wanted to have a word with him about comments Osborne had written. The two began to argue before heading into the dressing room, where they continued the discussion. The hot-tempered Sullivan demanded an apology from Osborne, who refused. Sullivan responded by calling Osborne a "vile" name, striking him in the face, and knocking him to the ground, then following up with several more blows. Hecker, who was nearby, pulled Sullivan off Osborne and restrained him until the sportswriter left the dressing room. The local papers were unanimous in their support for Osborne. "Mr. Osborne's strictures on Sullivan were just," wrote the *Courier-Journal,* "and they were endorsed by the large majority of the base-ball element of this city. Sullivan is known by both his intimates and others to be a drinking man, and he has not supported Hecker in the majority of games he has played this season."[23] The local papers were equally unanimous in their contempt for the perceived inaction of Hart, who allowed the incident to take place and then helped Sullivan avoid the police. "A manager who permits such an outrage in his own presence, without the slightest effort to prevent it, shows himself utterly wanting in the qualities which go to make a good manager," scolded the *Courier-Journal.*[24]

Sullivan, who had been with Louisville since the team's 1882 debut in the AA, was released two weeks later on June 9. He soon signed with St. Louis but lasted only 17 games before being released. He played one game the following season with Pittsburgh, which was the last of his career. Sullivan's tumultuous career included the highlight of catching the sixth and seventh no-hitters in MLB history (by Tony Mullane and Guy Hecker, respectively) eight days apart on September 11 and 19, 1882.

The 1885 season appeared to be devolving into the same kind of mess experienced in 1883. And as they had in 1883, local sportswriters, though recognizing the impact of the players' off-field habits on the team's performance, heaped much of the blame on the club's management. "The impression grows stronger here every day that the trouble with the Louisville Club is more with management than with the players. They are constantly losing games they should have won with ease, and if the Directors properly understand their own interests they will try if a change of management will not produce better results."[25]

Rumors persisted throughout the summer about both Hecker and Pete moving to new teams. Hecker openly expressed an interest in signing with Pittsburgh, which offered him a huge salary increase—from the $1,800 he was making in Louisville to an impressive $5,000. Pete was being pursued by Cincinnati, but despite regular chatter about Pete leaving Louisville, neither he nor the club seemed interested in making the move. Pete was most comfortable at home in Louisville. Hecker's situation was different. Even though he had spent his entire career in Louisville and was a popular player, he had fallen out of favor with the local sportswriters, who continually wrote about his leaving like it was a foregone conclusion. In the end, neither deal materialized.

Louisville continued its inconsistent play for the rest of the season, as winning streaks were interspersed with losing streaks. The team spent the bulk of the season between third and fifth place in the standings, never gaining much ground on the first-place St. Louis Browns. The Browns were on their way to the first of four straight AA titles, establishing themselves as the league's premier team. Over the AA's decade-long run, the Browns would pile up a league-high 780 wins.

A disastrous monthlong road trip to end the season saw Louisville win only 4 of 19 games. Meanwhile, the *Courier-Journal* demanded that the club's directors undertake a thorough investigation to ascertain who the troublemakers were. A 13–8 blowout to last-place Baltimore on the last day of the season was the final humiliation in a frustrating season, dropping the team from fifth to sixth place, 26 games out of first.

The only consistent bright spot throughout the year was Pete's hitting. He had promised to lead the league in hitting, and his performance with the bat kept him on pace to do that. Pete's steel nerves and steady concentration at the plate, likely aided by his inability to hear the crowd or the opposing team trying to rattle him, allowed him to wait patiently for the perfect pitch. Once he got it, he unleashed his powerful swing, wreaking havoc on many a pitcher.

Following his early-season 29-game hitting streak, Pete followed up with another 12-game streak from June 27 to July 11. Tucked into that streak was another impressive run: he led off ten straight games by reaching base safely. During a monthlong home stand from June 30 to August 2, Pete was on fire, hitting .431. Then he cooled off, and there were whispers that "he had fallen into an old habit of his." There may have been reason for concern, as the *Courier-Journal* wrote in August, "Manger Hart should look to his men, who are indulging too freely in liquor. Part of the trouble with the Louisville nine lately is due to the fact that two or three men in it are drinking enough to run an ordinary base ball team a whole season."[26]

More stories about the team's bad behavior followed. One claimed that a promising young player was so intoxicated after a game that he had to be carried home in a carriage. Another reported that one of the club's mainstays was drunk and barely able to talk before the game on August 16. No names were given, but it seems unlikely that this was Pete, as he had played drunk many times before. If it was Pete, it just proved that he could handle his liquor, as he went 2 for 6 in that game, including a leadoff inside-the-park home run. With or without alcohol, Pete was more than 20 points ahead of second-place Dave Orr in the contest for the batting title. League standings at the end of August showed Pete batting .369, just behind Tip O'Neill's .373. But O'Neill was hurt for much of the season and played in less than half the games. He returned in September but played poorly that last month, and his average plummeted 20 points.

Pete's dominance in 1885 was no doubt aided by the size of his bat. It was a massive piece of lumber, "an unwieldy, bologna-shaped bludgeon with a handle as thick as an elephant's trunk."[27] His bats were 37-inch, 46-ounce tree trunks that tapered only slightly from the barrel to the handle, requiring big hands to hold and swing them comfortably. They dwarfed the average-sized modern bat (34 inches and 32 ounces) and came in just behind Babe Ruth's legendary 54-ounce club he ordered from Hillerich & Bradsby to use in spring training to build his strength. The size of Pete's bat may have given him an advantage, but few players were capable of swinging such a massive club over the course of an entire season.

In 1962 single-season home run record holder Roger Maris took part in an experiment to determine what type of bat was best for hitting home runs—the slim, light, tapered bat of the modern game, or the large, cumbersome tree trunks of yore. Maris believed he knew the answer before even taking a swing. "There's no doubt," he said, "that I get a better piece of the ball and have better timing with the new slender bats than I ever did with the heavier, fat-handled models." The five models used in the experiment were Pete's behemoth, which Maris called "nothing but an overgrown milk bottle"; a Babe Ruth model; a Ty Cobb model; a John "Home Run" Baker model; and the bat Maris used during his record-setting 1961 season.[28] The overgrown milk bottle proved effective, finishing third in overall distance (the total distance traveled by five balls hit with each bat and pitched with "robot-like precision" by Yankees pitching coach Spud Murray). It bested the Ruth and Maris bats but finished behind the Cobb and Baker models. Maris's bat finished last among the five. Still, Maris said he preferred a lighter bat, claiming it was necessary to keep up with the speed of modern pitching. That sentiment is still a common argument for using lighter bats, as the physical demands of swinging a huge bat countless times every day for an entire season are daunting.

A 2003 study at Penn State University analyzed the physics behind bat size and its effects on a batted ball. It came to the same conclusion as the Maris demonstration: a heavier bat produces a faster batted ball speed. "This makes intuitive sense since a heavier bat brings more momentum into the collision," said Dr. Daniel A. Russell. "Doubling the mass of the bat results in an increase of almost 12 mph." Simply stated, using a heavier bat should result in a faster ball speed, which means the hit ball travels farther. But, like the Maris experiment, the Penn State study considered the physical demands of swinging a heavy bat versus a lighter one. Russell explained, "If a player can maintain the same bat swing speed with a heavier bat, the heavier bat will produce higher batted ball velocity and an increase in distance. But any player who has experimented swinging bats with widely different weights knows that it is easier to swing a light bat than a heavier bat. Put another way, it takes more effort to swing a heavy bat with the same speed as it does a lighter bat, and most players cannot swing a heavy bat as quickly as they can a bat which is half the weight." Russell brought up another issue with the use of heavier bats:

> All of the physics used to derive the optimum mass and the batted ball speed assume that the ball hits the bat at its center-of-mass. This very rarely happens—hits at the sweet spot are several inches from the center-of-mass. There is another very important parameter of the bat which affects how quickly you

> can swing a bat, and what the final ball speed is. This parameter involves the distribution of mass along the length of the bat and how that mass distribution affects the motion of a rotating object. In physics we refer to this parameter as the moment of inertia. It turns out that the moment-of-inertia (or "swing weight") matters more than mass.[29]

For Pete, the science didn't matter. Even though his bat weighed in at a colossal 46 ounces, he wanted it heavier. "Long" John Reilly, who played his entire ten-year career with Cincinnati and, like Pete, was a notorious bat hound, once picked up one of Pete's bats and said it seemed like it weighed 12 pounds. "It felt like it had an iron sash-weight in the end of it," quipped Reilly. He later gained insight into the weightiness of Pete's bats when he wandered into the Louisville clubhouse and saw a bat floating in a bathtub. Reilly inquired, "Whose bat is that?"

"It belongs to me," replied Pete with a smirk. "I put it in there so that it will get heavy."[30]

"Pete Browning uses the heaviest bat in the Louisville collection," wrote the *Dayton Herald* in 1887. "None of the other players attempt to strike with it."[31] "I use a 46-ounce bat," the cocky slugger declared in 1891:

> There ain't many players that like 'em so heavy. Besides, if any of those guys who are always borrowing sticks ask me how they [will] go on my bat, I say "rotten," and that settles it, they don't want to use it. I don't see how Jimmie Ryan of the Chicagos, or [Mike] Tiernan of the New Yorks makes so many long hits. They use bats not thicker than a broomstick and not much heavier. Old Pete couldn't do anything with a bat like that. He's got to have a heavy one, with good wood in it, that will make the ball bark when he hits it.[32]

The extra weight paid off, as Pete was said "to be the longest driving batter that ever played in the major league . . . he could certainly knock the ball a mile when he landed on it, and in consequence was the terror of the pitchers."[33]

Years after his retirement, his immense bats were still remembered and mythologized in the sporting press. In 1897 the *Buffalo Enquirer* remarked that future Hall of Famer "Wee" Willie Keller, on his way to his first batting title and a .424 year, would "get round-shouldered jest [*sic*] in trying to heft it."[34]

Even with an August slump, Pete's lead in the race for the batting title was never seriously challenged. He outhit runner-up Orr .362 to .342. He was as dominant in 1885 as he had been in his rookie season of 1882, leading the league in OBP (.393), OPS (.923), hits (174), runs created (100), and total bases (255). He finished second in slugging and doubles, third in home runs, and fifth in RBIs. More surprisingly, given Pete's history of illness and drunkenness, he tied for first in number of games played, with 112. Pete's second batting title in four years established him as the premier hitter of the AA and put him in contention for best hitter in the country. The *Courier-Journal* proclaimed, "Browning is undoubtedly the greatest batter in the Association."[35]

Pete's 1888 Old Judge Cigarettes baseball card. The Goodwin Company produced a series of cards from 1887 to 1890 depicting hundreds of ballplayers from more than 40 major and minor league teams. The cards were inserted in packs of Old Judge and Gypsy Queen cigarettes. Many of the iconic images of ballplayers from this era come from these cards. (Courtesy of National Baseball Hall of Fame, Cooperstown, NY)

Fred Pfeffer, one of Pete's oldest friends and a teammate on the semipro Eclipse. He played 16 seasons, mostly with Chicago as part of the famed Stonewall Infield, and is recognized as one of the greatest second basemen of the premodern era. (Library of Congress, LC-DIG-bbc-0141f)

Painting by Henry Sandham, 1887. (Library of Congress, LC-DIG-pga-04028)

City of Louisville as viewed across the Ohio River, 1872. (Library of Congress, LC-USZ62-103455)

Tony Mullane. Mullane was disliked by many of his teammates, but he posted five straight 30-win seasons and compiled 284 wins over his 13-year career. He played with Pete twice—with Louisville in 1882 and with Cincinnati in 1891–1892. (Library of Congress, LC-DIG-bbc-0412f)

Guy Hecker. A solid all-around player, Hecker is often considered the best combination pitcher-hitter of the nineteenth century. He is the only player to capture both a pitching triple crown and a batting title. He was teammates with Pete for eight years in Louisville. They were close friends and regularly roomed together on the road. (Library of Congress, LC-DIG-bbc-0433f)

Players on the 1877 Eclipse. This is the earliest known photograph of Pete. Depending on when during the season it was taken, he was either 15 or 16 years old. The 1877 Louisville Eclipse was an elite semipro team that was well on its way to becoming one of the best nonprofessional teams in the country. Back row, standing (left to right): John Reccius, John Pfeiffer, Tim Lehan, W. Zimmerman. Middle row, seated: Ed Quinlan, Pete Browning, Mike Walsh, Coleman. Front row: Charles Pfeiffer, Charlie Arny. (R. G. Potter Collection, P-02586-n, Archives & Special Collections, University of Louisville)

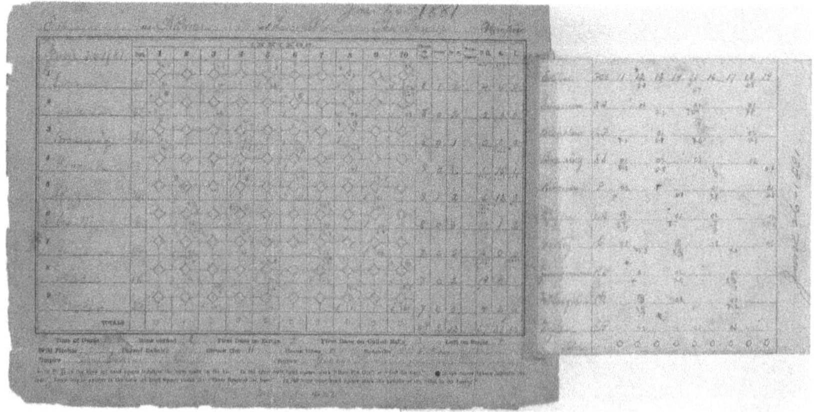

Louisville Grays, 1876. One of the original teams of the National League, the Grays *were* baseball in Louisville for two years. After a gambling scandal in 1877, in which four of the team's best players took money to lose games, the Grays were disbanded, leaving Louisville without Major League Baseball until 1882, when the Eclipse joined the new American Association. (Wikimedia.org; Wikimedia Commons)

Opposite: Score book from June 26, 1881, when Louisville and Akron—considered two of the premier nonprofessional teams in baseball—played to a 19-inning tie. Of the 18 men who participated in the game, 16 would go on to play at least one game in the major leagues, including a future Hall of Famer, two future batting champions, and a 284-game winner. (Used with permission; Louisville Slugger Museum & Factory)

Players on the 1882 Eclipse. Back row, standing (left to right): Leech Maskrey (left field), Pete Browning (second base), Tony Mullane (pitcher), utility player John Strick (far right). Middle row, seated: Dan Sullivan (catcher), player-manager Denny Mack (shortstop), Bill Schenck (third base), Guy Hecker (first base–pitcher). Front row: John Reccius (center field–pitcher), Chicken Wolf (right field). (R. G. Potter Collection, P-01086-p, Archives & Special Collections, University of Louisville)

Leech Maskrey, 1889. At the time, Maskrey was playing with Des Moines of the Western Association. He was teammates with Pete for four seasons in Louisville, and prior to that he was a member of the powerful Akron team. Though only average with the bat, Maskrey was known for his strong defensive skills. He played four seasons in the big league but was active in baseball throughout his life as a player and manager around the country, as well as a stint in England. (Library of Congress, LC-DIG-bbc-0507f)

Arlie Latham. He and Pete were teammates for one season (1891–1892) in Cincinnati. Latham stated in a 1937 interview that he, not Pete, had the first bat made by Bud Hillerich, but there is little evidence to back up his claim. (Library of Congress, LC-DIG-bbc-0478f)

Present location of the Louisville Slugger Museum & Factory. (Photo by the author)

The Louisville team, 1885. Top row (left to right): John Kerins (first base), Amos Cross (catcher), Norm Baker (pitcher), Al Mays (pitcher). Second row: Leech Maskrey (left field), Guy Hecker (pitcher–first base), Dan Sullivan (catcher), Chicken Wolf (right field). Center: Jim Hart (manager). Third row: Pete Browning (left field), Phil Reccius (third base), Joe Crotty (catcher), Monk Cline (third base–left field). Bottom row: Joe Miller (shortstop), Billy Geer (shortstop), Ed Whiting (catcher in 1884 but did not play for Louisville in 1885), Tom McLaughlin (second base). (Courtesy of National Baseball Hall of Fame, Cooperstown, NY)

The Louisville team, 1885. That year, Louisville limped to a 53–59 record and a sixth-place finish. (1) Tom McLaughlin (second base), (2) Al Mays (pitcher), (3) Joe Miller (shortstop), (4) Leech Maskrey (left field), (5) Dan Sullivan (catcher), (6) Monk Cline (infield-outfield), (7) John Kerins (first base–catcher), (8) Phil Reccius (third base), (9) Pete Browning (center field), (10) Guy Hecker (pitcher–first base), (11) Jim Hart (manager), (12) Norm Baker (pitcher), (13) Amos Cross (catcher), (14) Joe Crotty (catcher), (15) Chicken Wolf (right field). (R. G. Potter Collection, P-01156-n, Archives & Special Collections, University of Louisville)

Pete Browning, date unknown, showing off his dapper look. (Used with permission; Louisville Slugger Museum & Factory)

Toad Ramsey. A teammate of Pete's in Louisville from 1885 to 1889, Ramsey showed flashes of dominance over a two-year period when he won 75 games. Unfortunately, he burned out after only six years in the majors due to a drinking problem. (Wikimedia.org; Wikimedia Commons)

Iconic image of Pete Browning, the Louisville Slugger, from his Old Judge Cigarettes baseball card. (Library of Congress, LC-DIG-bbc-0580f)

Tip O'Neill. Canadian O'Neill was one of the leading hitters in the AA, along with Pete. In 1887, when Pete put up impressive numbers in almost every category, he failed to lead the league in any of them because O'Neill, who hit .435 that season, was even more impressive. (Library of Congress, LC-DIG-bbc-0593f)

John "Kick" Kelly. Kelly had a brief career as a player—just 16 games over one season—but he helped develop the modern role of the umpire. When Kelly, known as "Honest John," retired, he held the record for the most games umpired in the major leagues, with 587. He managed Louisville for a season and a half in 1887–1888. (Wikimedia.org; Wikimedia Commons)

The Louisville team, 1888. Standing (left to right): Samuel Smith (first base), Guy Hecker (pitcher–first base), Pete Browning (center field), John Kerins (utility infield-outfield), Paul Cook (catcher), Joe Werrick (third base). Seated: Thomas "Toad" Ramsey (pitcher), Elton "Icebox" Chamberlain (pitcher), Bill White (shortstop), John Kelly (manager), Scott Stratton (pitcher), Chicken Wolf (right field), Hub Collins (second base). (Courtesy of National Baseball Hall of Fame, Cooperstown, NY)

John Kerins. Kerins had a seven-year major league career, spending four of those years as Pete's teammate in Louisville. He also served as player-manager for one season. After leaving Louisville, he took on the same role for the St. Louis Browns in 1890. He was also an umpire for a number of years. (Library of Congress, LC-DIG-bbc-0435f)

had then struck out three batters, and allowed two men their bases on balls. When

the public the base-ball player is the most renowned, attracts the largest crowds, is more

leave for St. Louis to-night and open the championship season to-morrow. A

With Malice
TOWARD NONE
WITH
CHARITY FOR ALL

Francis Murphy

F. E. Murphy

I THE UNDERSIGNED DO PLEDGE MY WORD AND HONOR
GOD HELPING ME.
TO ABSTAIN FROM ALL INTOXICATING LIQUORS AS A BEVERAGE AND THAT I WILL BY ALL HONORABLE MEANS ENCOURAGE OTHERS TO ABSTAIN

L R Browning

BROWNING'S SIGNATURE, A FAC SIMILE.

the visitors took their batting turn at the

talked of and has more admirers than any other class of people. They talk of the crowds that go

large crowd should be present to-day to give the boys a good send off

Pete's pledge. A week after listening to evangelist Francis Murphy preach against the evils of liquor, Pete joined the rest of the team in taking a "solemn oath to never touch intoxicating liquor again." It proved to be only temporary. (*Louisville Courier-Journal,* April 17, 1888)

the Giants?" He has several nick names, but is generally referred to at home as the "Gladiator." Browning frequently creates a sen-

PETE BROWNING.

sation on the Louisville streets by appearing in a dude makeup that would make even Berry Wall envious.

Already there are rumors—as there have

Pete in action, as depicted in the *Lincoln Daily Call,* August 4, 1888.

Thomas John "Dude" Esterbrook. An eccentric player, Esterbrook broke into the majors in 1880 and then bounced around, playing with four different teams before signing with Louisville at the end of the 1888 season. His moments of brilliance were often overshadowed by his outlandish personality, so he was right at home in the Louisville clubhouse. (Library of Congress, LC-DIG-bbc-0211f)

John Ward. Future Hall of Famer Ward helped found the Brotherhood of Professional Baseball Players in 1885. He was a popular player, a brilliant and energetic leader, and a lawyer, which gave him the know-how to help players with contract issues. He was particularly interested in raising player salaries to reflect the popularity of professional baseball and the growing revenue generated by the game. (Library of Congress, LC-DIG-bbc-0576f)

Pete Browning, 1890. Photo by W. L. Erond, taken in his studio at 323 and 325 West Jefferson Street. (Used with permission; Louisville Slugger Museum & Factory)

Patsy Tebeau. The hot-tempered Tebeau was known for his rough and rowdy ways on the diamond. During the one season he managed Pete in Cleveland as part of the Players' League, he taught him how to "throw a jolt into the ribs of the baseman" to get him to drop the ball. (Library of Congress, LC-DIG-bbc-0176f)

John Reilly. Like Pete, Reilly was an obsessive bat hoarder. They played together for one season in Cincinnati and engaged in many conversations about batting. Pete padlocked his locker to protect his bats from the notoriously light-fingered Reilly. (Library of Congress, LC-DIG-bbc-0415f)

Louisville Colonels, 1890. In a season featuring three competing leagues, Louisville went from worst (in 1889) to first, capturing its only American Association and World Series titles. The reliable Chicken Wolf led the team to victory, finishing first in the AA in batting that season. (Library of Congress, LC-DIG-ds-09738)

Mike "King" Kelly. Future Hall of Famer Kelly managed Pete for half a season in 1894 as part of the Allentown team, which was packed with ex–major league players. Kelly, known as a baseball innovator, trickster, villain, and showman, drank himself to an early death at age 36. (Library of Congress, LC-DIG-ppmsca-18581)

7

The Dude (1886)

"Pete Browning in Tears," blared the *Courier-Journal* headline on February 12, 1886. According to the paper, "the pride of Louisville base-ball enthusiasts freely partook of sundry liquors," leading to a "state of wild and disorderly intoxication." Pete was arrested on Twelfth Street after creating a disturbance that required the intervention of two police officers. Upon being arrested, Pete "broke into tears and wept copiously."[1] His uncontrollable sobbing drew a crowd, which followed the patrol wagon as it took Pete to the police station. Once there, he "wept himself sober" and was eventually released on bail. The *Louisville Commercial* could not resist making a baseball analogy: "The champion batter of the Association had previously been run down and put out between bases, so to speak, by various and sundry drinks."[2]

The following day Pete missed his scheduled court appearance, claiming he was too tired to show up. Judge R. H. Thompson, awed by Pete's celebrity, declared, "I understand this is Mr. Browning's first offense of this character. He gave me and the members of the bar and the general public a great deal of pleasure last summer, so it gives me a great deal of pleasure in return to dismiss the case against him, as I understand he promises not to do so again. I am as patriotic as the next Louisvillian and may the Louisville Club win the pennant."[3]

If this were an isolated incident, it would have been easy to dismiss it, but it was not. It was the continuation of a troubling trend that found Pete drunk in public on a regular basis. The *Nashville Banner* reported, "Pete Browning is very sick," then added this sarcastic comment: "If trying to drink all the mean red-eye in Louisville will make a man sick, then Pete is very ill."[4] By 1886, Pete's boozy troubles could no longer be ignored or laughed off. Both the team and the city had grown tired of his transgressions. Local papers begged him to change his ways:

> Pete Browning should "take a drop" on himself, and shake some of his associates, and change his route and try to get himself in shape for the coming season. . . . Pete has a gang of followers in the West End who make a hero of him trying to impress on his mind that he is the greatest ball player in existence, and that such a player as he ought to be more appreciated by his club. They lead him to believe that he is abused, mistreated, neglected, and imposed upon by the club, until Pete thinks that something ought to be done.

The *Courier-Journal* implored Pete to heed its advice, reasoning that if he did, he could easily repeat as AA batting champion. It concluded, "He also ought to get the idea that the Louisville Club can't get along without him out of his head. Pete's salary has been gradually raised from what ice cream he could eat to the highest limit the rules allow."[5]

Since the beginning of his professional career, a few things had become clear. Pete was a hitter of incomparable talent who effortlessly wielded the bat in a way few other players could. He was also a man who wrestled with demons. *Sporting Life* suggested that Pete needed to change his ways and observed, "The truth is, . . . he is his own greatest enemy, and if he can once conquer himself he will find that he has at once conquered all his enemies."[6] The flaw with these arguments was that Pete did as he pleased and still produced at the highest levels. And these appeals only added to his belief that he was not treated fairly by the press.

Despite Pete's outgoing demeanor and all the attention he received, he was a fairly shy individual, overcompensating for his poor hearing and limited education with a braggadocious exuberance that masked his shortcomings and insecurities. His prickly standoffishness toward the press earned him a nickname that spoke to his combative personality: the Gladiator. It is unclear who came up with the nickname or when it was first used. One of the earliest appearances in print was in the May 3, 1887, edition of the *Courier-Journal:* "Even the gentle Pete Browning has begun to kick, and the Gladiator's voice is for war to the knife when there is a point to be made." Eventually, the nickname became as much a part of his identity as his hitting and drinking. The Gladiator was only one of many nicknames bestowed on Pete over the years, such as Old Warhorse, Line 'em out Pete, Distillery Pete, the Prince of Bourbon, and Red Light District Pete. He was also called Pietro, a nickname given to him by Harry Weldon, sports editor of the *Cincinnati Enquirer.*

Though outspoken in public, Pete was reluctant to grant interviews. The *Courier-Journal* noted that despite being "very bashful," Pete was "a great favorite among the fair sex." The newspaper also took notice of Pete's newfound interest in fashion and a more polished way of life, which he attempted to carry off with casual nonchalance. It wrote, "Of late he has become quite a dude [a nineteenth-century term for someone who values physical appearance, refined language, and leisurely hobbies], and has cultivated a passionate taste for flowers."[7] The *Lincoln Evening Call* said of Pete's new look, "[He] frequently creates a sensation on the Louisville streets by appearing in dude makeup that would make [celebrated New York socialite] Berry Wall envious."[8] Pete's stylish new look became part of his public persona, but it was purely a cosmetic change. At the end of the day, Pete was the same man he had always been. He "[did] not care much for poetry, theology, or metaphysics"; he liked his drink; and, most importantly, he was still "death on young pitchers."[9]

Once again, rumors of Pete's engagement floated around town. This time, he was reportedly going to marry a relative of William Shakespeare Hays, the renowned poet and songwriter from Louisville. But once again, no wedding took place, and Pete remained a bachelor for the rest of his life, although he had a well-known taste for brothels. *Sporting Life* also reported that Pete was supposed to be joining the bartending fraternity as the central figure in a Louisville barrel shop.[10] But this rumor never came to fruition either.

Pete started the 1886 season with an extended boozy bender. On April 10, following a preseason win over Detroit, Pete celebrated by "indulging in a glorious drunk," imbibing "unknown quantities of intoxicants after the game, and at night spread[ing] terror through the city. His victorious war whoop could be heard for several miles, and so frightened policemen that they took shelter in their hiding-places."[11] Manager Jim Hart tracked him down and fined him $25 on the spot. Pete did not show up for the next day's game against Detroit and was fined another $5. He was later spotted in the stands in tears. Although the monetary punishment meant little to Pete, preventing him from playing baseball cut him deeply. Baseball was his life.

It was an inauspicious start to the season for the reigning AA batting champ. Despite Pete's spectacular 1885 season, Hart was worried that his best hitter would succumb to the same issues that had plagued him in prior years. So Hart warned Pete that he would be fined $50 for his next offense and $100 for the one after that. The local papers were ready to write Pete off, noting, "One drunkard can ruin a whole team, and his example will spread, if not checked. Browning is not indispensable to this club, at any rate, and it is believed, besides that his best days are over."[12] Some thought that the only way Pete could be counted on to show up for games was if the distilleries closed early and forced him to stay home at night.

Meanwhile, the team had added left-handed pitcher Thomas "Toad" Ramsey at the end of the 1885 season. Ramsey had pitched for the Chattanooga Lookouts of the Southern League in 1885, compiling a 17–23 record. Despite losing more games than he won, Ramsey had exhibited moments of brilliance, including a no-hitter on May 30. His addition vastly strengthened the team's pitching roster, but it also added to the team's issues with problem drinkers. Ramsey was described as having "complete control over the ball, and pitches with the utmost ease. [He] possesses all the deceptive curves, and besides, is very speedy."[13] He is often credited as the inventor of the knuckleball, but that is not entirely accurate. Although Ramsey was indeed known for the extreme motion on his drop or sinker ball (partially due to a severed tendon in his index finger that did not allow him to straighten it), a knuckler is characterized by its lack of spin, slow speed, and difficulty to control. In contrast, Ramsey's pitches were known for their impressive movement. His drop ball "broke a foot and half," and he had an "in" curve that "jumped two inches," both delivered with a "shoulder motion [that] was free and easy."[14] At his peak, "he was the terror of the sluggers."[15]

Unfortunately, that peak was short-lived. Like Tony Mullane, Ramsey had the skills to be a generational pitcher and showed flashes of dominance over a two-year period when he won 75 games. However, he then had consecutive seasons with only eight, four, one, and three wins. Ramsey burned out after a six-year career in the majors due to a drinking problem that, in a league of celebrated boozers, was second to none. Ramsey's career was a perfect example of wasted talent. He was expected to "be a tower of strength for the Louisvilles," but his off-field behavior proved to be just another headache for management.[16] Ramsey has been described as "the hardest pitcher to handle that ever pitched. The only system that ever won with him was for the manager to say, 'Toad, you pitch today. After that you can go get drunk and stay drunk until next Thursday when you pitch again.' Then the great twirler would have a glorious three-day jag, sober up, and pitch a wonderful game."[17]

Hart, who suffered many sleepless nights trying to keep tabs on the nocturnal wanderings of his players, reportedly used this management style with Ramsey. For the most part, it was successful. Although Ramsey's out-of-control boozing could not be stopped, it could be curtailed, and he apparently drank less in 1886 than in any other season. The fact that he had a career-high 38 wins and led the AA in innings pitched and complete games lends credence to this belief. It was rumored that when John Kelly managed the team in 1887 and 1888 he took Ramsey to the bar underneath the grandstands on the days he was pitching and served him three "he-man sized" glasses of liquor to properly lubricate him and revive him from his inevitable hangover.[18]

Heading into the 1886 season, Guy Hecker took issue with the team's preseason trips to the South. He believed they were the primary cause of the team's early-season losses. In Hecker's opinion, regular gymnasium practice, combined with some basic on-field practice when the weather was warm, was adequate to prepare for the season. When Hecker got off to a slow start, his opposition to the preseason training regimen was heavily criticized.

Hecker was named team captain, but the local press questioned his leadership skills throughout the season. Yet his teammates had nothing but praise, saying, "Guy Hecker is baseball done up in a single package."[19] When Hecker slumped in the pitching box later in the season, however, an anti-Hecker clique took shape, spurred by the surly Ramsey, who was at odds with the gentlemanly Hecker. Ramsey claimed Hecker was jealous of his success and was spreading rumors about Ramsey's heavy drinking. Hecker didn't have to make up stories about Ramsey's boozing; his troubles were obvious. Ramsey argued that Hecker should be released. That didn't happen, although Hecker was eventually replaced as captain.

The Louisville roster was strong on paper and featured catcher Amos Cross, who was recognized for his strong arm and his unique method of throwing out runners at second. Most catchers stand and "take a step forward to give the arm more momentum as they send the ball down." Amos, "as soon as he caught the ball [would throw] it without moving out of his tracks and nearly always [nail] the runner."[20] The following year Amos was joined on the team by his younger brother Lafayette, better known as Lave. Lave went on to have a 21-year career in which he established himself as one of the game's best all-around players. Tragically, Amos's promising career was cut short when he died in 1888.

Overall, it was believed that the Louisville roster was a significant improvement over the prior season's. "Last year we were weak in batting and base running," said Hart, "but the new men [Bill] White, [Joe] Strauss, [Reddy] Mack, [Joe] Werrick, [Paul] Cook, and [Bones] Ely have strengthened all the weak points."[21] It seemed that such optimistic claims were made every year and never panned out. Despite the talent on the team, it was hampered by off-field distractions and end-of-season slumps.

The local papers claimed that Ramsey and Pete were the only drinkers on the team (not true) and that both had pledged to abstain. This was news to Pete, who had been on a "glorious drunk" a week earlier. Fueling the trouble was the addition of Irish-born second baseman Joseph "Reddy" Mack, who became Ramsey's drinking and nightlife partner. In an effort to control his team, Hart instituted new, stricter rules. Players were required to report each day by 8:00 a.m. and "retire" by 11:00 p.m. He warned, "Drinking players will be heavily fined, and if found incorrigible their salaries will be taken, while the men themselves will be blacklisted, and not released." The local paper supported Hart's plan, stating, "He has the right idea about discipline."[22] Still, team management had made these claims before, with little follow-through, especially when it came to Pete.

Despite his February arrest, Pete seemed to get his excesses under control, and in March the *Courier-Journal* praised his conduct as "particularly commendable."[23] The addition of Ramsey helped Pete's image. Ramsey, whose behavior was called a disgrace, was drunk every day of the team's southern tour and even more out of control than Pete. By comparison, Pete looked utterly angelic.

Yet the 1886 season marked the beginning of a change in the public perception of Pete from a good, solid fielder to an inept, worthless one. Although his defensive play had been criticized in previous seasons, he had more often been recognized for his strong play in the field. Some of the perceptions of Pete's defensive decline were true, however. He was making less of an effort and paying less attention in the field, perhaps because he was too busy calculating his batting average on his sleeves or perhaps because he was hungover. Still, he made some mind-boggling plays, reminding fans of his potential defensive greatness and what he was capable of.

Over the first two months of the season, Pete, who was now hitting cleanup after years of batting leadoff, continued his strong work at the plate from the year before. Yet his off-field actions were starting to overshadow his on-field performance, though sometimes they were good for a laugh. While on a road trip in St. Louis, Pete showed up at the team meal still bleary-eyed from the night before. When the waiter asked what he wanted to eat, Pete squinted at the menu before responding, "I ain't very hungry today. Give me some beaver eggs." The confused waiter responded that they had no beaver eggs. "The hell there ain't," answered Pete, who snatched the menu and emphatically pointed to the word over the wine card: "Beverages."[24] That same trip, Hecker, who roomed with Pete, arrived at the hotel late and sent a waiter into the dining room to inquire what room they had been assigned. Pete grabbed a menu and scribbled on it "Aity Ate." Upon receiving the note, Hecker turned and headed to room 88.[25]

Even though Pete was leading the league in hitting on June 9 with a .373 average and logged a 24-game hitting streak from May 15 to June 12—achievements that would normally put him above reproach—the local papers were in a full-throated scream about his declining skills and poor play in the field. Pete's streak (often incorrectly listed as lasting for 34 games) came to an end in a 4–2 win over Cincinnati when Pete "hit the ball hard and often, but the fielders always managed to capture his long drives."[26] The end of Pete's hitting streak is sometimes attributed not to great fielding or his declining skills but to the loss of a loaded die he kept in the hip pocket of his knickerbockers for luck.

Though reports of Pete's failures were greatly overblown, local sportswriters' concerns about his behavior and its impact on the team were not. On June 27 Pete went 0 for 5 in a 4–3, 11-inning loss to Pittsburgh that also saw him fall down like a "wooden man" while trying to field what turned out to be the game-winning hit. After that game, Pete was suspended indefinitely without pay for "incompetency."[27] His bad behavior off the field and his questionable play on it caused local papers to sarcastically refer to Hart as Pete's "best friend," given the lack of disciplinary action taken against the star player.[28] The *Courier-Journal* published a lengthy piece the same day he was suspended that functioned as an obituary for Pete's career up to that point:

> Wherever baseball is known, Browning's name is a household word. He began playing ball when a mere stripling, and now at twenty-five, he is a broken-down man, as a natural result of his intemperate habits. . . . At the beginning of this year Pete began to decline. He even now stands near the head of the batting list, but his record as a center fielder is the lowest ever known. He is partially deaf, is defective in his eyesight, while he is as stiff and slow as an old man. Pete has lost several games for the club this year, and it was only a matter of dire necessity that he was suspended without pay. Pete for many years has been a great favorite both in Louisville and all over the country. A few think that he will now take care of himself, and soon be the pride of the home team. Manager Hart will give him a chance if he ever demonstrates capability. It is doubtful, however, if Browning will benefit by the lesson administered to him last night, as it is now thought too late, and his best friends think his days of usefulness are numbered.[29]

Pete was not the only one playing poorly and out of control. There had been a "continuous outcry against the loose discipline Manager Hart allowed in the Louisville club" over the first few months of the season. The foremost offender was Ramsey. "He is insolent to everyone," wrote the *Courier-Journal* in May, "and thinks that his services are indispensable. It is well known that he is a champion lusher and has well-nigh demoralized the whole team. The question is how long can this be endured?"[30] At the end of June he went on an extended bender, resulting in no disciplinary action. Instead, Hart and team management tried to whitewash his delinquent behavior and publicly defended him. Ramsey rewarded management's faith by "masquerading with a strawberry blond on Green Street until 4 o'clock in the morning."[31] Ramsey's late-night carousing clearly had a negative impact, as the next day he was "not sober when the game was called" and "was wild in his throwing, and listless in his playing."[32] In Ramsey's defense, the good times had started earlier in the day at a team fish fry, and the surly pitcher was not the only player to show up for the next day's game less than sober. Hart maintained his timid stance toward disciplining the team. Team president Zach Phelps finally stepped in, demanding that players totally abstain from the use of intoxicants, as provided in their contracts. There were mutterings against enforcement of the rule, but Phelps assured the players that he meant what he said.

Louisville was not the only team with drunken players, although Browning and Ramsey were two of the most notorious. Two of the team's best players were also two of its biggest headaches. Whereas Louisville did little to curb the players' excesses, other teams tried a variety of methods to rein in their players' drinking. While managing the NL's Philadelphia club, Hall of Famer Harry Wright went so far as to hire private detectives to watch the players and make sure they weren't drinking. Still, the hard-living, hard-drinking lifestyles of baseball players presented a conundrum: how did management curb the alcoholic excesses of its players without benching the best players on the team? This dilemma led to inconsistent enforcement of the rules, as management punished and suspended lesser players while looking the other way when stars misbehaved.

Pete's indefinite suspension for incompetent play lasted all of three games, and he returned on July 1. He batted ninth and went 1 for 4 with a triple in a 14–2 win over visiting Brooklyn. The following day, in a 15–7 loss to Brooklyn, Pete played "in the most discerptible style, and piled up errors until the spectators lost all sympathy."[33] Frustration with Pete was boiling over among fans, the press, and team management. Over the next two games he went 0 for 8 and was benched for the second game of a doubleheader on July 5 after playing a "rotten game" in the opener.[34] It was the last game he played for a month, as he was suspended the next day. "It is plainly evident to everybody here that, apart from his disposition to drink hard, Browning is physically unable to play ball," wrote the *Sporting News*.[35] He watched the game from the stands, commenting on the play and telling a nearby reporter he would give $5 to be in the game.

Pete left the next day for the West Baden Hot Springs in French Lick, Indiana, to rest, renew, and sober up. At the time, he was seventh in the league in hitting. Originally, his suspension was supposed to last only two weeks, but it was extended. A reporter from the *Sporting News* visited Pete and interviewed him at West Baden. Pete apparently had a hard time drinking the water, as he was unaccustomed to that beverage, so "he had the picture of a distillery hung in his room, [and] it seemed to afford him much pleasure." The reporter found Pete in good spirits and preparing for a return in August. Pete struck an optimistic tone, saying the rest had done him a "world of good" and he would be batting and fielding in his "old style" when he returned.[36]

While Pete was away, Pittsburgh expressed an interest in obtaining his services and offered $500 for them. The sportswriters in Louisville would have been happy to see him go. When it was rumored that Pittsburgh manager Horace Phillips was in Louisville looking to sign him, the *Courier-Journal* wrote with a palpable sense of exasperation, "For heaven's sake take him along."[37] Pete was adamant that he did not want to leave Louisville. He even claimed to have heart disease and warned he might die if he moved away from home. A more plausible explanation is that Pete was uncomfortable in new situations due to his worsening hearing and did not want to leave the comforts of home, where people understood his needs and limitations. The rumored move did not happen, and Phillips later claimed, "The Louisville club [wanted] the earth for him."[38]

Pete finally returned to the field after missing 22 games. In his absence, his teammates went 17–5, including having their best road trip of the season (8–3). Hart said, "The rest of the boys naturally joshed him a good deal about it, and gleefully referred to their splendid record while he was away." Pete, reluctant to admit he had no role in the team's success, claimed he had scratched out a baseball diamond in the dirt behind his hotel, and on game days he went through his good-luck routine of touching third base, thereby influencing the team's wins.

Upon his return, Pete said he felt "as new as a school boy" and quickly returned to his dominant form of years past.[39] In his first appearance on August 5, he played a first-class game in the field and went 1 for 3 at the plate. This proved to be only the prelude to what Pete would accomplish. After a rain-shortened game on August 7, he exploded. The following day in front of a home crowd estimated at 4,000, he logged his first career cycle—hitting a single, double, triple, and home run in the same game. It was the eleventh cycle in major league history at the time but only the second natural cycle, meaning that the single, double, triple, and home run happened in that order. As of 2021 there had been 334 cycles, but only 17 were natural cycles. The local papers gushed with praise: "This is a glorious record of ten bases per game and is unexcelled for the number of times at the bat."[40]

A batting race was developing between Pete and Hecker, and ten days later Hecker went 6 for 7, with three home runs and seven runs scored. He also pitched a complete game, a four-hitter, in the 22–5 win over Baltimore. Hecker became the first pitcher to hit three home runs in a game—a feat equaled only once when Boston's Jim Tobin did so in 1942. Hecker's seven runs scored in a game is still the record today.

In the next four games after his cycle, Pete came back with a vengeance, going 11 for 21, including a triple and two doubles, and erasing the memory of his month at the hot springs. The praise poured in. "Louis Rodgers [*sic*] Browning the reformed man is doing some tall batting," hailed the *Courier-Journal*. "Seven hits in two games . . . is about as effective work with the bat as any man was ever known to do."[41] His work with the bat was also applauded by *Sporting Life:* "It is worth the price of admission to see Browning make some of his long, low, terrific drives. He usually begins with a few long fouls which strike the fence with enough force to tear off a plank and then whacks the ball for three bases."[42]

Brooklyn player Ed Swartwood, who had edged out Pete for the 1883 batting title, called him "the greatest batter on the diamond" and declared, "He is hard to fool, has a long reach, and plenty of strength to back it."[43] Swartwood predicted Pete would overtake teammate Hecker, who was leading the league in batting at the time, and win the title at the end of the season.

Pete's hot play drew interest from Baltimore, and rumors of a trade involving Joe Sommer surfaced in the papers every few days. Sommer had played with the semipro Louisville Eclipse during the 1881 season after the NL dropped his Cincinnati team for refusing to ban alcohol sales in league parks. When Cincinnati joined the AA as the Reds in 1882, Sommer rejoined that team. He ended up in Baltimore when he tried to hasten the departure of John "Pop" Corkhill and Chick Fulmer from the Reds in 1883. The Reds were not happy with Sommer's underhandedness and shipped him, along with teammate and fellow schemer Jimmy Macullar, off to Baltimore. As discussion of a potential trade heated up, it was suggested that Pete and Sommer would be part of a three-way swap that would send Pete to Baltimore and Sommer to Louisville; then Louisville would trade Sommer back to the Reds in exchange for outfielder Corkhill. The proposed trade seemed unlikely, as Pete, who was on fire at the plate, was allegedly going to be traded for two players who were defensive standouts but accomplishing little with the bat. Sommer set the record for the lowest single-season batting average by a player with more than 500 at-bats (since broken) in 1886, hitting an anemic .209. In mid-September Baltimore papers reported that the deal had been finalized, with the Orioles now receiving second baseman Reddy Mack in addition to Pete. Despite constant speculation, the deal never materialized, and Pete remained with Louisville.

After being bashed by the local papers for weeks, Pete finally won them over with his hot hitting. "Despite the opposition to Pete he continues to be one of the most valuable men in the Louisville club," conceded the *Courier-Journal.* "He led the battery on the Eastern trip, and now on the home grounds promises to make Hecker, Orr, and O'Neil work like beavers to keep him from winning the Association batting honors for the third time. Browning may be a fielder of the most indifferent type, but his value to the club lies in another sphere. The talk of his release is folly."[44] His stellar batting was not going unnoticed nationally, as the *Sporting News* declared, "A few weeks since the Louisville management would have traded Browning for Joe Sommer. Now they would not trade the warhorse for the whole Baltimore club."[45]

Even with Pete's magnificent play, the team was still a streaky mess, and once again it ended the season disastrously. Between July 4 and August 22, Louisville won 28 of 35 games. Then it managed only 6 victories while dropping 30 games, including 7- and 13-game losing streaks and losses in its final 6 games. Pete's glorious play at the plate was countered by his return to "speculating in rye and corn" and a seemingly endless string of intoxicated jaunts around town.[46] "Browning is doing extensive business with the willow," wrote the *Sporting News.* "It is also alleged that he again gazes frequently upon the beer when it is amber colored."[47]

The team's poor play was attributed to the off-field behavior of its two biggest stars and inept management. "Jim Hart can't handle his men properly," wrote the *Courier-Journal* after a 7–6 loss to Brooklyn in which Louisville outhit the opponent but committed eight errors. As the season fell apart, a longtime Louisville baseball observer who had "seen the game rise from a crude imperfect sport to the dignity of a scientific pastime" remarked, "Browning could easily be the greatest player on the diamond, but he is allowed to get drunk. Ramsey is the greatest pitcher in the world, but his vicious habits are given free reign [*sic*] and allowed to run riot; the result is that he is a wreck . . . while the rest of the men do as they please."[48] A truer assessment could not have been spoken.

Louisville's season mercifully came to an end with a 66–70 record and a fourth-place finish, 22½ games behind the first-place St. Louis Browns. It was the team's second straight year under .500. Louisville's up-and-down season is represented by two bizarre plays. On August 22, in a home game versus Cincinnati, Louisville picked up the win on an eleventh-inning inside-the-park home run by Chicken Wolf, aided by a small dog that ran on the field and kept interfering with center fielder Abner Powell as he attempted to retrieve the ball and throw Wolf out as he rounded the bases. The other play took place on September 5 during a home against St. Louis when Pete was tagged out in a rare unassisted pickoff by pitcher Dave Foutz. Pete, who had taken a healthy lead off first base, had his back turned toward second base and was staring at first baseman Charles Comiskey as he "pranced back and forth to show the crowd that he was not afraid to steal off a bag."[49] Foutz, seeing that Browning was not paying attention, dashed over from the pitching box and tagged him out before Pete knew what was happening.

Pete hoped to find solace in his individual accomplishments, and when *Sporting Life* released its end-of-season statistics, it had Pete at the top of the batting leaderboard, one point above Hecker. The *Courier-Journal* said that although *Sporting Life*'s figures "may not exactly tally with those of [AA] President [Wheeler] Wikoff, [they] are probably about correct."[50] Given the tight race for the batting title between Hecker and Pete, no one knew who was actually on top for a few weeks. When the AA finally released its official statistics, it told a different story. Atop the leaderboard was New York's Dave Orr with a .346 average, followed by Hecker and St. Louis's Bob Caruthers at .342. Pete and St. Louis's Tip O'Neill were tied for third at .339. Decades later, as statisticians researched and corrected baseball records for inclusion in the *Baseball Encyclopedia,* they revised the averages for 1886. Their new statistics put Hecker on top with a .342 average, followed by Pete (.340), Orr (.338), Caruthers (.334), and O'Neill (.328). Additional research put Hecker's league-leading average at .341. But there was controversy over Hecker's first-place finish. As a pitcher, he was not an everyday player, and even though he occasionally played first base, Hecker appeared in only 84 games (with 378 plate appearances), well below the 100-game standard used by the *Spalding Baseball Guide,* the premier baseball publication of the era, for inclusion on its leaderboard. By comparison, even with the 25 games Pete missed due to his suspensions, he still logged 28 more games and 126 more plate appearances than Hecker. Regardless, Hecker is now recognized as the batting leader for the 1886 season, making him the only player in history to win both the triple crown of pitching and a batting title. Hecker's win denied Pete a shot at consecutive batting titles and his third crown in five years. Pete's only honor was the dubious distinction of being the only player to lose a batting title to a pitcher.

For Pete, his second-place finish raises the question of what if? How different would his career legacy have been if he had four career titles, with back-to-back titles in 1885 and 1886? He lost to Hecker by less than one percentage point. If he had gotten just one more hit, one more of what Kevin Costner's character Crash Davis famously calls "a gork, a ground ball—a ground ball with eyes, a dying quail" in the classic baseball movie *Bull Durham,* he would have surpassed Hecker. Football is said to be a game of inches, but for Pete, inches might have made the difference between three batting titles and four. One "ground ball with eyes" that snuck through the infield and Pete would have won back-to-back titles. But even with a second-place finish, Pete's season was remarkable, especially considering his monthlong suspension. His second-place finish in 1886 was his fifth straight finish in the top three and fourth overall in the top two. He also finished fourth in OBP, fifth in slugging, and, despite missing 25 games, fifth in doubles.

The 1886 season also marked a turning point for Pete, as he seemed to have lost all interest in the defensive side of the game. In his second full season in the outfield, he led all outfielders in errors and posted a miserable .791 fielding percentage, well below the league average of .906. Still, as Pete made abundantly clear, he was there to hit the ball, not to shag flies and run down grounders.

The 1886 season also marked a turning point for Pete and his drinking. While he had long been a heavy drinker and regularly showed up to games drunk and hungover, there had been few consequences for his behavior. That changed in 1886, as he was hit with the first extended suspension of his career, and the local sporting press was no longer willing to ignore his problems. The *Sporting News* summed it up best: "No matter whether Pete Browning loves the bottle or the bottle loves Pete, he is still hitting the ball for all it's worth."[51]

The Gladiator (1887)

After the end of the 1886 season, Pete was holding court with fans on a street corner in downtown Louisville, "musing quietly over the glory of the ballfield and the inestimable laurels that he won on the green diamond." While Pete was waxing philosophical on past achievements, a sports reporter for the local *Courier-Journal* walked by. "Say, look here," bellowed Pete at the passing scribe, who stopped in his tracks. "Do you know that the newspapers have not treated me squarely? I stand at the head of the batters of the Asociashun again, but I ain't seen my photegraf in the papers yit. I'm going to make a quiet kick. You know it ain't treating a man fair, considerin' the amusement I have given the people who like the nashun'l game." Pete was proved wrong on one point a few weeks later when teammate Guy Hecker was named AA batting champion, but that was the least of his complaints. Pete craved the adoration of fans and the press and was more than a little annoyed when he didn't get the coverage he thought he deserved, especially as he (rightly) believed he was head and shoulders above the rest of the hitters in the AA. Pete continued, "These common players can't bat. Look at me! I beat 'em all this year and didn't half try. You know I was sick half this season, and then downed the sluggers like babies. It takes a man to play ball. . . . I'm the lad that can line 'em out to center field. You just say ter-morrer that Petey can give 'em all lessons when it comes to playin' ball."[1]

Pete's rant exposed his capricious relationship with the local papers and his combative attitude toward the press. "Pietro is like the politician who went to the editor and said, 'Write what you please about me. I don't care what you write, just so as you write something,'" observed the

Cincinnati Enquirer in 1891. "He didn't want to be ignored. Neither does the Gladiator. The Gladiator has been misrepresented and maligned frequently. He has been the victim of many a joke and the central figure in many an escapade, but many of the stories in print about him had their foundation only in the mind of the person who wrote them."[2] The press could be Pete's biggest fan and sing his praises but then turn against the mercurial star in an instant. For Pete and his fragile ego, this was too much, especially after he built up some liquid courage. The *Courier-Journal* reported on the exchange between Pete and its reporter the following day and went on to observe, "[Pete] takes notoriously poor care of himself, and has strong proclivities to strong drink, but even when handicapped he is the king ball player. Pete is 28 [actually, he was 26] years old and has played ball all his life. He was laid off twice during the past season on account of bad physical condition, but he triumphed as usual in the end."[3]

Some of the surliness Pete exhibited can be attributed, like many issues in his life, to the ongoing effects of mastoiditis. A common symptom is increased irritability, which Pete displayed both on and off the field.[4] Of course, Pete's drinking also contributed to his irritability. But no matter how bad Pete's drinking and off-field behavior got, it was hard to argue with the results he achieved on the diamond. The first five years of his career put him firmly in contention for best hitter of the decade, along with Cap Anson and Dan Brouthers.

Following his second-place finish behind Hecker in the contest for batting title in 1886, Pete spent the off-season at the nearby hot springs preparing for his sixth season, which was arguably the greatest statistical outing of his career. He set career highs in batting average (.402), slugging (.547), OPS (1.011), runs scored (137), hits (220), total bases (299), triples (16), RBIs (118), and runs created (137), yet he didn't lead the league in any of these categories. Pete ran up against the even better year of James Edward "Tip" O'Neill, known for his ability to stay alive at the plate by fouling off pitches until he got one he liked. O'Neill is one of the greatest Canadian players in the history of the game, capturing back-to-back batting titles in 1887 and 1888.

The statistics of batters like Pete and O'Neill were greatly influenced by several rule changes enacted in 1887 to stimulate hitting. Most prominently, batters were aided by the change from three to four strikes for an out (it reverted to three strikes the following season) and five balls for a walk. More curious was the decision to count a walk as both a hit and a time at bat, which created some interesting stat lines. On April 27, in a 5–0 loss to Cincinnati, Pete's batting average for the game was 1.000, yet he didn't get a hit. He stepped up to the plate four times and was hit by pitcher Tony Mullane once and walked three times. The rule lasted for only one season, but it had a significant effect on batting averages. Having an even greater impact, though often overlooked, were changes in the pitching rules.

For the first time, the pitcher was required to start his delivery with one foot on the back line of the pitcher's box. Prior to 1887, the pitcher could take as many steps as he wanted before delivering the ball to the batter, as long as he remained in the pitcher's box. The front line of the pitching box was a mere 50 feet from home plate, while the back line was 55½ feet from home. By requiring the pitcher to keep his rear foot on the back line of the box, the first standard pitching distance was established. For pitchers, this was a tremendous adjustment; rather than getting a running start, they had to throw the ball from a stationary position, and it had to travel 5½ feet further to reach home plate. The changes in distance and delivery were not the only ones that affected pitchers. In 1887 the pitcher was required to present the ball to the batter before delivering it to home plate, with a pause before each pitch, pickoff attempt, or fake pickoff attempt. In addition, the strike zone was established, extending from the batter's knees to the shoulders, and batters were no longer able to call for high or low pitches. These changes created a monstrous offensive season the likes of which had never been seen before. For the first time, two hitters would reach the fabled .400 plateau in the same year—one of only five times in MLB history that a season produced multiple .400 hitters.

When asked about the new rules' impact on hitters, St. Louis Browns pitcher George "Jumbo" McGinnis, the first ace of the fabled franchise, thought that of all the batters in the AA, Pete would handle the changes best. "Pete don't seem to care a cent whether the ball is up under his chin or down in the neighborhood of his ankles," he explained. "He'll paste it in the nose just the same. I've tried harder to fool this man than any other batter I ever faced, but he cannot be fooled. . . . Dave Orr of the Mets is very hard to 'draw on,' but as I said before Pete has the quickest eye in the American Association."[5]

Proving McGinnis right, Pete seemed unfazed when asked about the new rules. "No, they won't hurt me however, for I can hit any kind of ball—high or low. But the new rules will save a good many players from being fined, for hereafter when a man who always bats a high ball chances to strike at a low one, the manager can't yell out, 'Ten dollars!'"[6]

Louisville entered the 1887 season with a new manager. The ineffectual Jim Hart, who had guided the team to consecutive losing seasons, was replaced by John "Kick" Kelly. Kelly had a brief career as a player, lasting only 16 games over one season, but his most important contribution to baseball was as an umpire. Known as "Honest John," he helped develop the modern role of the umpire. When he retired, he held the record for most games umpired in the major leagues, with 587. He was coaxed to take over the reins of the Louisville team in 1887 but did not give up his other role entirely, umpiring the 15-game World Series at the end of the season. Some were surprised that Kelly accepted the job of managing the club. Longtime baseball fixture O. P. Caylor, who worked as both a manager and a sportswriter, speculated that if umpires were paid better, Kelly "would have been umpiring this season instead of chasing Ramsey and Browning away from the dangerous localities of red lights."[7] Oddly enough, Kelly believed the new rules instituted in 1887 would actually aid pitchers and not increase batting averages.

The Louisville organization put tremendous faith in Kelly, giving him exclusive authority to impose fines, decide who would be released, and designate the positions of all the players. Kelly's power to control the roster and dispense discipline was greater than that of any other manager in the country, and the hope was that he could get the most out of the talented but poorly behaved team. His objective was to rein in the players' worst impulses and avoid the headaches caused by their drinking. He also planned to implement an enthusiastic and lively "hurrah" approach, informing the team, "When the bell taps for a game the players will run out to their positions and when the contest ends they will run back." This idea was based on the "dash and vim" style of play of the NL champion Chicago White Stockings. Kelly believed that "this spirit not only pleases the audiences, but also gives the men confidence in themselves."[8]

Kelly planned to have a roster of 14 when the season started, which seems minuscule compared to modern rosters and their conveyor belts of pitchers. Pete, holding court in Hecker's sporting goods store and fashionably attired in a green suit, a tie emblazoned with a gold letter *B*, and a gaudy silk handkerchief stuck jauntily in his coat pocket, was asked about the new skipper. He replied, "Kelly and I always get along friendly. If he gets down on me, I'll take him out and get him drunk. No man is worth a cent if he doesn't get drunk once in a while."[9] Pete claimed Kelly tried to motivate the team with some pretty persuasion, promising "a new suit of clothes and a five-gallon keg of whiskey" for each player if the team won the championship.[10]

Louisville opened the season on a high note with an 8–3 win over the St. Louis Browns, the defending AA and World Series champions. They were led by Toad Ramsey, who pitched a strong game and got two hits, and Pete, who helped put the game away in the seventh inning with a two-RBI double. This win stirred the emotions of the Louisville faithful, who thought this might be their season. Predictably, Louisville returned to earth, losing the next two games against St. Louis.

As was often the case with Pete, highs and lows went hand in hand. Following an early season 8–4 win over Cincinnati that pushed Louisville's record to 7–4, one game out of first, Pete celebrated by doing a somersault and hurt himself when he landed on his back. Despite fears that he might have to miss multiple games, Pete, bad back and all, played a remarkable game in center field the next day, making a number of brilliant catches and going 3 for 4 with a double at the plate. A few days later, on the evening of May 9, police were summoned when Pete created a disturbance while riding a streetcar at the corner of Thirteenth and Walnut Streets. He persisted in trying to pay the fare with a check, which was not allowed after 6:00 p.m. When police arrived, he was arrested for public drunkenness and refusing to pay his fare. Pete claimed he was not drunk but was under the influence of quinine, an antimalaria drug, and said he had witnesses who could attest to his sobriety. Pete was fined $5 for drunkenness and disorderly conduct, given a lecture on the evils of intemperance by the judge, and ordered to keep the peace for six months. Despite Pete's promise to conduct himself temperately, Kelly fined him for being out at such a late hour. Still smelling of booze, Pete responded by going 0 for 5 the next day in a 10–5 win over Philadelphia.

Pete recovered and reeled off a 14-game hitting streak to close out May. After a one-game skid, he followed up with a 40-game hitting streak that included 15 doubles, three triples, two home runs, and a stretch of 10 of 14 games with an extra-base hit. His 40-game streak was interrupted after 36 games, when he missed two games with an injury, but upon his return he hit safely in four more games. Even with the new rule that counted a walk as a hit, Pete continued his aggressive approach at the plate, always swinging away. "I never saw Browning do anything but hit," praised the *Courier-Journal.*[11]

Even with his stellar hitting, Pete continued to stumble off the field. On July 11 he and Wolf had been excused from practice to attend a local picnic. Wolf conducted himself in a reserved manner, but Pete got howling drunk. The *St. Louis Globe Democrat* blamed Pete's behavior on a poor sense of direction, claiming he got lost on the way to the picnic and "made several stops in bar-rooms to inquire. He stopped too often and by noon was drunk as a lord."[12] After the picnic Pete did not want the good times to end, so he headed out, "painting the town all Monday night."[13] He failed to report for practice the next morning. Kelly fined him $110 and warned that if it happened again, the fine would be doubled.

Prior to the debacle at the picnic, Kelly had been hesitant to punish Pete, as he was playing well, so the manager had always let him off with a warning and extracted a promise that he would behave better next time. "It is Browning's misfortune that he can get drunk one night and play good ball the next day," wrote the *Courier-Journal.* "His bad habits do not seem to interfere in the least with his work. The moral effect is bad however."[14] Time after time, Pete proved that he was not worried about the moral effect, and the team was often willing to overlook his behavior off the field as long as he played well on it. The local paper saddled him with the nickname "Mr. Pete Brownjug Browning" and warned that he and fellow boozer Reddy Mack "had better wake up and look to their laurels."[15]

In an effort to scare Pete sober, one night while he was out "clinking glasses," Kelly and a few of his teammates broke into his room and redecorated it. "From the ceiling we hung bats, stuffed owls, Chinese dragons with green eyes, paper boa constrictors, and skulls," explained Kelly. "Then we got a lot of toy animals, painted the elephants pink, the giraffes purple, and the lions gaslight green, and arranged them in a wonderful parade that began at the keyhole of the door and ran along the footboard of his bed. We got a couple of dark lanterns with green and red flashes and then we rounded up Pete and put him to bed in the dark." After letting Pete get a few hours of sleep, Kelly and his teammates woke him up by making as much noise as possible. As the lantern lights flashed, Pete got glimpses of the "improvised inferno" in his room and turned a little gray.[16] Kelly said his plan worked, at least for a while. Pete, who thought the scene in his room was an alcohol-induced hallucination, refrained from drinking for a short time.

Much like Pete, who excelled on the field despite his drunken transgressions off it, Ramsey was on his way to a 37-win, 355-strikeout season, good for second and first place in the AA, respectively. He had a number of memorable games, including retiring the Brooklyn side on three consecutive pitches in the fifth inning on May 25, "when he made the batters who faced him look ridiculous"; a 16-strikeout outing against St. Louis on June 30; and an even more impressive 17-strikeout game on June 21 in a 21–1 whitewashing of Cleveland.[17] Despite the positivity generated by Ramsey's performance and the win against Cleveland, the *Pittsburgh Chronicle* reported that Kelly was contemplating resigning. Like Hart, Kelly found the Louisville team an unmanageable bunch who spent as much time pushing back against discipline as they did preparing to play ball. Louisville was in the bottom half of the standings, one game below .500, and the players expressed more interest in drinking than winning. The *Chronicle* wrote, "[Kelly] claims he cannot make his men play good ball. It is probably a case of boycott by the players, who have been thumbscrewed and tied down by John until they have secretly revolted."[18] A headline in the *Courier-Journal* summed up the frustration: "The Louisvilles Losing Games with Exasperating Regularity."[19]

One bright spot came on June 24, when Louisville finally got the best of longtime tormentor Mullane and knocked him out of the game after four innings, getting ten runs off him on the way to a nail-biting 10–9 win over Cincinnati. A month earlier the *Courier-Journal* had written: "The Louisville Club has an extensive reputation for playing a most uncertain game of ball. One day the men will work with a fiery enthusiasm, coach like wild men, and field in faultless style; but the very next contest the men will probably play like sleepy heads, and pile up more errors than any amateur club in the country. Manager Kelly says that he cannot account for this state of affairs but affirms that the club's reputation is founded on truth."[20] Kelly hoped to improve the team's lackadaisical attitude by encouraging the players to be more aggressive. "Louisville has the reputation of being the quietest club on earth, and I want the boys to change their tactics," he explained. "They never kick when the umpire gives it to them. That ain't right. Whenever they see an umpire trying to give 'em the cheese they're going to march right up and kick."[21]

By mid-July, Kelly's motivational style was starting to work. The team found its footing and was playing the best ball of the year. Pete was performing spectacularly. Following a 5–4 win over rival Cincinnati in which Pete dominated, going 2 for 4 with a triple, two runs scored, a stolen base, and a couple of defensive gems in center field that saved runs, the *Courier-Journal* adoringly called him "The Old War Horse." The moniker was quickly adopted and added to Pete's growing list of nicknames. Pete was only 26 and far from the oldest player on the team (that was Hecker, at 31), but the nickname spoke to the perception that he had been around baseball for a long time, having first achieved national recognition as a teenager before making his professional debut at 20.

Louisville went 17–8 in July and then started August with a 7–3 record. "Second," proclaimed the *Courier-Journal,* "that's where yesterday's victory over the tail-enders placed the Kentucky team. Two months ago the Louisvilles were struggling along in sixth place, with gloomy prospects for the future, but Tom Ramsey, Guy Hecker, Pete Browning, Reddy Mack and the rest of the nine swore by the whiskers of the great prophet that they would do better." It was a remarkable turnaround for the team, but it still faced an uphill battle, trailing the streaking St. Louis Browns by 12½ games. Kelly's winning smile after defeating Cleveland 7–1 on August 6 "bespoke victory, fine weather, and fair sailing for the Louisville club."[22]

Kelly's smile proved premature, as the high times did not last. Even as the team was reeling off a six-game winning streak to close out August, the club's annual tumble in the standings was already being touted in the papers. "Will history repeat itself and the Louisville club go to pieces?" questioned the *Courier-Journal.* "Will the collapse come?"[23] Though the team managed to avoid a complete collapse, its hot play cooled off, leading to a 14–16–2 record over the remainder of the season. The team's poor play coincided with Pete's return to some serious boozing. He had been relatively sober during the preceding month, raising a chicken-or-egg question that plagued Pete's entire career. Was the team's poor play caused by his increased drinking? Or did his drinking increase because of the team's poor play? On August 25, in a 15–8 loss to Philadelphia, Pete was obviously still saturated with whiskey and clearly had not sobered up from his "debauch" the night before. He fell down twice in the field while chasing fly balls and struck out three times at the plate. Kelly fined him $50 and threatened to suspend him for the remainder of the year if things did not improve. It was a troubling trend, as ever since the Louisville club had moved into second place, Pete was "spreeing frequently, keeping irregular hours, and indulging in bad company."[24]

For fans in Louisville, it was another frustrating year as the team's late-season nosedive left them wondering, what if? They watched other teams in the league improve from year to year, while Louisville stayed in the middle of the pack, never terrible but never great either. Local sportswriters took a different view of the team's lackluster end-of-season play. While they heaped blame on the team owners, poor off-field decisions by Pete and Ramsey, and a multitude of other factors, they also held the fans accountable, noting, "Louisville is a poor ball town, and has too great a club to be playing to small crowds." When rumors surfaced in August that the team would be sold, the *Courier-Journal* speculated, "What a fine drawing card, for instance, would the present Louisville Club be if it were planted in New York city! It would prove a gold mine to the stockholders. The team compares favorably with the League club of that city, while Ramsey, Hecker, Browning, Kerins, and the rest would create the greatest enthusiasm."[25]

Even with all the distractions, many of them self-imposed, Pete continued to murder the ball, proving that "whatever may be his shortcomings, Pete never forgets that he is a slugger."[26] With a drink in his hand and a drunken stagger in his step, Pete got his swagger back. In an 11–9 win over Brooklyn on August 28 in which he laced five hits, Pete sauntered over to Brooklyn manager Charles Byrne and asked to borrow a chew of "old Virginia twist." Byrne was clearly irritated by the question and Pete's cocksure manner and replied indignantly that he "didn't use the damned stuff in any shape or form."[27]

On a road trip at the end of July, Pete, whose confidence was in overdrive, warned O'Neill, who was leading the AA in batting, "Say, Tip old man, I'll make you hustle 'fore the season's over; I'm hitting big."[28] Pete's swagger was warranted, as he clubbed 15 hits over the final four games in August and moved up to third in the AA in batting. Pete even revealed to a Chicago sportswriter the secret to his success at the plate. "When men fight, they look each other in the eye, don't they," Pete lectured the attentive writer. "Now, when I bat, I watch the pitcher's eyes and I can tell where he's going to pitch the ball. It works first rate. I'm lining the ball out for all it's worth, and the pitchers can't understand it."[29]

At the end of August, after Pete had posted another remarkable month at the plate, Kelly remarked, "See what you can do when you take care of yourself old man." "That's right," Pete replied, "Old Petie can line 'em out when he's in shape."[30] Of course, Pete was not really taking better care of himself. On August 21, after Ramsey pitched Louisville to an 8–3 win over Baltimore, he and Pete celebrated with an all-night bender. The win was special to Ramsey because he had defeated Matt Kilroy, who was challenging Ramsey for pitching supremacy in the AA. At the end of the year they finished first and second in almost every important pitching category, with Kilroy topping Ramsey in everything but strikeouts, where Ramsey outpaced Kilroy 355 to 217. Kilroy and Ramsey had been battling it out since the previous season, when they finished first and second in strikeouts—Kilroy's 513 is still the record, and Ramsey's 499 is still good for second place. As a reward for their all-night binge, Pete was slapped with a $50 fine and Ramsey was hit with an indefinite suspension. Ramsey returned August 31 but pitched only two innings due to a sore arm. Ramsey, who had been a workhorse and overused all season, finally broke down and sat out for a week before returning to action and posting a five-game winning streak.

Even with his hot bat, Pete was never a serious threat to overtake O'Neill, who was having the best year of his career. Both men's impressive seasons are often viewed as statistical anomalies due to the odd rules implemented in 1887. They finished the year with O'Neill hitting .495 and Pete hitting .421. Years later, their batting averages were adjusted to .435 and .402, respectively, by removing the walks counted as hits. Still, they are two of the most impressive seasons in the history of baseball. Pete finished the year with career highs in a number of categories yet finished no better than second behind O'Neill's slugging average (.691), hits (225), and runs (167). This was the second consecutive year Pete lost the AA batting title in odd fashion. He was just a whisker away from winning three consecutive batting crowns.

Louisville finished fourth, the same as the year before, although Kelly coached the team to a ten-win improvement over the prior year. St. Louis captured its third straight title, finishing 14 games ahead of second-place Cincinnati. Louisville's better win record was not the only thing Kelly was praised for; he was credited with playing a role in Pete's success as well. Kelly exerted an almost fatherly influence. On the road, he kept an eye on Pete after games, and when he seemed headed for the bottle, Kelly would place a stern hand on his shoulder and, with a few quiet words in his ear, steer Pete away from trouble. "John Kelly can do more with Pete

Browning than any other manager," wrote the *Courier-Journal*. "Pete has been intoxicated fewer times this season than in any other year."[31]

Pete's exceptional hitting was no surprise, but he also led the team on the base paths. The *Courier-Journal* noted that he "continues to pilfer bases with the same astonishing regularity that he lines out base hits." Pete swiped 103 bases, finishing fourth in the AA in steals and posting his best single-season steal total.[32] Even so, local sportswriters criticized his baserunning and refusal to slide. Although O'Neill led the way in every major hitting category, Pete's work with the bat and on the base paths placed him in rarefied company. He became one of only three players in MLB history with 50 or more extra-base hits and 90 or more stolen bases in a season, along with Tom Brown in 1891 and Tim Raines in 1983. And he was one of only three players with 220+ hits, 55+ extra-base hits, and 55+ stolen bases, joining Ty Cobb, who accomplished the feat three times in 1911, 1912, and 1917, and Jose Altuve in 2014.

Louisville's collapse, which saw the team drop from second to fourth place over the final month of the season, led the *Globe Democrat* to write, "Louisville cannot hope to win the pennant race until it purges its team of the drunkards, who are a great drawback to its success." This assessment was proved accurate when Pete indulged in an extended multiday bender to close out the season. He actually started the bender a few days before the end of the season in St. Louis. After the team's last game there, he proceeded to get massively drunk and refused to travel home with the team. He missed the next day's game and was expected to miss the final game of the year, but he made it back from St. Louis on his own and took the field to jeering and hissing from the crowd. After the game he left the grounds, "got out his bucket of paint," and proceeded to paint the town, driving up the street in a carriage and stopping at every saloon along the way.[33] At 9:00 p.m. he was in the East End with a baseball bat in hand, belligerent and crying because he was not at the top of the AA batting list.

A few days later, Pete played in a charity game and then got hammered again. He was found wandering the streets of downtown Louisville, asking police officers for protection and claiming, in his drunken stupor, that O'Neill was threatening his life and pursuing him with a knife (O'Neill was 250 miles away in St. Louis at the time). The police took pity on the well-lubricated Pete and did not arrest him. The headline in the *Courier-Journal* summed up Pete's state of mind, simply calling it "A Lively Imagination."[34] The *Globe Democrat* could not resist taking a shot at Pete, remarking, "Now, only if O'Neill would scare the Detroits, and not a worn-out Louisville player, the Browns might win something."[35]

Pete's drunken run-in with the specter of O'Neill was not his last public misadventure of the year. Pete and Ramsey, who had the reputation as "the greatest lushers in the base ball profession,"[36] hired horses and a buggy to take them to New Albany, Indiana, just over the river from Louisville, to call on a lady friend of Pete's. As they set off from the stable, Pete suggested they "get their load on the Kentucky side, because Indiana tangle-foot always made him see large animals, while the bluegrass fluid reduced the size of the carnivora very materially." By the time they neared the river, "they were both willing to run for president." Pete then made the sage decision to stop for one more drink before continuing on their journey. While the two were enjoying some of Kentucky's finest "tonsil varnish," drunkenly complimenting each other on being the best pitcher and best center fielder in the world, former Louisville manager Mike Walsh walked by the establishment and noticed their horses and buggy parked outside. Walsh was a painter at a local carriage shop and happened to have some paint with him. He proceeded to paint the horses' ribs in alternating red and green stripes. He planned to paint the buggy too, but the besotted players "decided to give up their sour mash for their sweet mash over the river" and headed out of the saloon. Walsh hustled around the corner to avoid being seen. He thought the pair would be too embarrassed to drive the gaudily painted horses and would head home, so he was astonished when they unhitched the horses, climbed into the buggy, and continued their journey. As they crossed into New Albany, Pete and Ramsey were blissfully unaware of the state of their horses, despite the curious crowd that was now following them. As the crowd grew, so did the two men's egos. "They all know me," gushed Pete to his drinking partner.

"Me too, Petah," slurred Ramsey.

"Yeah, they know us," Pete agreed.[37]

Upon arriving at the young lady's mansion, the well-sauced players wobbled up the steps and rang the bell. The young lady heard the commotion and looked out her window, where she saw two staggering drunks on her porch, a pair of freshly painted horses, and a jeering and laughing crowd. She immediately asked her steward to fetch the police, who arrived and bundled Pete and Ramsey into a patrol wagon and took them to jail, where they spent the night. Not until the following day did

Pete and Ramsey learn what all the commotion had been about. They paid their fines, gathered their horses, and sadly headed back to Louisville.

A few weeks later, a Philadelphia publication reported, "Pete, as the readers of *The Sporting Life* know, is something of a drinker at times, and a considerable portion of his money goes for that purpose. He keeps a slate at several places, but he never fails to pay up at the end of the season."[38] After the season ended, Pete settled his bills with all the saloons in the West End. With $300 in hand, Pete went from saloon to saloon, paying as much as $100 at one place. When he was done, $45 remained. He carefully folded the money up and put it in his vest pocket, saying he was going to buy a new suit of clothes. Summoning a group of friends, he announced, in a most earnest manner, that he was quitting liquor forever.

The *Louisville Commercial* summed up his options with this simple statement: "Pete will either have to play ball or drink whisky next year. He cannot do both."[39]

Gutter Fishing (1888)

"He got roaring drunk Monday," reported the *Courier-Journal,* "but he was put to bed before he had a chance to show what a large sized ass he is under the influence of liquor."[1] The team had wrapped up a two-game series in Kansas City on Sunday night, so Pete overindulged on Monday and then repeated his "roaring drunk" on Tuesday. The players were due to leave that evening for a four-game series in Cincinnati, but Pete refused to go, saying the whole team was jealous of him and he would never play ball with the club again. Instead, he got hammered. "His sense of humor developed with each drink he took," lambasted the *Courier-Journal.*[2] Instead of accompanying the team to Cincinnati, Pete washed down his beer with more beer, wandered into a local store, purchased some fishing tackle, and returned to the hotel. It had rained heavily, and the gutters out front were filled with water. Pete found a good spot and cast his line into the gutter. Sportswriter John B. Foster recounted the scene: "He lighted a long black cigar, took a lounging chair from the hotel and fished in solitary grandeur. Curious-minded persons by the score watched him and giggled. Oblivious to all, soaked to the skin, keeping his cigar alight against the water falling and wind blowing, Pete cast his line and swept the current, re-baited his hook, amused himself until he was tired of it and finally withdrew in discomfiture because of his ill luck." He went into the hotel and announced, "No luck," addressing no one in particular. "They ain't running very well today. Thought I'd get a fresh fish for dinner. Tired of these hotel doodles."[3]

Like many tales about Pete, this one has been exaggerated. Foster's account did not appear until years later, and contemporary reports lacked some of the more colorful images in his version. It was originally reported that Pete wrapped up his fishing excursion only after the hotel had received several complaints about the ruckus he was causing and threatened to call the police. A few weeks later, a simpler, more plausible story emerged, although it was missing the humorous spectacle of Pete fishing in the rain gutter. According to this version, Pete had planned to go to a nearby fishing spot but never made it to his destination, as the heat and the excessive alcohol he had consumed proved too much for him. He was found passed out in a doorway, along with all his fishing tackle, and was carted back to his hotel. This version speaks to the darker reality of Pete's alcoholism.

While in Kansas City, Pete also got suckered into a game of three-card monte and lost $40. "Browning has not turned a card since, and is willing to acknowledge with all due humility that he knows nothing about gambling," chided the *Courier-Journal*.[4] This is complete conjecture, as humility was not a trait Pete was familiar with.

Pete's multiday bender followed two games in which he went a combined 6 for 8, with three doubles, underscoring an important point: Pete's drinking was never triggered by any specific event. His embarrassing episodes of public drunkenness followed games in which he had played great and games in which he had played poorly. There was no discernible pattern.

Whereas the Louisville papers had grown used to Pete's antics and tended to downplay his behavior, the *Kansas City Star* did not hold back: "It is a good thing for base ball that but very few of the players disgrace the profession as Pete Browning does. The members of the profession in this city, who are all gentlemen, for Dave Rowe [player-manager of Kansas City] will tolerate no other kind, are highly indignant at the notoriety Browning has attracted towards ball players." The paper quoted an unnamed teammate of Pete's who said, "Browning had better play ball with the Louisvilles, because no other management on earth would tolerate such a drunken loafer."[5] The anonymous player's comment spoke as much to Pete's drunken indifference as it did to the team's failure to discipline its star player.

After sobering up for two days and missing the first two games of the series with Cincinnati, Pete rejoined the team on Friday night and was in the lineup on Saturday. He was welcomed back with a $100 fine, which, though hefty, was nowhere near the hollow threat made by team management at the end of the 1887 season: "His first drinking offense will be promptly met by suspension for the remainder of the season."[6] Pete argued that the fine was unfair, as it was his first case of "backsliding" that season.

Upon arriving at the field, Pete was dubbed the "Lone Fisherman" by a gaggle of kids in the stands. While striding to the plate for his first at-bat, he was heckled by a local saloon owner who cried, "Hurrah for John Barleycorn."[7] Despite seeing double, Pete hit for a triple, lining the first ball delivered by pitcher Billy Serad into deep center. As he stopped at third, he doffed his cap to the crowd with a sly smile. Even though he went 3 for 4 at the plate, Pete was described as looking "nervous and pale" and struggling defensively: "He couldn't see a balloon in the field . . . and almost every hit in his territory got away from him."[8]

Heading into 1888, Pete had a busy off-season. In November 1887 he ran unsuccessfully for councilman in the Eleventh Ward. There were a couple of other election losses over the years, but there is no evidence of what, if any, political positions or ideologies he held, other than a brief mention that he was a Republican. It would not be unfair to assume that Pete's desire to run for office was driven more by his ego and less by any desire to enact social and political change in the community. Following his election loss, Pete spent most of his time drinking hard cider and playing seven-up, although he did umpire a local baseball game, receiving praise for his fairness, honesty, and judgment on the field.

As the season neared, it was the same old story for Pete. He delayed signing his contract until the last moment. The local paper praised his decision to hold out by offering a backhanded compliment:

> Mr. Peter Browning has not yet affixed his autograph to a contract with the Louisville Club, and in withholding he is displaying a great deal more judgment than people generally give him credit for. As long as Mr. Browning refrains from signing, so long as he is his own master, the more money he saves. He cannot go to the club for an advance unless he signs; he cannot spend the money unless he gets it; he knows if he signed he would want money, and he is certain he would spend it if he had it. In a word, Mr. Browning has not much confidence in his ability to resist the temptation to go out with the boys, and he knows that as soon as he places himself under orders he will

> have to toe the mark. He will sign in due time, but he will have as much fun as possible in the interim.[9]

Pete held out for the entire month of March and missed preseason training. His explanation for the holdout was straightforward, claiming he was "constitutionally different from all other players and did not need any preliminary work to fit him for good ball playing."[10] At its core, Pete's refusal to sign was much simpler: he did not want to take part in the team's training regimen. Every afternoon, after a morning spent in the gymnasium "swing[ing] iron wands, clubs, and dumb bells," the team traveled to nearby Churchill Downs to "work off all extra fat and get sound wind staying qualities" by running around the track several times.[11] "[I] won't sign because [I] don't want to be converted into a race-horse and made to run five or six miles a day around the racetrack," explained Pete.[12]

During Pete's holdout, the club threatened to replace both him and pitcher Elton "Ice Box" Chamberlain, who hadn't signed yet either.[13] The club was promising fans a surprise acquisition that would make "the signing of Chamberlain and Browning [not] matter a snap of the finger." The team claimed to be in negotiations with the National League for the release of one of its "tip-top" fielders that other AA clubs were also eager to sign. "We will have to pay a nice sum of money for him, but he is worth it," said the club, "and then let dissatisfied players be on the lookout. This man ranked high up last season in the league fielders, was among the first half dozen in batting, and is able to go into the box regularly and pitch two winning games per week. Our negotiations are progressing smoothly, and we hope to have the big man's name on a Louisville contract within the next few days. [We] . . . regard the man we are after as Browning's superior in fielding and batting, to say nothing of his ability to pitch a winning game of ball."[14] The player was eventually revealed to be Pittsburgh's John Coleman—a solid player, but nowhere near the caliber of Pete or Chamberlain. Coleman never signed with Louisville and remained with Pittsburgh. Pete's holdout lasted another week; Chamberlain's lasted another month.

The day after Pete signed his contract, manager John Kelly unveiled the team rules for the season. Players were required to be in bed by 11:30 p.m. or be fined anywhere from $5 to $50. All players were expected to practice temperance: drinking was not allowed. The first offense would result in a $25 fine, the second a $50 fine, and the third a suspension.

Kelly added, "I sincerely trust that it will not become necessary to inflict penalty upon any player during the season, but it is proper that I announce any violation of the requirements and spirit of these rules will be punished."[15] Kelly's enforcement of the rules would soon be tested when star pitcher Toad Ramsey found himself in court after being charged with drunkenness.

Upon joining the team, Pete wasted no time in regaining his form. A week after his monthlong holdout he had already "commenced to swing his club with old time vigor and skill."[16] A week later, after listening to evangelist Francis Murphy preach against the evils of liquor, Pete joined the rest of the team in taking a "solemn oath to never touch intoxicating liquor again." Fellow warriors of booze and base hits Guy Hecker, Toad Ramsey, and Reddy Mack joined him in the pledge. Ramsey claimed he "was never more earnest in his life and will live up to his word."[17] Pete was so moved by the evangelist's speech that he headed to the local magistrate to take a second oath. Given the club's history, it could not have been a more positive start to the season. Two weeks later, "Prohibition Pete" was hailed for his strong play in April, when he hit .395.[18] Despite his hot bat, the nickname seemed a bit premature, as two weeks of sobriety did not make Pete a teetotaling prohibitionist.

The positivity and sobriety were fleeting. In an 18–1 shellacking by the St. Louis Browns described as "the worst exhibition of ball playing this season," Louisville committed 14 errors, with Ramsey contributing eight (surprisingly, Pete had none).[19] Before the game, Ramsey and Kelly had gotten into an argument over the manager's refusal to give the pitcher advance money. Ramsey showed up late for practice the following day, at which point Kelly suspended him indefinitely. Ramsey disappeared for several days and was believed to be on a drunken spree. He returned a few days later and was reinstated, but he cast aside the blue ribbon that marked him as abstinent and went back to his old ways. Teammates said Ramsey had "swallowed his pledge and [that he] drinks simply to keep his pledge down."[20] Soon after, a visitor to the saloon at Fifth and Jefferson in downtown Louisville noticed a ribbon hanging behind the bar. When asked what it was, the barkeep said Ramsey had given it to him as security for a drink. Upon closer inspection, it was identified as the temperance ribbon Ramsey had been awarded by evangelist Murphy. The club, as usual, showed no spine in dealing with the destructive behavior of one of its star players.

Pete, who claimed to be sober, was not hitting the ball up to his usual lofty standards. Sportswriters around the country took note of his slump, commenting that since he "signed the pledge he cannot hit the ball."[21] This made Pete question his decision not to drink. Whether drinking was the cause or not, the undeniable fact was that Pete was not hitting well. Through the month of May he hit only .250, going hitless in eight games. It was only the fifth time in six seasons that he had hit less than .300 in any month (one of those months was July 1886, when he was suspended and played in only four games).[22]

Pete's troubles at the plate give credence to one of the most famous quotes attributed to him: "I can't hit the ball, until I hit the bottle." It highlights the dark side of Pete's life, the sad reality of a baseball legend who could not escape his demons. The quote first started appearing in articles during the 1888 season, but it is an inaccurate representation of what Pete said. On May 20, 1888, more than a month before the line first appeared in the *Courier-Journal,* the *Philadelphia Times* ran a short story quoting St. Louis catcher John "Jocko" Milligan, who had played with Philadelphia for four seasons. Milligan was talking to a local sportswriter about the Browns' recent four-game series against Louisville, in which Pete had gone a miserable 3 for 15. "Pete Browning looks as pale as a ghost," said Milligan, "but he was never in such fine form. He can't hit the ball though and the other day said to me, 'Jack since I joined the temperance gang I can't bat. I think I'll have to hit the bottle again, so that I can hit the ball.'"[23] This minor change transforms Pete's statement from the definitive to the speculative. It can be taken as a halfhearted jest, easily laughed off, but given Pete's struggles with the bottle, it can also be read as a cry for help.

Pete did indeed start hitting the bottle again, but his slump continued. He would have spurts of greatness that quickly vanished. A 3-for-4 day on May 22, featuring standout defensive work and hailed as "the greatest game of his life," sparked hope among the team and the Louisville faithful, but it was short-lived.[24] It was preceded by a game in which Pete had been fined $5 for "napping at second," and it was followed by four hitless games.[25] On an eastern road trip stretching from the end of May to the first week of June, Pete was criticized mercilessly for his poor play. "Browning, who is at present the weakest man in the nine at the bat, played in the field like a blind man. . . . Big Pete is disappointing his Eastern admirers this trip," wrote the *Courier-Journal* after Pete went 0 for 4 in a 6–5 loss to Brooklyn.[26]

June was no better. The team entered the month with an awful record of 9–23, 15 games out of first place. Kelly, looking to motivate his players, threatened them with fines for poor play. "I don't want to deprive any player of his money," he said, "but henceforth the man who fails to play good, lively ball will find a hole in his package when payday comes."[27] Kelly's tough approach didn't work, and the team started to chafe under his strict leadership. An article in the *Baltimore Sun* alleged that certain members of the Louisville club, believed to be Hecker, outfielder-catcher John Kerins, and Ramsey, conspired to oust Kelly and refused to play ball for him. Pete, speaking on behalf of his teammates, refuted the allegations, stating, "There [is no] truth in the story." Team president and co-owner William Lyons responded even more forcefully: "If I were satisfied that players in the club were throwing off for whatever purpose, I would not hesitate to blacklist them. . . . While matters do look queer, I don't share the opinion of some that the playing of the club is purposefully bad. That is, I think a mere opinion, a deduction from their circumstances. The people are disappointed, and reasonably so. I have been disappointed myself. I was led to believe that our club is stronger than it is."[28] Lyons's bluster and denials rang hollow when the team was sold a few days later on June 6 to team secretary and treasurer Mordecai Davidson. Davidson was a local businessman and Civil War veteran who had served in Company A of the Seventeenth Indiana Regiment of the Union army. He claimed to have a noble purpose in purchasing the club, explaining that he was inspired by local pride and believed "he could lift the club from its sorry financial and artistic plight through the application of sound business methods and strict disciplining."[29]

Having a new owner did not change the team's fortunes, as it posted a 7–15 record in June and dropped 21½ games behind first. Davidson planned to install Hecker as the new manager but was shocked when half a dozen of his teammates said they would not play for him. Davidson was surprised, as Hecker was well liked, loyal, and hardworking. One of the other players spoke up and explained, "Hecker is a Republican, we're all Democrats, except Hecker and Browning, and no so-and-so Republican is going to push us around."[30] The following day Davidson himself replaced Kelly as manager. The team was riding a five-game losing streak but won in Davidson's debut before promptly losing two more. Davidson then named Kerins as manager. He led the team for seven games before Davidson resumed the managerial duties for the remainder of the season.

Davidson's leadership and baseball knowledge were immediately questioned. "He doesn't even know the difference between a base hit and a bass viol," lampooned one writer.[31] This was unlikely, as Davidson was a man of elegant taste in music and surely knew what a bass viol was. A 5–1 loss to Kansas City led the *Courier-Journal* to ask, "Is this a professional club or a set of third-class amateurs?" as the team took a firm hold on last place.[32]

For Pete, the sale of the team marked an important yet often overlooked change in his status with the Louisville club. For his entire career, Zach Phelps had been involved with the organization as both an owner and team president. Phelps and Pete had a long-standing friendship, having gone to school together as youngsters. Their relationship impacted the way Pete was disciplined (or not) over the years, and he recognized this. "Phelps and I used to play ball together when we were kids," he slyly explained, "and I know how to go about him when I want a favor."[33] With Phelps no longer involved, Pete lost one of his biggest supporters in the club.

The beginning of June found Pete third on the team in hitting and a distant eleventh in the league. The *Courier-Journal* misquoted him again, writing, "Pietro Browning is the originator of the remark, 'I can't hit the ball until I hit the bottle.' Well, he has hit the bottle, it remains to be seen what he does with the ball."[34] The month ended with Pete's drunken fishing adventure in Kansas City. The *Courier-Journal* declared, "It is too bad that Gladiator Browning can't resist the temptation and went back to his old bibulous habits."[35] Things only got worse as Pete's drinking drew comments from around the country. The *St. Louis Globe Democrat* wrote, "They call Pete Browning 'Dr. Jekyll and Mr. Hyde' down in Louisville. Whenever Pete runs up against a distiller, he carries out the 'Hyde' idea."[36]

The season was not going well for the rest of the team either. Ramsey was excused from pitching with an unknown "illness," while shortstop Bill White was suspended indefinitely for poor play. For Ramsey, things only got worse. After he missed the train for a series in Cincinnati, Davidson left a ticket for him at the station. But when Ramsey arrived he felt a thirst coming on, so he sold his ticket to another traveler for half price and went out for drinks. Davidson suspended him immediately. A few days later, Ramsey was arrested for not paying his bills and spent the night in jail. Much of the blame for the team's poor performance and behavior was heaped on Davidson and his failure to hire a real manager. And all this happened despite the team's abstinence pledge.

As Pete's off-field behavior deteriorated, the rumor mill was in full swing. Stories popped up regularly claiming that he was going to lose his spot in the starting lineup or be traded or released, only to be followed the next day with an article refuting the previous one. These rumors persisted even though, after a miserable month of May, Pete rebounded at the plate, hitting over .380 in June and pulling himself up to seventh in the league batting race by mid-July. Pete's performance was even more impressive when he hurt himself doing something he was loath to do: he scored the winning run in a game against Brooklyn on a "daring slide to the plate."[37] He was forced to leave the game in the first inning on July 6, suffering from a fever and an unspecified illness. As the outside temperature crept into the upper 90s, Pete missed the next two games as well, since the summer heat exacerbated the symptoms of his mastoiditis. He returned to the field on July 10, and it seemed that "the Gladiator was himself again." He had a number of "circus" catches and a 2-for-4 day at the plate, including a triple.[38] Over the next few games, Pete continued his standout play, but it would not last.

The end of July was a negative turning point in Pete's season. During a three-game series in Cincinnati, he complained to Red Stockings pitcher Mike "Elmer" Smith about the press's coverage of him. "It's an outrage Elmer," blustered Pete, "that we can't drink our beer occasionally without the papers roasting us."[39] He failed to show up for a game on July 21 and was believed to be out drinking. Davidson went to Pete's mother's house and found Pete "stretched full length in bed. [His] mustache curl[ed] and droop[ed], and his brow [was] swathed in bandages and ice."[40] The doctor confirmed that Pete was too ill to play, but he missed only one game. A few weeks after his return, on August 8, Pete left the game after suffering a foot injury and missed a week. His time away from the field seemed to push him toward the bottle. Just when he seemed ready to rejoin the team for a monthlong road trip, he was arrested for disorderly conduct after getting into a fight. At the time of his arrest, he was "well loaded with whiskey," but Pete claimed he had merely taken an "internal application of rock and rye" to ease the pain in his foot.[41] At his booking, he said he had no memory of getting drunk. Pete promised never to use such remedies again and was released until his court appearance the following day. He didn't show up and was fined.

When Pete heard that the team was planning to leave for the eastern trip without him, he asked to meet with Davidson and Kerins at Hecker's sporting goods store. He showed up with two fresh black eyes, which he claimed were the result of a fall a few days before. Kerins spoke first: "Now look here, Pete, you said you had a sore foot, and we gave you time to get it healed up. Your pay wasn't stopped and for nearly three weeks you have been drawing your salary for no work. You have imagined yourself Prince Peter, and have lived like a lord, and instead of staying at home and nursing your foot you have been making a racehorse out of yourself and got out in the jug." Kerins's words stung Pete, and it took him a moment to realize the gravity of the situation: he would not be joining the team on the road trip. Pete wiped a "suspicious moisture" from his eyes and then, in his usual cocky manner, tried to appeal to Kerins: "What's dat Kerins? Ain't I no more good? Ain't Pete a ballplayer? You're no good unless I'm going. In Philadelphia all the town comes to see the Gladiator line 'em out and if I ain't along you'll play to empty benches. When Pete's away Louisville ain't got any club." He ended with a warning to Davidson: "This is my home and I want to stay here, but I've got to play ball."[42]

The team left for the East Coast road trip without Pete, heading for Philadelphia. Pete was "the saddest man in Louisville," having been "left at home to get drunk and entertain the small boys of the West End with wonderful tales of how he is wont to line 'em out."[43] Get drunk is exactly what he did.

A few days after the team departed, Pete boarded a streetcar in downtown Louisville on a rainy night. He was drunk and disheveled, soaking wet, still sporting two black eyes, and shirtless under his coat, much to the amusement of his fellow passengers. He noticed a man smoking a cigar and plopped down next to him. That individual was a city councilman, a "dignified and respectable member of society" who "[did] not patronize saloons, [and was] unfamiliar with saloon slang." He was also unfamiliar with Pete. Pete commanded the councilman to "gimme a spark," and he obliged, lighting the wet, misshapen, cheap cigar stump Pete was chewing on. Pete eyed the councilman's cigar and told him, "Throw it away." Again, the man did as he was told. Pete pulled another wet, cheap cigar from his coat pocket and thrust it into the councilman's mouth, and he smoked the stogie in dignified silence, hoping not to offend his obnoxiously drunk seatmate. Pete tried to strike up a conversation with the councilman, talking about two of his passions: poker and gambling. The councilman politely responded, "You are a stranger to me sir, and I never played poker in all my life." Pete, undeterred by the weak protest, continued his rant.

The councilman tried to take a more assertive stance, defiantly saying, "I never bet." At that, Pete pulled the streetcar bell, got off at the next stop, and dragged his new friend into the nearest saloon, where he forced the councilman to "drink stale common beer and learn the mysteries of poker dice" for the rest of the night.[44]

This was only one of several troubling incidents, and Pete's friends were alarmed by his behavior, which they attributed to his suspension from the team. "Many think that sorrow is causing him to lose his mind," reported the *Courier-Journal*. "Pete's intellect, except on the ball field, was never of the strongest, and since his suspension he seems to be growing childish and playful. He imagines that everybody he meets wants to chuck poker dice, and he holds out his ragged $50 and tries to get a bet that he can or can't beat three deuces and two trays. He never varies the combination but sticks religiously to his three deuces and two trays."[45]

For once, the team stood firm and refused to take Pete on the road. Still, Pete was proved right: without him, "Louisville ain't got any club." The team was steamrolled by Philadelphia 16–2 and 11–1 in the first two games of the series. "I told them they couldn't get along without Petey," he boasted as he puffed away on a cheap cigar and watched the scoreboard at baseball headquarters in Louisville.[46] Despite losing six straight games without Pete, it seemed that the team was finally ready to move on from him. It was reported that Pete's suspension would be extended to the end of the season.

Regardless, Pete's talent outweighed his off-field shortcomings. Even while suspended he was in demand, and trade rumors swirled daily. One involved a swap with Cleveland for outfielder Gus Alberts and his weak .197 career batting average. Louisville demanded an additional $1,000 and another player, rumored to be Cleveland second baseman Cub Stricker, as part of the deal. After days of negotiations, the proposed trade fell through, and Pete remained in Louisville.

While suspended, Pete spent time at the nearby hot springs resort in French Lick, whose waters were "famous for correcting too much liquor." Upon his return to Louisville, not much changed. Pete was spotted at the local saloons making "strenuous efforts to get the taste of mineral water out of his mouth."[47]

In between trips to saloons and distilleries, Pete was spied in the stands at home games, looking sad not because Louisville was losing but because he was not playing. At one game Pete approached Davidson to ask about returning to the team. "Can't do it," responded Davidson flatly, "until you stop drinking and bring me a certificate from your physician saying that you are in good physical condition and then I will talk with you."[48] Pete and his physician eventually convinced Davidson of his (relative) sobriety, and he returned to the team for a doubleheader on September 23. Pete wasted no time in returning to form. After a pedestrian first game in which he went 1 for 5, he went 3 for 4 in the second game. His return was hailed in the *Courier-Journal:* "Lewis [*sic*] Rogers Browning made his appearance in a Louisville uniform, after a short sojourn among the Louisville taverns, [and] the Gladiator received cheer after cheer for his great work. Besides wielding his willow with effect, Pete made a one-handed circus catch, and after that the crowd would not condescend to refer to him as the Lone Fisherman or Distillery Pete, but he was the Gladiator from that time on, and Pete showed his delight by doffing his cap, even when the beer rushers would hollo 'beer, cigars, lemonade,' mistaking it for applause."[49]

For Louisville, the season was all but over when Pete returned. The team was buried in seventh place, 40 games out of first. And that was where it finished, 44 games back. Pete's hot play continued, however. At the time of his suspension, he was eighth in the league in hitting. Upon his return, he hit .368 over the season's final 20 games, putting himself back in the race for the batting title. Eventual champion Tip O'Neill, who was on pace to win back-to-back batting titles, was out of reach, but Pete clawed his way back to third, with a .313 average. St. Louis also won its fourth consecutive AA title. It was Pete's seventh straight year finishing in the top three in hitting, an unmatched run of consistency at the time. Cap Anson, Dan Brouthers, and Dave Orr had all recorded three consecutive top-three finishes, falling far short of Pete's seven. Even with the turmoil of the 1888 season and missing 36 games due to a combination of suspensions, injuries, and drunken misadventures, Pete salvaged a more-than-respectable individual season. In addition to his third-place finish in hitting, he was third in OBP, fourth in slugging and OPS, and ninth in RBIs.

At the conclusion of the season, sporting goods mogul Albert Spalding organized an around-the-world goodwill tour with two teams: Spalding's Chicago White Stockings and an All-Star All-American team made up of players from both the NL and the AA. Although some of the game's bigger names were asked to play, the roster also featured a number of "fourth-rate" players, as Spalding was too cheap to offer the kind of money that would attract the best. Spalding reportedly asked Pete to participate, but given the six-month commitment needed, Pete's reluctance to leave home, the poor pay, and Spalding's desire to bring men of "clean habits," it is not surprising that Pete did not go on the tour.[50]

After the season, Pete again found himself at the center of trade rumors, as a move to Cleveland was suggested. Some believed that Pete was the scapegoat for Louisville's troubles and underachievement, and perhaps a change of scenery would benefit both Pete and the team. Much like the earlier rumors, this one lived in the papers for a few weeks before fading away. Pete remained silent on the matter, busying himself in the off-season with opening a small notions store in downtown Louisville. And, as in past seasons, Pete's imminent marriage—this time to a young lady from the West End of town—was reported. This announcement seemed to answer the question of why the grandstand had been the recipient of so many "sweet smiles" from Pete as he trotted on and off the field. More important for the team, Pete supposedly made a New Year's resolution for 1889. "Mr. Browning has most emphatically expressed himself on the drinking questions," wrote the *Courier-Journal,* "and from the first day of January Lewis [*sic*] will abstain from all intoxicating drinks and lead a temperance life."[51]

10

The Worst Team in Baseball (1889)

Beyond the individual success of some of its players, most notably Pete Browning and Guy Hecker, dysfunction and underachievement were the hallmarks of Louisville baseball. Since its first season in the American Association, not much had changed for the luckless franchise. Over its first seven years of existence, the team exhibited moments of near greatness, but more often it was dominated by mediocre play, unruly behavior by its best players, and late-season collapse. It got worse in 1889—much worse.

There have been some horrendous teams in the history of Major League Baseball. The 1899 Cleveland Spiders had an anemic record of 20–134 and finished 84 games out of first place. The 2003 Detroit Tigers embarrassed themselves by setting an American League record of 119 losses, only a whisker away from the 1962 New York Mets' all-time modern record of 120 losses. Recently the Baltimore Orioles established new levels of miserable play, reeling off 100 losses in three of four years from 2018 to 2021 (the only non-100-loss season being 2020, which was shortened due to the COVID-19 pandemic). Even with all that ineptitude, the 1889 Louisville Colonels (as they were now known) can proudly claim to be one of the all-time worst teams.

The Colonels became the first team in MLB history to lose 100 games, finishing an abysmal 27–111, 66½ games out of first place. Their record was 9–65 on the road, a .122 winning percentage, which is the third lowest in MLB history for a minimum of 60 games. They still hold the record for the longest losing streak, dropping 26 straight games from May 22 to June 22, 1889. This was followed by a 14-game losing streak from August 7 to August 20 and a 13-game nonwinning streak (one game was a tie) from

September 22 to October 10. The 1889 Colonels lost five or more games in a row eight times, never won more than three consecutive games, and won back-to-back games only six times throughout the season. In addition to the on-field misery, the team got trapped in a flood and was feared lost, suffered through the first players strike, and saw unpopular owner Mordecai Davidson relinquish control to the AA in midseason, before the team was sold. There were no bright spots. The pitching was awful, the offense was average at best, and the defense mishandled about one in ten chances. Bad management, poor play, and losing were the norm.

At the center of much of the turmoil was Pete. Despite his New Year's resolution of temperance, his excessive drinking became disruptive. Even given his many difficulties in the 1888 season, he had managed to finish third in the batting race. The local paper noted, "It mattered little whether he came in contact with [a] quarter or a schooner [a type of beer glass] he came out victorious. He drank nothing but schooners, and it was not infrequently the case that half a dozen 'kegs' were 'laid away' in one sitting."[1] As he had proved so many times in his career, a drunk Pete still played at a level far beyond that of most other men.

As usual, it was reported in the preseason that Pete and fellow lush Toad Ramsey, while "not strictly temperate, have behaved themselves in an improved manner."[2] That improvement was merely an illusion. Upon signing his contract for the year, Davidson said to Pete, "You have been drinking a great deal this winter and I do not propose to have you drink any this summer."[3] In response, Pete thrust up his right hand and swore that he would abstain from liquor. He had pledged not to drink countless times before, and as usual, he meant it this time too. But the sporting press did not take his declaration seriously. "It may be safely assumed that the Gladiator has a bigger stock of shattered resolutions on hand than any other player in the league," chastised the *Omaha Daily Bee.*[4]

With Pete supposedly bidding farewell to "cocktails and spiked lemonades," the season seemed to be off to a promising start, but his claim of abstinence was nothing more than a momentary calm in the titanic rift developing between him and Davidson.[5] The off-season negotiations between the two had been particularly contentious, as the notoriously cheap owner was reluctant to acquiesce to Pete's salary demands. Davidson's tightfisted approach resulted in combative negotiations with several players, causing ill feelings and distrust between the team and management before the season even began. In Davidson's defense, the team was severely short of cash. Although he and the other shareholders were wealthy, they did not have an abundance of capital to invest in the club and struggled to make payroll each month. To enhance the team's revenue, Davidson decided that ladies would be admitted to games free with an escort, in the hope of increasing attendance and concession sales. He also sold players throughout the season to raise funds. He had resorted to this tactic the prior season by selling three of the team's better young players—pitcher Ice Box Chamberlain, outfielder Hub Collins, and catcher Lave Cross—and bringing in cheaper, less talented replacements.

The lack of money was not the sole reason for the team's poor performance. Davidson may have been a shrewd businessman, but his ability to run and manage a baseball club was questioned—and rightly so. He was misguided in thinking that a team could win without quality (and expensive) players and in believing that hard work could overcome a lack of talent. The release of Chamberlain illustrated another of Davidson's misguided beliefs. He thought the average pitcher didn't work enough, so rather than replacing Chamberlain, he relied on a scaled-down pitching staff. These ideas led to not only a dearth of talent on the roster but also overworked pitchers who broke down late in the season.

As the train wreck of 1888 rolled seamlessly into the disaster of 1889, everyone was playing their expected roles. Pete was claiming to be sober (a farce); Davidson was the evil, overbearing owner; Hecker was complaining about off-season workouts; Ramsey was drunk; Chicken Wolf was his quiet, reliable self; and the local papers were spinning their annual fantasy about how great the team looked. In stark contrast to the *Courier-Journal*'s upbeat, hopeful outlook was new manager and first baseman Thomas John Esterbrook, who flatly stated that Louisville would not win the pennant. Esterbrook's negative attitude set the tone for his short, confrontational tenure as manager.

Esterbrook, known as "Dude" for his sartorial perfection, was an eccentric player who broke into the majors in 1880 with the National League's Buffalo team. He then bounced around, playing with four different teams before signing with Louisville at the end of the 1888 season. He exhibited moments of brilliance throughout his career, but they were often overshadowed by his outlandish personality. In other words, he was right at home in the lunacy of the Louisville clubhouse.

The season got off to a contentious start when the penny-pinching Davidson announced the end of a long-standing practice: he would no longer give players advance money. "I have come to the conclusion," he said, "that base ball managers make a mistake in advancing players' money before the regular season opens, and hereafter none of the Louisville players will be paid for their services until they are rendered. They go under contract April 1, and each player will receive his first pay the 15th of the month, provided none of them are fined for drunkenness or indifferent playing."[6] The relationship between Davidson and the players was already tense, and this announcement, along with the owner's tendency to fine players with a harsh, callous hand, only made things worse. Further angering players was Davidson's habit of walking the streets late at night and poking his head into various drinking establishments to make sure they were home by their 10:00 p.m. curfew. He often found players in the back room of a little bar at 323 West Liberty Street (near the present location of the Hyatt Regency), which for years was the city's baseball hub and the rumored location of the preliminary meetings that led to the formation of the National League in 1876. Players who were out after curfew were fined on the spot, and Pete was regularly one of those players. On one occasion Davidson found Pete and John Kerins at a table in the back room of the bar on West Liberty after midnight, a pair of tall beers in front of them. After a moment of awkward silence, Pete spoke first. "Mr. Davidson," he said with a smirk, "me and Jack just dropped in here to get a sarsaparilla; you know it's so hot we couldn't sleep."[7] Davidson, who was not amused, personally escorted both men home. He alienated players further when he informed them that he would travel with the team on road trips to enforce discipline.

Davidson's appointment of Esterbrook as manager proved to be another misguided decision, as Esterbrook's confrontational approach immediately caused trouble. He insisted that players do things his way and fined those who did not take his advice to heart. Team morale, already on shaky ground, deteriorated. On April 21, during pregame practice for the opening of a three-game home stand versus St. Louis, Esterbrook fined second baseman Dan Shannon $10 for failing to obey his ball-throwing instructions. Two days later, the even-tempered Wolf and Esterbrook engaged in a heated argument over Shannon's fine, and Esterbrook dropped a $10 fine on the popular Wolf. As more words were exchanged, the fine escalated to $40, and Wolf stormed off to air his grievances to Davidson. Esterbrook's heavy-handed style was clearly not working with the temperamental Louisville team, which started the year

0–6. His extreme, out-of-control demeanor on the field led Louisville fans to question his sanity. (That assessment of Esterbrook's mental health may have been spot-on, as he died in 1901 when he leaped from a train transporting him to a mental hospital.) The end came when the entire team refused to take the field as long as he was manager. Finally, after ten games and a 2–8 record, Esterbrook was relieved of his managerial duties and replaced with Wolf. Esterbrook played one more game with Louisville before being released on May 8.

Just ten games into the season, the Colonels already appeared to be on a sinking ship. Things did not improve. A 13–3 loss to Brooklyn on May 7 was followed by an even less impressive 21–2 drubbing, about which the *Courier-Journal* wrote, "Louisville attempted to play against Brooklyn. The details are too horrible to mention."[8] That same day, only 19 games into the season, there were reports that a disgusted Davidson was trying to sell the team.

The appointment of Wolf as manager seemed a logical choice. He was a reliable player known for his steady, calm demeanor. He was quiet by nature and gladly let his more loquacious teammates such as Pete, Hecker, and Ramsey deal with the press. He was rarely mentioned in the newspapers except for accounts of his play on the field. He was never known to hold out during contract negotiations, always signing before the first of the year. To many, Wolf's demeanor and approach to the game marked him as the anti-Pete. He was described as someone who "doesn't have to be petted and fed with a silver spoon, as an inducement for him to play ball, like . . . some other ball players. He does not regard it as a great condescension on his part to let people see him play but goes in and works like a man who thought it was his duty to earn the salary paid to him."[9] The *Columbus Post* stated, "Jim Wolf is the best player and one of the nicest gentlemen in the Louisville club. He is worth two-dozen such players as Pete Browning."[10] Despite the gushing praise, and although Wolf had a solid career, he never reached the heights Pete did.

Wolf took his new role seriously. Shortly after taking over as manager, he disciplined two of the biggest personalities on the team when he scolded Pete for poor baserunning and swore at Hecker for being lazy defensively. When Hecker argued back, Wolf fined him $25. Even as he tried to discipline the team, Wolf himself was not immune from Davidson's punishment. One on occasion, in an effort to motivate Pete to play harder, Wolf told him, "I'll smash your face if you don't brace up and play ball."[11] Davidson fined him $25 for that friendly advice. Still, Wolf's usually easygoing personality and the deep respect his teammates had for him eased some of the tensions that were building.

Contributing to the team's awful start was Pete's horrendous play and what was described as the downfall of Ramsey. Pete started off the year with a thud, going 0 for 4 in the opening game. He went hitless over the first three games of the year and in five of the first eleven, hitting a meager .214 in April. May started off with a $25 fine when he, Shannon, Kerins, and Phil Tomney were caught playing cards in the back of the White Elephant Saloon after curfew. The local paper proclaimed, "Pete Browning's days of usefulness are about over."[12]

Even more disastrous was Ramsey's early season. In his first start of the year, a 14–9 loss to Kansas City on April 20, he gave up six runs in two innings before being replaced. He would not pitch again until May 7, which was another embarrassing performance that "thoroughly disgusted the 1500 spectators . . . [as] most of the time he was unable to get the ball in the vicinity of the plate, and when it did happen to land there it was sent spinning all over the field." He was removed after giving up nine runs in three innings. The next day the *Courier-Journal* was frank in its assessment: "It is becoming painfully apparent that Ramsey's pitching days are gone."[13] Ramsey missed a month of starts before returning with another loss on June 1. Over the next month he reeled off 14 losses and just one win. By mid-July, the team was so desperate to get rid of Ramsey that it traded him to St. Louis for dead-armed pitcher Nat Hudson, whose best years were behind him. In keeping with the disastrous nature of the season, Hudson refused to report.

Despite the poor play of Pete and Ramsey, the team's fortunes changed—slightly—after Wolf's appointment as manager. After a 3–14 start, Louisville rebounded a bit, going 5–8 over the next 13 games. On May 21 the Colonels won their third game in a row, an 8–4 defeat of Baltimore. It seemed to portend brighter days ahead, but unfortunately, it did not. That was Louisville's last victory for a month and the end of the team's longest winning streak of the season.

Louisville's swift return to defeat coincided with a terrible streak by Pete that ended with him being benched on May 23 against Baltimore. He returned two days later in an 8–7 loss to Cincinnati, going 0 for 4. Pete then had his best run of the year with three consecutive three-hit games, but it was all for naught, as Louisville's losing streak stretched to six. Despite his hitting streak, Pete, who prided himself on coming through in the clutch, was getting a reputation for being unable to hit with men on base. But to be fair, there were not many batters getting on base ahead of him.

Losing was becoming the norm for Louisville. One of the few bright spots was pitcher Scott Stratton's grand slam off Cincinnati pitcher Lee Viau on May 27. Stratton became one of the youngest players (at 19 years old) and just the third pitcher to hit a grand slam. But Stratton's heroics didn't matter, as Louisville went down 10–9 to keep the losing streak alive. After Louisville lost four straight games to Columbus by a combined score of 38–12, the *Columbus State Journal* wrote, "The game yesterday was a clear case of assault and battery, and the Columbus team should have been taken into custody for attacking a party not near their size. The Louisville team may pose as ball-players in the Bluegrass region, famous for its pretty women, fast horses, and red liquor that hath a bead upon it, but in this part of the country it is liable to indictment for traveling under false pretenses."[14]

Following the losses to Columbus, the team was a no-show for its games in Philadelphia on June 3 and 4. For 36 hours there was no word from the team, and the *Courier-Journal*'s headline speculated that they were "Lost Again."[15] When the Louisville players eventually arrived in Philadelphia on June 5, they explained that they had been stranded when the Conemaugh River washed over the train tracks, making them impassable. This was the famous Johnstown Flood, which occurred in Johnstown, Pennsylvania, on May 31 when, after days of heavy rain, there was a catastrophic failure of the South Fork dam that killed 2,209 people and caused $17 million worth of damage (about $490 million in 2020 dollars). The Louisville players had left Columbus on June 2 and then got stranded in a small train station halfway between Erie and Pittsburgh when the flood stopped train and telegraph service throughout western Pennsylvania. The *Louisville Times* joked that this might be a positive turn of events: "There is some slight consolation in the hope that the members are lost in the mud in the Conemaugh Valley and may not be able to extricate themselves until the season is nearly over."[16] When they finally made it to the City of Brotherly Love, they dropped another four games to Philadelphia, followed by four more losses in Brooklyn.

As the losses piled up, so did the fines from Davidson. The team's money was running out, so he stopped trying to win games and focused on assessing and collecting fines as a way to meet the payroll. He instituted a series of fines for poor play and petty offenses. As the team prepared to leave for a monthlong road trip, Davidson informed the players, "I expect to get about $1000 of your salaries on this trip." In Columbus he fined Pete, Wolf, and third baseman Harry Raymond $25 each for arguing at the train station. He fined Hecker $25 for muffing a thrown ball. When shortstop Phil Tomney took the blame and admitted he had thrown the ball too high, he was slapped with a $25 fine as well. Catcher Paul Cook was fined for two passed balls on a pair of poor pitches, and when he explained to Davidson that pitcher Red Ehret could not see the signs because it was getting dark, Davidson's response was as expected: "It will cost Red $25 for not seeing better." After a poor showing in the Brooklyn series, a frustrated Pete threw one of his bats into the river and was promptly hit with a $100 fine. He protested that the bat was his property and he could do whatever he wished with it. When an angry Pete threw another bat in the river, Davidson fined him another $100. Pete accumulated a third $100 fine when he returned to the hotel that night at 12:45 a.m.—loaded. His claim that he was only drinking soft drinks was to no avail.

Even during the ongoing disaster, Pete still exhibited moments of greatness. On June 7 against Philadelphia, Pete hit his second career cycle when he went 5 for 6, with two singles, a double, a triple, and a three-run homer. He was only the fourth player in major league history to hit for multiple cycles, and as of 2021, he was still one of only 34 players to record two or more.[17] Despite Pete's standout day, Louisville lost its fourteenth straight game, going down 9–7 in 11 innings.

To address the team's dire financial situation, Davidson relocated a home series to Cincinnati and was seeking league permission to move all home games to the road. He was vilified in the press for this plan and ultimately dropped the idea. Davidson then tried to sell players' contracts, as they were the only valuable assets he had left. The other owners, recognizing what this would mean for the Louisville franchise, prevailed on the league office not to recognize any of the sales. Davidson was also actively looking to sell the club, but his asking price was too high and he had no luck finding a buyer.

After the four-game sweep in Brooklyn, Louisville was scheduled to play four games in Baltimore. It suffered its nineteenth consecutive loss to Baltimore on June 13, and Davidson fined Shannon and Cook for a couple of errors and "stupid base running."[18] Davidson had been traveling with the team but would be attending a league meeting in New York to discuss the team's financial woes. The players had finally had enough of Davidson's heavy-handed tactics and rebelled. Confronting him before he left for New York, they presented Davidson with a round-robin (a written protest with their signatures affixed in a circle to disguise who had signed first) stating that if the fines were not dropped, they would not report for the game against Baltimore the next day. Every player, with the exception of Wolf, signed the protest. Wolf had been fined and mistreated by Davidson just like the rest of the team, but as manager, he felt a sense of responsibility to his boss. As expected, Davidson's response was defiant. He informed the players that if they failed to win the next day, the entire team would be fined $25 each, and anyone who didn't show up for the game would be fined an additional $100. The following day six players—Pete, Cook, Ehret, Hecker, Raymond, and Shannon—refused to play, while Bill Gleason, Ramsey, Stratton, Farmer Vaughn, Farmer Weaver, and Wolf played. The first players strike in Major League Baseball was on. Louisville filled its roster with three semipro players from the Baltimore area—Walter Fisher, Mike Gaul, and John Traffley, who were making their first and only appearances in a major league game.[19] The game was rained out after two innings, with Baltimore ahead 5–0. It was replayed the next day, again minus the striking players, and again with the same outcome, as Baltimore won 4–2 in a rain-shortened five-inning game. The trio of semipro pickups went a combined 1 for 6. Knowing that Davidson's only goal at this point was to collect fines to keep the team afloat, one of the striking players said, "Nothing could have pleased Davidson better, than when we refused to play ball in Baltimore."[20]

The next day the striking players tried to negotiate with Davidson, saying they would return if he remitted all the fines. He did not. However, other team owners urged the striking players to play and let the league office determine the outcome of the dispute over the fines. The strikers heeded that advice, but the losses continued to pile up. In 1877 the Louisville Grays had collaborated with gamblers and thrown games because the owners did not pay the players. A decade later, Louisville watched another season go down in flames as the owner and players fought over pay and fines again. Hecker told the press that it had been a month since they had last received paychecks. The players were viewed sympathetically in the national sporting press, while Davidson was universally viewed as the villain.

Louisville closed out the road trip by losing all 21 games and running its consecutive loss streak to 23. The team returned to Louisville and lost another 3 games before, mercifully, the 26-game losing streak came to an end on June 23 with a 7–3 win over St. Louis. Ramsey picked up the win over ex-Louisville pitcher Chamberlain. The losing streak lasted a month, stretching from May 22 (an 11–2 loss to Baltimore) to June 22 (a 3–2 loss in 11 innings to St. Louis). It was feast or famine for Louisville during the streak; it lost 12 games by two runs or less but 8 games by nine runs or more. To prove the losing streak was no fluke, the day after it ended, bringing the team's record to 9–46, Louisville proceeded to lose 9 of the next 12 games. All told, the team lost 35 of 38 games. On July 1 Louisville had a 10–52 record. It was 32½ games out of first place and 15 games behind the team ahead of it. It was an astonishing run of bad baseball.

The losing streak may have ended, but the troubles between the team and Davidson did not. June 21, the day before the streak ended, was payday, and after the game the players trudged to Davidson's office to collect their checks. One by one they were called in and given their pay—minus the fines assessed on the hellacious road trip. Only two players drew their full pay, while five of the six strikers owed the team money. Hecker, the only striker to get any pay, received the paltry sum of $1.95. Pete owed the most, at $325, but surprisingly, he only argued over a single dollar. "That $1," bellowed Pete, "is for a bat that was stolen from me at McKeesport, where we played an exhibition. I have bought all my sticks this season. . . . At McKeesport someone stole one of the bats out of my bag, and now Davidson has charged me $1!"[21]

Hostilities between Davidson and the players increased, and several said they would not play. Third baseman Raymond threatened to quit baseball altogether and go home to California. None of that happened, but the players did establish a Louisville chapter of the Brotherhood of Professional Baseball Players. Over the next few weeks other teams followed suit, and eventually all the AA teams had chapters, except for Columbus. The Brotherhood was a union-like organization founded in 1885 by Hall of Famer John Montgomery Ward. It was becoming a force in baseball, and with a growing labor dispute on the horizon, it would take on even greater importance the following season.

Rumors persisted that Davidson was going to sell the team, and a collective of local businessmen led by the oldest Reccius brother, Bill, was poised to buy it. At the last minute, however, the miserly Davidson turned down their $5,000 offer. Finally, out of money and out of options, Davidson surrendered control of the team to the AA on July 2, leaving the franchise in limbo. The fear in Louisville was that the team would be dissolved or moved to another city. The players' futures were even more uncertain. Pay had been sporadic over the past month at best. That, combined with Davidson's outlandish fines, meant that some players had received no money for three paydays. At the end of June, during a seven-day road trip to Kansas City and St. Louis (during which the team went 1–6), players were forced to borrow money from opposing players and pawn their possessions so they could afford to eat and do laundry while on the road.

On July 3 the team was sold to a group of ten Louisville businessmen led by George Reiger. The sale did not settle the disputes between Davidson and the players, who had appealed to the AA over the excessive and unnecessary fines. At a July 5 meeting attended by Davidson, the new owners, several players, and the AA's board of directors, the league ordered that $735 of the $1,435 in fines collected in June be returned to the players. The league office noted, "These men had been very arbitrarily and unreasonably treated in many ways, were behind in compensation due them by the Louisville Club and were lacking the presence of a manager or any one representing their club to whom to look for guidance or to protect them in their rights."[22] The $700 in fines upheld by the league office consisted of the $100 fines levied against each of the six strikers who refused to play in Baltimore and Pete's $100 fine for his drunken late-night outing in Brooklyn.

Despite being ordered to do so by the league office, the petty and vengeful Davidson refused to return the players' fines in a timely manner. He procrastinated for days and then wrote one check to the players' spokesman, Hecker. But the check was written on a nonexistent bank account in Baltimore. In the space for the dollar amount, Davidson had written, "Any sum he wishes to collect," and the check was unsigned.[23] After dragging the drama out for a few more days, Davidson finally remitted the players' money. Wolf, who was emotionally drained from the stress of trying to run the team with the overbearing Davidson looming over his shoulder, resigned as manager on July 21 so he could focus on playing baseball. He was replaced by second baseman Shannon.

The new owners tried to improve morale by covering the players' back pay, even though they were not obligated to do so. The day after the sale, Louisville split a doubleheader with Philadelphia. Things appeared to be looking up, but a return to the awful was on the horizon. Pete sat out the first week of July with a charley horse and then went missing. He finally showed up at the ballpark on July 11. When asked where he had been, he casually replied that he had been spending time at home with his mom. Pete did not return to the lineup for another four days. Upon his return he was cheered by the fans, proving that no matter how poorly he played or how badly he behaved, he was still a favorite of the crowd in the bleachers. He responded by pounding out two hits and scoring two runs. The team responded by losing its fifty-eighth game of the season. The return of the Gladiator sparked optimism for the cellar-dwelling Colonels, as he batted .324 with six doubles over the remainder of the month. Unfortunately, optimism did not translate into wins. Although the club won nine games in July (nearly matching its ten wins for the entire season), the players were beset by injuries at the end of the month, setting them up for another miserable run. On July 24 against Baltimore, the lineup was already thin, with Hecker out of town to be with his sick wife. Both Raymond and Shannon were injured and had to leave the game, so Louisville called on amateur Harry Scherer to make his one and only major league appearance. Unsurprisingly, Louisville was walloped 17–3.

Meanwhile, Pete was "winning distinction with his willow," starting August with a seven-game hitting streak.[24] Then, just when it appeared that Pete had found his swing again, he reeled off a string of clunkers, going hitless in 8 of the next 15 games and batting only .145. On August 17, in a 10–0 whitewashing by Brooklyn, Pete "shattered the spectators' confidence by making three ineffectual strikes at the wind," going 1 for 4 with a strikeout and an error.[25] The following day he went hitless. It was his last appearance of 1889, as he was laid off without pay for the remainder of the season. Pete thought his layoff was unjust. Teammates and local sportswriters agreed, one of the latter writing, "The Louisville Club . . . without Pete Browning is like a steamboat without a pilot. The Gladiator is missed everywhere."[26] Management did not agree and claimed Pete had been laid off for drunkenness. Whether Pete was drunk or not, his suspension was really about the club preparing for next season. There were two factions on the team, and if the club wanted to be successful, those players viewed as disruptive had to be released, regardless of their on-field performance. The club also wanted younger players for the next season. It signed four new players at the start of September and hired veteran manager Jack Chapman, who had played with and managed the

Louisville Grays in 1876–1877, to helm the team in 1890. A week after Chapman was hired, Hecker was released. He ended up as Pittsburgh's player-manager for the 1890 season, his last in the major leagues.

Louisville ended its season on October 14 with a 7–5 loss to Kansas City. The Colonels finished the season with two consecutive losses, dropping 14 of their final 16 and finishing with a record of 27–111. Statistics tell the story of the 1889 team, and it was truly terrible. The Colonels were 9–65 on the road and an abysmal 6–20 in one-run games. Individually, the team did not produce a .300 hitter, the only team in the AA not to do so. The best hitters were Weaver and Wolf, at .291. Pete finished the season with a .256 average. It was the first time he did not hit at least .300 in a season and the first time he was not among the league's top three hitters. As disastrous as the season was by his lofty standards, and despite playing in only 83 games with 358 plate appearances, Pete finished right around the league average in many statistical hitting categories. Even with those underwhelming numbers, the team's offense was surprisingly mediocre, but its pitching was downright ugly. The leading pitcher was Ehret, with his 10–29 record and 4.80 ERA.

The legacy of this horrific season became part of Louisville baseball lore. For years, old-time baseball cranks told stories about how bad the 1889 team was. One of the most well-known tales involved the famous Laclede Hotel in St. Louis, where the Colonels were staying. Late one night, guests were awakened by someone yelling, "Help! Police! Help!" Policemen and hotel porters broke down the door to the room from which the screams were emanating. They gazed inside and were startled to see Pete wrestling with a pillow. One of the officers asked what was going on. Pete, with tears in eyes, turned and said, "I dreamt that Louisville won a game."[27]

At the end of the season, Pete's status for the following year was unclear, but many thought a return to the club was unlikely. Thus, it was a shock when he played in a number of exhibition games with Louisville and even more of a shock when he was reserved for the 1890 season and the man hired to replace him, John Galligan, was released. Chapman addressed his potential starting lineup for the upcoming season: "I have noticed Browning's playing since I came here, and in my opinion, he is capable of doing great work still. I don't think there is any doubt of his playing good ball if properly treated and I shall put him in center field."[28] Chapman's praise and attempt at diplomacy were too little, too late for

Pete. In December he sued the club for $650 in back pay, claiming it had violated his contract by keeping him on the bench when he was physically able to play. Despite daily stories of his return to the Louisville lineup in 1890, that was never a realistic option for Pete. The only question was where he would swing his Louisville Slugger in 1890.

The disastrous 1889 season would have a lasting impact on Pete's legacy. It stands out—and not in a good way—from the rest of his career and leads one to speculate how Pete would be viewed if that season had never happened. Another top-three finish in the batting race would have given him ten straight years in the top three, an impressive feat in any era. Removing the 1889 season from Pete's career would increase his lifetime batting average six points, from .341 to .347. The 1889 season was merely an aberration, but it seemed to convince many that Pete's career was over, and anything good that happened afterward would be a comeback.

The departure of Hecker at the end of the season and the eventual exit of Pete left Wolf as the only player remaining from the original AA Eclipse team of 1882. Wolf, always loyal, stayed and guided Louisville from its worst season to its first World Series championship in 1890, the city's first and only major title. The championship was made possible by the youth movement started at the end of the 1889 season by the team's new owners. It was also aided by a growing labor dispute that shattered the near-decade-long status quo and splintered the baseball universe into three recognized major leagues for the first and only time in history. The "Brotherhood War" was coming.

11

The Brotherhood War (1890)

"You bet your sweet life it's true," an excited Pete gushed when asked if he had signed with the newly formed Cleveland Infants of the Players' League (PL). "I have been waiting for this chance for the last four years. They ain't treated me right here [in Louisville] since 1886. Why I used ter play great ball for 'em till they put the screws to me; then I just quit, don't yer see? I don't mean ter say that I didn't play honest ball for 'em see? But I just got discouraged and I couldn't do it."[1]

To prove that his excitement was real, Pete took the Cleveland club's secretary, J. J. Coleman, into the back room of his house and proudly showed off three bats hanging on the wall. "I have just had dem sticks turned," said Pete. "Just watch 'em next season. I'll make those pitchers wish they had never been born. I'll break their hearts with them."[2]

Team owner Al Johnson was equally excited about signing his old friend, saying, "Pete is eccentric, but a great batsman and a clever fielder."[3] "This calls for $3000," he told Pete upon his arrival in Cleveland, "but you don't get it if you touch a drop of liquor." Pete reassured him and said, "I've been trying to drink Kentucky dry for ten years. I guess I can let the stuff alone for a year."[4]

Pete's declaration rang hollow to some, who sarcastically whispered that the only reason Pete wasn't drinking was because he hadn't received any advance money from the team. But Pete made a tremendous effort throughout the season to stay sober and was mostly successful. He even claimed that he had approached Louisville management the season before to ask for help in his quest for sobriety. He proposed that the club pay him only if he didn't drink. "I went to these people several times and I says, I'll sign a contract just this way," said Pete. "If I keeps sober I gets so much and I get it regular, but if youse ever smell anything on my breath or if youse ever hear of my takin' a drink, why I plays the rest of the season for nuthin'."[5] Louisville management did not take Pete up on his offer.

Pete signed with Cleveland on January 22 following a tumultuous off-season that included a war of words with the Louisville club. "See how they have been lyin' about me?" lamented Pete. "I know that I have gone wrong sometimes, but if they had come to me and talked to me like a gentleman I would have done anything for 'em. But they don't do it. They run off to the papers with another story of Pete being on a tear. That only made me worse. Don't you think I have got no feelin's left? Well, I have. I don't say nuthin', but it hurts just the same."[6] In addition, Pete sued his former club for money he felt he was owed after being benched and released before the end of the 1889 season. His lawsuit was a clear sign that he would not be returning to the only team he had ever played for professionally.

Pete lost his appetite for playing in his hometown after the hellish 1889 season in which the team finished a dismal 27–111 amidst unrelenting dysfunction and hostility. It was no surprise when Pete signed with Cleveland for 1890. He left the AA after eight seasons with a .345 career average, which stands as the best mark by any player with more than one season in the league.

Pete's decision to join Cleveland was heavily influenced by Al Johnson, a wealthy businessman and one of Pete's oldest and closest friends. The two grew up together playing baseball on the lots in the West End of Louisville. Johnson was one of the driving forces behind the new PL, which was born from the Brotherhood of Professional Baseball Players. The Brotherhood was formed in 1885 by Hall of Famer John Montgomery Ward and eight other members of the New York Giants as a fraternal organization. As stated in its charter, its purpose was "to protect and benefit its members collectively and individually, to promote a high standard of professional conduct, and to advance the interests of the National Game." The Brotherhood originated from sportswriter and minor league manager William Voltz's idea to create a benefit fund for needy players. Voltz, as a non–major leaguer, possessed little clout, so Ward and his Giants teammates co-opted the idea and built on Voltz's original concept. Ward was a popular player and a brilliant and energetic leader. He was also a lawyer, and he used that background to help players with contract issues. He was particularly interested in raising players' salaries in conjunction with the growing popularity of professional baseball and the increased revenue generated by the game.

Though not expressly viewed as a labor union and not referred to as such, the Brotherhood served many of the same purposes, without the negative connotations prevalent at the time. The Brotherhood took issue with the reserve clause, which was an integral part of the business of baseball. Under the reserve clause, teams owned players' contracts indefinitely until they were sold, traded, or terminated; they even retained control over players whose contracts had expired, including the right to reassign, sell, trade, or release them. Players' only recourse was to hold out and refuse to play. Because of the reserve clause, players' movement was restricted, and their salaries were limited. By 1887, the Brotherhood counted 107 players in its membership and held its first national meeting in New York on August 28. The stated goal of the meeting was to help players remedy contract abuses. Despite the Brotherhood's desire to meet with representatives of the National League to discuss new contracts, the NL did not recognize the Brotherhood as a legitimate organization and refused to negotiate with it. The NL argued that it had already conferred with preexisting committees that included players who were part of the Brotherhood, so there was no need to associate with what it viewed as a rebel organization.

In June 1889, in response to a new plan meant to severely limit players' salaries, the Brotherhood, led by Ward, was rumored to be planning a strike that would "be the biggest thing ever heard of in the baseball world."[7] The players were upset by the owners' desire to implement the Brush Classification System, which was the brainchild of John T. Brush, owner of the NL's Indianapolis Hoosiers. It proposed to divide players into five groups based on "habits, earnestness, and special qualifications," as determined by the previous season.[8] The owners wanted to base players' salaries on not only their performance on the field but also their conduct off it. These proposed changes were in addition to new NL policies requiring players to buy their own uniforms and providing only 50¢ per diem (roughly $14 in 2020 dollars). Despite continued protests from the Brotherhood and rumors of a strike, the NL ignored requests to negotiate. The NL viewed itself as an all-powerful entity and was not worried about the rumblings of some discontented players.

Despite the NL's attitude, Ward was opposed to the idea of a strike on principle. Strikes, like unions, were viewed negatively by middle-class society, and Ward shared those views. He made it clear that the Brotherhood's purpose was to encourage entrepreneurship and improve working conditions; the organization's activities were not defined by greed and disloyalty. As the dispute turned ugly, newspapers were filled with accusations and name-calling by both sides. Johnson publicly defended the Brotherhood and its leadership. "I see that Ward and [Fred] Pfeffer are termed 'Anarchists,'" he said. "I can hardly see how the term fits them, for it is not a division of profits gained in the past they ask for, nor is it the wild, visionary scheme of socialism that this struggle is for."[9]

The rumored work stoppage never materialized. Instead, Ward proposed a radical idea: he wanted to change the status of players from employees and assets to equal partners in the business of baseball. On July 14, 1889, he asked players to investigate the feasibility of securing capital in their own cities for the purpose of starting a new major league. This endeavor, which some sportswriters referred to as the "scheme," was kept a secret as Ward sought financial backers. Chief among them was Johnson, who believed owners were taking advantage of the players. He also saw the potential for personal financial gain if a new league were created. He owned a number of streetcar lines around Cleveland and realized that ownership in a nearby ballpark would give him two businesses, each enhancing the profits of the other. Johnson spent a fair amount of his own time and money traveling to other cities to help organize the new league.

At its core, the Brotherhood wanted to challenge the idea that players were simply contract employees with no voice in league operations and no say in whether they were traded or sold to other teams. To this end, the PL was created to function as a co-op, where players were investors in their clubs, trades required the players' consent, and owners' profits were shared with the players.

The idea for the PL was born on Albert Spalding's around-the-world baseball tour at the end of the 1888 season. On the long trips in between stops, Ward and fellow players Jim Fogarty, Ned Hanlon, and Fred Pfeffer discussed the NL's perceived mistreatment of players and "how the League had broken faith with them." They discussed "getting capital in each city to build the grounds for [new teams]," with the players receiving "a portion of the profits and . . . if possible . . . liberat[ing] themselves from the tyrannical rule of the League."[10]

Based on those conversations, Ward set in motion plans to establish a new league, christened the Players' League, to begin play in 1890. The NL gave the proposed new league little chance of getting off the ground and was shocked when the PL announced teams for the 1890 season. The NL continued to ignore players' complaints and exhibited a complete lack of understanding of the source of their anger. As a result, almost the entire NL and many of the top players in the AA, including 15 future Hall of Famers, defected to the PL. The NL was left with few established stars and had to fill its rosters with young players and rookies for the 1890 season.[11]

The AA was not hit as hard as the NL in terms of player defections, but thanks to financial uncertainty and the departure of the Brooklyn team—the 1889 champs—to the NL, there were many unknowns heading into the new season. The AA placed new teams in small markets, adding clubs in Syracuse, Toledo, and Rochester, weakening the AA and leading to an unstable season. A new AA team was also formed in Brooklyn to replace the departing champs.

In Louisville, Mordecai Davidson's poor treatment forced the players to establish a chapter of the Brotherhood in June 1889—the first AA team to do so—but it was dissolved soon after Davidson sold the team. This decision to disband the chapter benefited the Louisville team going forward. When the PL became a reality and players started joining it, there was no local Brotherhood to pressure the players to jump ship, so Louisville lost fewer players than other teams, although it did lose its superstar Pete. However, his decision to leave was rooted in years of perceived mistreatment by the team and the press. "I tell you it makes a great difference in your playing is how you are treated," he explained. "Last season I was used shamefully. I was fined without reason, and there was no redress for a player. I would have left Louisville long ago had I been able, and I thank heaven that deliverance from baseball bondage has come at last."[12]

The Brotherhood War, as the conflict between the leagues came to be known, mostly involved the larger and richer NL and the PL, with the AA caught in the crossfire between them. The PL was composed of a majority of ex-NL players who adhered to the same conservative, middle-class values espoused by the NL: no Sunday baseball, 50¢ tickets, and no alcohol sales. Despite the potential need to expand its audience by including the common-man ideals of the AA, the PL was not willing to engage in immoral practices such as breaking the Sabbath. Ironically, by the end of the season, many of the best players in the PL were refugees from the "immoral" AA. Despite their philosophical differences, the PL and the AA might have been ideal partners in a fight against the NL, but many of the former NL players who made up the PL's power structure retained their negative attitude toward the AA. The AA was regularly ignored, as the PL wanted to directly challenge the established NL and placed seven of its eight franchises in cities that already had NL teams: Boston, Brooklyn, Chicago, Cleveland, New York, Philadelphia, and Pittsburgh (the eighth PL team was in Buffalo). Brooklyn and Philadelphia, which also hosted AA teams, had three major league teams competing for the fans' attention. Parks were situated next to each other, and games were often scheduled on the same day and at the same time, forcing fans to choose which team to support. In Chicago, the NL White Stockings and the PL Pirates shared 48 conflicting dates out of 70 home games. In Philadelphia, the schedule featured 32 days when all three clubs played at once.

Pete thought he knew who would come out on top in this war between the leagues. "The Players' League is in its first season, yet in the few months of its career has provided the finest organization, the greatest collection of players, and the most magnificent grounds the game has ever known. It has moved on smoothly, strongly, and successfully, despite vehement opposition, and I know what I'm talking about. Drink to our success."[13]

Freed from what he called "baseball bondage," Pete was happy to be playing in a positive, supportive environment. His attitude reflected this change. He claimed he was going to break some of his bad habits on the field. "I will slide this season if it breaks my leg or neck," said Pete. "The Old War Horse is not played out as they say. If he don't keep some of the youngsters guessing, he knows nothing about baseball." To help with his sliding and protect him when he hit the dirt, he wore pants "padded until he look[ed] like the fat man in a dime museum."[14]

Early in the year, on March 27, a massive cyclone tore through downtown Louisville. Pete was in St. Louis when the twister hit, and a friend informed him what had happened. Pete looked surprised and quickly corrected his friend: "You must not be up to date in baseball if you don't know that Cyclone Duryea [pitcher Jesse Duryea] has signed with Cincinnati." After this misunderstanding was cleared up, Pete coldly said, "The cyclone could have been forgiven if it had only hit the Louisville team"—proving that his animosity toward his former team was still intact.[15]

Pete started the season hitting safely in 22 of 28 games, with nine doubles, back-to-back home runs on May 16 and 17, and an 11-game hitting streak. This helped him regain his swagger and confidence from years past. When asked about his play, Pete responded with his old vim: "Oh, I'm hittin' 'em right along, old man. My lamps are great, and dey can't fool Peter."[16]

On May 8 Pete was hit by a pitch from George Haddock in a 14–4 win over Buffalo. After the game, he claimed he had not been hit by a pitch in ten years. This statement evolved over the years to include the myth that he was never hit by a pitch in his entire career or that he was hit only once. In fact, Pete was hit many times throughout his career, most famously the first time in 1883, which sidelined him for eight games, and in 1891 when Kid Gleason broke his wrist with a fastball, ending his season. Pete finished tenth in the AA in being hit by pitched balls in 1886, when he was plunked seven times.

Pete was playing with the joy and freedom of his younger self and excelling both with the bat and in the field. On June 4 he wowed the Chicago crowd when he chased down a long fly ball that looked like a sure three-bagger, "springing three feet in the air and pulling the ball down with one hand."[17] The crowd responded with a standing ovation lasting several minutes and compelling Pete to doff his cap several times. After witnessing Pete's acrobatics in the field, Chicago team president John Addison remarked, "That fellow is seven feet high and he jumps six feet into the air to pull down home runs. What does he want to do? Kill off the sport entirely."[18]

Given Pete's impressive return to form, Cleveland sportswriters regularly questioned why Louisville had released the slugger. Pete was enjoying the new league and reveling in his success. "I was never in such fast company in all my life," he said of his new team and new league. "It is the greatest organization, with the best array of players, ever known." Teammate Henry Larkin agreed: "The game as played by the Players' League, will accomplish its own work. All other organizations are minor leagues compared with ours and not in it."[19]

Despite his success at the plate, Pete was suffering regularly from the effects of mastoiditis. He missed four games in June due to a fever, probably connected to his worsening condition. "If not properly treated," wrote Dr. Pasquale Cassano in 2020, "acute mastoiditis can lead to extracranial and intracranial complications, which are sometimes very serious and even life-threatening."[20] Pete dealt with these serious complications his entire life.

The 1890 season was the first time Pete publicly commented on the negative impact the summer heat had on his health. Cleveland's ballpark had a clump of trees near left field, casting long shadows over the deep part of the field. On hot days, Pete played deep in the outfield so he could stand in the shade, the result being that any balls landing in shallow left field were hits. Manager Patsy Tebeau instructed Pete to move in, which he did, but after a few moments he moved back to the cool comfort of the shade. At the end of the inning, Tebeau confronted Pete and asked, "Why don't you play for the batters? You missed three hits today by playing deep, Pete. If you can't play as I tell you I will yank you out." Pete's response was as expected: "That's all right Cap, about yanking old Pete out of the game, but you will miss Pete's batting. I'm subject to headaches and I can't play in the sun. If I play out in the sun and get sunstruck what would you do for a batter who cracks out those singles. Pete cannot afford to play in the sun. But he will locate himself in any place that you ask, Cap, on cloudy days."[21] Later in the year, in a close game against Chicago on a hot summer day, Pete called for a time-out in the eighth inning and jogged to the bench, where he plunged his hand into the water cooler and pulled out a cabbage leaf. He removed his hat, put the wet leaf on his head, and replaced his cap before retaking his spot in the shade of deep left field. After the game, when asked about the cabbage leaf, Pete, who had knocked in the winning run in the ninth, explained, "You see it cooled off old Pete's head and braced Pete's batting lamps. There is nothing like a cabbage leaf for the head and lamps."[22]

Despite his pledge to avoid alcohol, Pete struggled to stay sober. The *Cincinnati Times Star* wrote about a recently invented bottle stopper with a bell attached that rang every time someone took a drink. "Pete Browning has one of them," wrote the *Star*, "and now, whenever the Cleveland Brotherhood team strikes a town on their travels everybody inquires, 'Who's dead?' They think it is a church bell tolling."[23] Still, Pete managed to stay mostly sober, and he regularly attended temperance meetings. During the season he lived at Kennard House, and scarcely a night passed that he was not asked half a dozen times to have a drink while relaxing downstairs in the lounge. Even teammates going out for the evening tried to coax him into having a taste, but for the most part, Pete drank nothing but seltzer lemonade. Some nights were even more of a struggle when he was surrounded by adoring fans who tried to shame him into having a drink for old times' sake. He was known to refuse a glass from a stranger out of fear it might be spiked. When asked about his sobriety in July, Pete said, "I never knew what it was to go to bed sober until the 14th of last August. . . . Some men know when they have plenty; I did not, and since I have stopped drinking, I feel like a new man. I sleep better, have an awful appetite, can hit the ball harder and more often than ever, and when salary day comes I have more to my credit than I ever had before. . . . A player cannot drink beer and play ball."[24]

Pete continued to slug away. As good as he was at the start of the season, he was even better in July. He hit safely in 25 of 27 games, with hitting streaks of 10 and 15 games, and blasted 16 extra-base hits over the month, with nine doubles, five triples, and two home runs. He also stole 11 bases. It seemed like nothing could stop Pete. As his confidence grew, every single looked good for a double, every double looked good for a triple, and every triple looked like he could make it all the way home. Teams resorted to anything they could think of to stop him. In one game, after Pete lined a shot to deep center and started to round the bases, the center fielder took off to retrieve the ball. The center-field fence in Cleveland was lined with apple trees that regularly dropped their fruit onto the field. The ball rolled toward a clump of apples, and the center fielder, hoping to catch Pete off guard, picked up an apple and fired it to second base. Pete saw the incoming fruit, mistook it for the ball, and stopped running. The fielder finally located the ball amongst the apples and relayed it in, holding Pete to a double with his deviousness.

Papers across the country were taking notice of Pete's season and writing about him in glowing terms. The influential *New York World* wrote, "Pete Browning, the old iron-faced Thracian, is well known for his ability to hit impossible balls. He can pick a ball off his right ear and send it howling over the outer walls quite as often as he can hit one over the plate." In what amounted to modesty for the cocky slugger, Pete declared, "I've been the best batter and fielder in the country for ten years, but I didn't know it until this season."[25]

Pete's well-known mania for his bats was still intact. At the start of the season he boasted about a new bat he had custom-made in Louisville (likely by the Hilleriches) during the off-season. As Pete's success at the plate continued throughout the season, his attachment to that bat grew. In a late-season showdown in New York against the Giants, the game was delayed in the third inning when Pete couldn't find his treasured bat, which had been hidden by some fans. It was eventually returned when Pete refused to go to bat without it.

While Pete was enjoying a resurgence after the disaster of 1889, the Brotherhood War continued. It was a war of attrition, with each side trying to bleed the other dry financially while losing money itself. As the season dragged on, each side took its case to the newspapers, inflating attendance figures to give the impression that it was the more popular league. In July, Cap Anson, one of the most prominent players who remained in the NL, spit venom, stating, "The Brotherhood is making a wonderful bluff, but it can't last. They will have rag carpet hereafter instead of velvet, and the interest will sag like a clothesline attached to a three-ounce kite. I don't believe their plums made them enough profit to pay half their lumber bills for the grandstand. When the crash comes you will hear it a mile off."[26]

Sportswriters saw through the charade perpetrated by both sides and penned opinion pieces begging for the war to end. "To carry on the war is only proving financially disastrous," pleaded the *Sporting News*. "With conflicting dates all over the country the crowds to one or the other must be diminished as the season progresses. . . . Have not the rival forces had enough of the losing fight to change their dates and avoid any further trouble?"[27] The two sides did not heed the warnings and continued to lose money at a rapid pace, while making public proclamations that all was fine. The NL offered Brotherhood players large contracts as an inducement to defect from the PL, but this tactic had little success.

The end of the season was a financial bloodbath for all three leagues, as attendance and concession sales were down for every team. It is hard to estimate how much revenue was lost, as the teams inflated their numbers all season, but the amounts were clearly significant. The PL likely lost about $125,000, and the NL lost between $300,000 and $500,000. The AA was in even worse shape, as in addition to its financial losses, two of its franchises declared bankruptcy during the season. An editorial in the *Courier-Journal* highlighted the negative aspects of the season: "Base-ball has undergone a severe strain this season, and it is probable that the formation of the Players' League had considerable to do with it. The National game has enjoyed a substantial and phenomenal growth up to the present season, but that it has declined this year cannot be denied. More base-ball organizations have met their death this season than ever before."[28]

It can be argued that the PL won the war, with a more exciting season, better baseball, and larger crowds. But it lost the off-season negotiations, bringing the upstart league to an end. The PL's failure was largely due to the dubious dealings of the NL owners in their negotiations with the PL and their superior business savvy. By the end of the season, the NL was in bad financial shape, but the Brotherhood did not realize how serious its rival's troubles were. Most of the PL's financial backers were inexperienced and new to the business of baseball, and they did not understand what constituted acceptable losses for a season. Ward and the Brotherhood offered a compromise to the NL and the AA, in the hopes they could find a way to coexist. But the PL's financial backers sabotaged Ward's plan when they were outmaneuvered by Albert Spalding, the influential owner of the Chicago White Stockings, and the rest of the NL owners. When asked about their league's financial situation, the PL owners answered honestly, disclosing their true losses for the season. Spalding sensed weakness and pounced, convincing the PL owners that only the PL had lost money. The *Sporting News* compared the PL owners to a fly that, upon being invited into the spider's parlor, walked right in.[29] Instead of trying to negotiate a compromise with the NL, the PL owners looked for a way to salvage their own investments. The Brotherhood's players were hung out to dry. In the end, it did not come down to some principled stand. It came down to what it always does: money. The PL's backers began consolidating their franchises with rival teams in the same cities. Johnson, who was believed to have an investment stake in five of the PL's eight clubs, was fed up with the drama and withdrew his financial support, effectively bringing the league to an end.

The players of the Brotherhood returned to the NL, which proceeded to destroy what remained of the AA over the next season, swallowing up four of its teams in the process. By 1892, there was only one 12-team league. That monopoly ended nine years later when the American League was founded, establishing the modern two-league system. Baseball would have to wait until the middle of the twentieth century for a successful attempt to unionize players.

Despite its short life, the PL should be recognized for the vision of Ward and the Brotherhood and their attempt to improve the power structure in baseball. The Brotherhood War was the first and only challenge to the organizational structure of professional sports. It attempted to create a true business partnership between the skilled laborers (the players) and their capitalist bosses (the owners). Modern work stoppages and strikes revolve around contractual issues; they do not address the players' role in the structure of the sport. Although it ultimately lost the war, the Brotherhood had some long-term successes, such as driving wages upward and improving certain playing conditions. Ward tried to bring about change not through strikes and confrontation but through an orderly system of cooperation between players and owners, albeit owners who were more open to cooperation and more player-friendly. The *Sporting News* provided a fitting epitaph at the end of the 1890 season: "Goodbye Players' League. . . . Your life has been a stormy one. Because of your existence many a man has lost thousands of dollars. And before long all that will be left of [you] is a memory—a sad, discouraging memory."[30]

The collapse of the Brotherhood and the PL was of little concern to Pete. His participation in the new league had not been some principled stand against an unfair system. Although he was vocal in his support of the PL and its ideals, at the end of the day, he simply wanted to play baseball and get paid as much as possible for it. Once, when asked about the Brotherhood, a smile crept across Pete's face as he reached into his pocket and pulled out a big roll of money. "See this long green?" he asked. "Well the Brotherhood is full of it."[31]

For Pete, 1890 ended like many seasons before it: he had a standout year playing on a bad team, as Cleveland finished seventh in the eight-team league. Initially, it was thought that Dave Orr led the league in hitting, besting Pete by .001, but that soon changed when Pete, with a .373 average, was officially declared the batting champion. This was his third career batting title, making him the first player (and one of only four) to win titles in two different leagues.[32] He led the PL in doubles and OPS+ and finished second in OBP, second in runs created, and fifth in slugging and hits. It was a return to form after the disastrous 1889 season. Pete viewed his success in the PL as validation of his skills, as he competed against and surpassed the best players in baseball, proving that he was among the game's top hitters and adding to his resumé as one of the top players of his generation. While his accomplishments in the AA are often derided due to the perceived lack of talent in that league, Pete's sole season in the PL proved that perception wrong. Even though the AA provided only about a quarter of the players in the PL (the rest coming from the NL), those players disproved the existence of a talent gap between the two leagues. Pete and Orr had played their entire careers in the AA and finished first and second in hitting in the stacked PL. In addition, the top three winning pitchers in the PL—Mark Baldwin, Silver King, and Gus Weyhing—all played the 1889 season in the AA.

Pete credited much of his success in 1890 to his long, heavy, unwieldy, custom-made ash bat, which he claimed to swing in every at-bat. The normally generous Pete was particularly protective of this bat and denied his teammates use of it. Unfortunately, after smoking a hit in his last at-bat of the season, he laid the bat on the grass near the bench, and when he returned a few minutes later to retrieve it, the bat had disappeared. Neither the bat nor the thief was ever found.

The 1890 season was one of redemption for the Louisville team, as it was rewarded with both an AA and a World Series title. Its World Series win marked the first time a team went from worst to first in a season, and it was Louisville's one and only World Series title. The 1890 season was also a breakout year for Pete's childhood friends Chicken Wolf, who led the AA with a .363 batting average, and Hub Collins, who led the NL in runs scored.

The 1890 season also played a role in an oddity that is unlikely to be repeated: two teams winning back-to-back titles in different leagues in consecutive years. The Brooklyn team, which left the AA after winning the title in 1889, repeated the same feat in the NL in 1890. The PL champion Boston Reds were asked to join the AA the following season and won the AA championship in 1891. Boston also became the only team to win the pennant in every season of its existence, as the AA disbanded after the 1891 season, and the team folded along with it.

Once the season ended, Pete took the train home to Louisville. He arrived at the station looking fit and healthy, dressed in a fashionable three-button cutaway coat, with a large diamond pin adorning his scarf. A crowd immediately surrounded him, and reporters approached, asking questions. Pete couldn't resist the chance to boast of his accomplishments. "I told the people here if I could get away from this town, I would show them how to play ball," crowed Pete. "Well, I did it. . . . You ought to have seen me line the ball out. I led 'em all. Dan Brouthers, Dave Orr, Mike Kelly, Roger Connor, and all those sluggers were not in it with Pete, the Gladiator."[33] He claimed he hadn't touched a drop of liquor all season, though that is up for debate. Flush with confidence, Pete held court with fans and reporters, talking about his favorite topic—himself—and how the press mistreated him and the public didn't show him enough respect:

> You see when Pete was here, he wasn't nobody and he had to go away from Kentucky to get recognition from the people. They didn't know Pete anymore. Now Pete comes back here, and everybody calls him, "Mr. Browning," and tells him he's fine as silk. 'Cause why? Cause he led Brouthers, Orr, Stovey, and Connor, and all them big batters, and got an average of .391, see? In 1882 and 1885 Pete was something here, but the papers pulled him down and the people called him "Red Eye" and "Distillery Pete," and hadn't no respect for him. But when he got with good people, he got to be good people himself.[34]

12

Final Seasons (1891–1894)

The argument can be made that if the Louisville Grays' game-fixing scandal of 1877 never happened, Pete likely would have played the bulk of his career, if not all of it, with his hometown National League team. Instead, he took a circuitous route to get there. After years dominating the American Association, followed by a move to the highly competitive Players' League, where he continued his dominant ways, Pete finally ended up in the NL in 1891, his tenth year playing Major League Baseball. After his 1890 batting title in the PL, Pete was once again an in-demand player and received many offers. The *Philadelphia Inquirer* chalked this up to not only his impressive season at the plate but also his improved off-field lifestyle. "Ball players should take example from Peter Browning," the paper wrote. "Two years ago, he was laid off from the Louisville Club for indifferent playing caused by excessive indulgence in alcoholic stimulants. ... Total abstinence brought out all his good qualities.... This year Peter's services are in great demand. He has been offered as high as $3800, and the Louisville Club, with which he formerly played for about $1800, has offered him double that salary.... Total abstinence has given him a bank account and made a man of him."[1] Despite this praise and Pete's bluster, his final seasons in MLB were frustrating. He struggled to find a consistent home, bouncing from team to team even though, as he regularly pointed out, he was still in top form as a hitter. He was also battling the headaches and vertigo that had plagued him most of his life, negatively affecting his performance on the field and making life in general more difficult.

Following his year in the PL, Pete split the 1891 season between the two worst teams in the NL: the Pittsburgh Pirates and the Cincinnati Reds.

He signed with Pittsburgh in March for $4,000, having been persuaded to do so by former teammate Guy Hecker, who had managed the team the season before. After winning the PL batting title, Pete's confidence, which had taken a hit after the nightmare of 1889, returned in force. He told a Louisville reporter:

> Pittsburgh has agreed to my terms and I am only waiting on my $1000 advance money. . . . I ain't very pretty and the women don't go wild over me when I appear in public, but when a ball player is wanted, I just about fit the bill. I only asked for $500 advance at first, but I changed my mind. I want $1000 now and won't stir a peg out of this place until it comes. They want me awful bad, but they don't like to forward the sugar. Your Uncle Peter's no fool. He served long and well in the ranks of John Barleycorn. I am a passed graduate now, a genuine up and up gem of the first water.[2]

Pete's signing with Pittsburgh angered some fans in Kentucky, who were shocked when he didn't return home. "The whole state will, of course, sympathize with Louisville in the loss of her beloved Pete Browning," wrote the *Owensboro Messenger,* "the drunken bum whom the base ball idiots of that town slobber over so disgustingly. Louisville is Kentucky's idol, and what grieves Louisville grieves the State, even if she has to hold her nose while manifesting sorrow."[3]

Former teammate Tony Mullane, whose relationship with Pete was rocky at best, recognized his talent and rebirth as a hitter and had high praise for him: "Old Pete Browning is undoubtedly a great batter," Mullane commented prior to the season. "He is a natural born hitter and since he has quit boozing is better than ever. They tell me he has got to be a great bunter. If that is so he is a dangerous man, because he can tap 'em down and pull the infield in, and then let out the ball with all his might, and anyone who tries to stop it at short range will lose a leg or an arm. Yes, I believe the old gladiator will stay sober and make his mark."[4]

Pete had indeed added bunting to his arsenal, after being opposed to it for so long. But his time in Pittsburgh got off to a rough start when he bunted into a triple play on May 5 against Chicago. In the sixth inning, Pittsburgh, which had struggled to get runners on base, finally had runners at first and second. Pete "made an artistic bunt" that "dropped gently" into former teammate Fred Pfeffer's hands.[5] Pfeffer fired the ball to shortstop Jimmy Cooney, who was covering second, and Cooney then relayed the ball to first baseman Cap Anson, catching both runners well off the bag for a 4–6–3 triple play. "The crowd yelled itself hoarse over the play," reported the *Chicago Tribune*. For Pete, it was the culmination of a miserable inning. In the top half of the sixth he had misjudged a long fly ball and chased it around the outfield like it was a "toy balloon," allowing the winning run to score.[6]

The triple-play bunt was a rarity, but it presaged Pete's tenure in Pittsburgh. Although he was hitting decently—he clubbed four home runs over the first three weeks of the season and was tops on the team in hitting—he was unhappy with his play and observed, "I am just batting hard enough to keep me from getting blue."[7] His well-known independent streak was beginning to run afoul of manager and future Hall of Famer Ned Hanlon. Accustomed to the long leash and the freedoms afforded him in Louisville, where he had been allowed to do pretty much as he pleased, Pete chafed under Hanlon's rules. And the manager was growing tired of some of Pete's more ridiculous eccentricities. At the start of the season, Pete had shaved his eyelashes off. When asked why, he nonchalantly explained, "So they wouldn't obstruct my lamps."[8] On another occasion, Hanlon fined Pete $5 for not having spikes on his shoes, which caused him to fall while chasing a fly ball. According to baseball historian David Nemec, Pete was the last player on record to be fined for not wearing spikes.[9] Pete, of course, was ready with an explanation: "They say I'm getting old and that I drink. Lies, all lies. Sore feet is my complaint. My feet have been sore under the bottoms all season. I took the spikes out of my shoes to make it easier on them."[10] Another time he hit into a double play after ignoring Hanlon's order to sacrifice. Pete was also troubled by a large yellow sign on the center-field fence and asked that it be taken down, claiming that this Jonah was interfering with his hitting. He said the same thing had happened the season before in Cleveland, and once the advertisement on the center-field fence had been removed, he began to "smite the leather."[11]

Some of Pete's issues may have been due to an illness he apparently picked up on the team's preseason trip to the South at the beginning of April. A month later, he was reportedly not a "well man" and "hardly in shape to play ball." This illness lingered into June, when Pete admitted he was not fit to play and asked to be laid off without pay until he was feeling better. The newspaper called Pete's illness a "cold" that had "settled in his face" and left his eyes weak. The length of this illness, which lasted more than two months, indicates that it was probably mastoid related.[12]

All this led to Pete being released on June 26 after 50 games with Pittsburgh. Given that the team was 11 games out of first and battling Cincinnati for the title of worst team in the league, this was a bit surprising, as Pete was still leading the team in hitting at .291. After Pete was released, the *Pittsburgh Press* reported that "the club was hard up for players and . . . started out to pick up whatever they could find," eventually settling on a couple of local youngsters.[13] Neither panned out. One never played a game, and the other made only three appearances before being cut.

Pete took his release in stride, knowing he wouldn't be out of a job for long and happy to be away from the dysfunction in Pittsburgh. The Pittsburgh papers were aghast at the move. "[Pete] was just beginning to get his second wind when he was given his walking papers," wrote the *Pittsburgh Daily Post.* "Before the season closes the local club will probably have cause to regret the unceremonious release of Browning."[14] Four days after being cut, Pete signed with Cincinnati for $3,800—a move that took him from one horrible team to another. Still, Pete expressed excitement, saying, "I have always wanted to play in Cincinnati, and I am satisfied."[15]

Pete arrived in Cincinnati in time for a three-game home stand against Pittsburgh. His arrival at the stadium caused a stir when he loudly announced his presence. "The Gladiator, who usually talks in a voice several times louder than a sea captain uses in a storm, was in high glee," reported the *Cincinnati Enquirer.* "Pietro is a little deaf and he seems to think everybody else is. When he cleared his throat and turned himself loose, the policeman on the beat thought there was a riot in the brickyard back of the park." New teammate Bug Holliday's 21-pound bulldog pup was seen running for cover at the sound of Pete's bellowing voice. After praising the team's selection of bats, Pete declared, "Cincinnati is the town for me, and I have been working eight years to get here. That's straight. Watch the Gladiator. He'll pull 'em out from now on. Pittsburgh is a dead Jonah town. No good for Pete. I always could hit 'em here."[16] He then retired to the clubhouse to spend the rest of the afternoon oiling his bats in preparation for the game.

Pete's move to Cincinnati reunited him with former teammate Mullane. He also crossed paths with "Long" John Reilly, a similarly obsessed bat hoarder. Pete replaced Reilly in center field, allowing Reilly to move to his more natural position at first base. The two engaged in many odd conversations about batting, and Pete, who was worried that his sticks might end up in the possession of the notoriously light-fingered Reilly, padlocked his locker.

Pete entered the three-game series against Pittsburgh with revenge on his mind. He felt he had been mistreated by the Pittsburgh papers, and he held a personal grudge against pitcher Mark Baldwin, whom he had overhead disparaging him. In the opening game of the series, the Cincinnati fans welcomed Pete with an ovation lasting several minutes. He torched Baldwin for two hits and two RBIs in a 6–4 loss for Cincinnati. The next day, Pete went 0 for 4 but rebounded in the final game, going 2 for 4, with two RBIs and a double, in a 10-inning 6–5 win. The *Cincinnati Enquirer* hailed his arrival: "At last he is ours, Pietro Redlight Distillery Browning is a full-fledged Red Stocking, and a right good Red Stocking he is. . . . The Gladiator's initiatory appearance in the historic red and white apparel of the Queen City was a success."[17]

Pete flourished in the positive environment in Cincinnati. Despite being a cellar dweller in the standings, the team never devolved into the dysfunction that had marked his brief time in Pittsburgh. Pete remarked that he no longer had anything to complain about and was "satisfied with the world and himself."[18] "I like Cincinnati better than any other city in the League," he told an *Enquirer* reporter. "I not only like the city, but I like the management and the players."[19] He continued to do what he had always done: hit the ball and theorize on the best way and the best bat to accomplish that. "I am going to get out my old sash-weight bat tonight," said Pete to no one in particular. "I have been using a light stick. They're no good. No, you want to kill 'em when you got a light stick in your hands. . . . They are pitching curves all the time and you can't kill 'em. . . . No more light sticks for Petey."[20]

After years of alcohol abuse, Pete was sober and relishing in it, attributing much of his success to his nondrinking ways. "No, I ain't blowed one off since a year ago last August," he proudly proclaimed, "and you can bet it will be many more years before I touch another. There is nothing in it. Just look at me now. I am lining 'em out. It don't take old red-eye to give you courage to go up against 'em."[21] Still, it was sometimes a struggle to maintain his sobriety. He was, after all, Pete Browning, the Prince of Bourbon, and fans clamored to have a drink, share a cigar, and spend time with the legendary slugger and (former) boozer. The *Chicago Inter-Ocean* wrote, "Very few people realize what courage and firmness of character it has taken to carry out the Gladiator's determination to let booze alone. Fully fifty times I have seen him surrounded by a crowd of half-inebriated sportsmen laughing at him sarcastically and begging him to come to the bar. 'All right,' Pete would say, 'I'll take a seltzer lemonade.'"[22]

Cincinnati was looking to improve on its fourth-place, 77–55 finish in 1890 and have a better season in 1891, but an early slump seemed to sap the life out of the club. It was hoped the midseason addition of Pete would provide a spark. A three-game winning streak soon after his arrival gave credence to this notion, but the club slipped back into its old ways, playing with little heart and no fight until the August 18 game against the Cleveland Spiders. In the eighth inning, after completing what they thought was an inning-ending double play, the Cincinnati players were heading off the field when umpire Phil Powers ruled otherwise. Cincinnati captain and third baseman Arlie Latham charged at Powers to argue the call, leaving Pete, who had come in from left field, standing on third with the ball. While Latham argued with Powers, Spiders second baseman Clarence "Cupid" Childs, who was coaching third base, snatched the ball out of Pete's hand and threw it into his vacant spot in left field. Immediately the Spiders base runners ran for home, instigating another round of arguing. Childs's actions were not surprising, as the Spiders were managed by the notoriously hot-tempered Patsy Tebeau, who, according to baseball historian Lee Allen, "was the prototype of all hooligans and his players cheerfully followed his example."[23] Order was eventually restored, and the two runners returned to their bases, but tensions remained high. After the Spiders got a couple of hits that scored three runs, outfielder Jimmy McAleer ended up on second base. Another hit sent McAleer toward third, and Latham, seeing that the umpire wasn't watching, attempted to block McAleer from rounding the bag and heading for home. McAleer responded by punching Latham in the side, and when Latham continued to block his path, McAleer kicked him twice in a "vicious manner." Latham retaliated with a hard right to the jaw that "staggered" McAleer, causing him to fall to a "sitting posture." As a dazed McAleer got to his feet and wobbled away, Cleveland catcher Charles Zimmer "rushed Latham like a mad bull." Then McAleer came to his senses and grabbed a bat. "Half frenzied with rage and with the bat brandished above his head in a threatening manner he bore down on Latham," wrote the *Enquirer*. "McAleer had murder in his heart" and chased Latham to the outfield with a host of Spiders in pursuit. Realizing that he was not going to catch Latham, McAleer threw the bat at him. "It sped through the air with terrific force, but Latham was lucky enough to dodge."[24] The park police, as well as members of the city police force who were in attendance, raced toward the outfield to help, as spectators swarmed onto the field. A melee ensued as players, police, and spectators jostled one another out on the field. It took the police a full half hour to restore order, allowing play to resume. Cleveland went on to win, 6–2.

The following day, Latham, while chasing an overthrown ball from Pete that had rolled near the Spiders' bench, found his path blocked by McAleer in clear provocation. "Had Latham been the least bit pugnaciously inclined there would have been repetition yesterday of the disgraceful brawl of the day previous," wrote the *Enquirer.* "Latham sensibly declined the challenge. It was not through fear that he did not, however, for Latham is physically capable of whipping two McAleers."[25]

As the summer wore on, Pete started to heat up at the plate, reeling off a ten-game hitting streak in August and creeping back into the race for the batting title. Pete defiantly declared, "They are all dead easy for me to catch. I have caught my second wind, and watch me from now."[26] The day after a four-hit game in which he smacked a double and a triple, the *Enquirer* wrote, "Pete Browning's sole ambition is to lead the League in batting. He has had the honor of heading the premier's place in the American Association and the Brotherhood and if he would show the way to Roger Connor, Billy Hamilton, Harry Stovey, Bug Holliday, and the rest of the League batters he would be puffed out to such a degree that you wouldn't hand him a ripe peach or a fishing pole. His slashing work with the bat yesterday tickled him greatly. Four safe drives give the Gladiator a big boost in the right direction."[27] The sporting press realized how impressive it would be if Pete led the NL in hitting. It would be the third league in which he topped the batting list, a feat never achieved before and one that could never be replicated in the modern era. Pete's quest for baseball immortality came to an end on September 6 when Philadelphia pitcher Kid Gleason threw the ball high and inside and Pete fended it off with his hand to avoid being beaned.[28] It was a violent impact. Pete's teammates thought he had been struck in the head as he rolled around on the ground in pain, and a sympathetic crowd of players gathered around to help him. Pete's hand was broken, and he was sidelined for the final month of the season.

Pete batted .343 in 55 games for Cincinnati to raise his season average to .313, good for third in the NL, behind Billy Hamilton's .340 and teammate Holliday's .319. The top three NL batters had all started their careers in the AA, once again refuting that league's perceived lack of talent. Pete's third-place finish at age 30 was impressive, but he believed he had been "jobbed" out of the batting title. He was known to record his batting average on his cuffs and claimed he actually had a higher average than league leader Hamilton. "The old Gladiator put down all his hits on his collars and cuffs after every game so he wouldn't get them mixed. My home average shows me .336 and you know dabgasted well I was hitting 2 to 1 better on the trips. I had all the third basemen scared of me. I kept their think-boxes going. They didn't know whether I was going to cut off their legs with a hot one or just dump and run." He would have been able to prove this, except that "a chambermaid gathered up all Pete's cuffs and collars and sent them to the laundry. What's the consequence? Pete is jobbed, and he can't help himself. His batting average has been washed out."[29] Regardless, it is reasonable to believe that if Pete had spent the entire season in Cincinnati and remained injury free, he might have become the first and only player to win batting crowns in three different leagues, guaranteeing him a spot in the Baseball Hall of Fame.

In 1892, for the first time in a decade, MLB found itself with only one league. The PL had folded after the 1890 campaign, and the AA closed shop in 1891 when it could no longer afford to operate. The NL absorbed four teams (Baltimore, Louisville, St. Louis, and Washington) from the AA, and they joined four other AA teams that had moved to the NL over the years (Brooklyn, Cincinnati, Cleveland, and Pittsburgh). Of those eight teams, four still exist today: Brooklyn, as the Los Angeles Dodgers; the Cincinnati Reds; Pittsburgh, as the Pirates; and the St. Louis Browns, as the Cardinals. Ironically, despite its struggles to be competitive on the field, Louisville was one of only three teams that played in the AA throughout the league's ten-year existence, and Chicken Wolf was the only player to play in the AA all ten years.

With Louisville joining the ranks of the NL in 1892, Pete had a chance to play at home, which he preferred. But despite pressure from longtime friend Pfeffer, who was now player-manager of the Louisville squad, Pete hesitated to return. He still had a deep well of resentment stemming from the disastrous 1889 season and the club's disrespect, not to mention the money he believed the team owed him. When asked by a Louisville sports reporter about returning home to play, Pete's response was forceful: "No I ain't signed no contract. I don't sign wid none of them till the spring. When I get ready, I'll play with whoever gives me the most money, except in this shit-town. They owe me $650 now, and they better pay their debts before they talk about running any club."[30]

Pete, as usual, delayed signing a contract all winter, waiting until the spring to decide where to play. During that time, the rumors swirled: would he return home to Louisville; move to Baltimore, Chicago, or St. Louis; or perhaps sign with a team in California? Pete spent his time at the hot springs readying himself for the season, wherever he ended up playing. He eventually signed with Louisville, only to be released before the season started over a contract dispute. The two sides resolved their differences, and Pete re-signed a week into the season. Louisville started out 11–3 but quickly returned to form and played like the below-average, ninth-place team it was. Pete struggled over the first month, hitting only .247, nearly 100 points below his career average. He was unusually negative when talking with Cincinnati sportswriter Harry Weldon. "I guess I am rotten. I guess I ought to be out of the business. 'Old Gladdy' ain't to his speed yet, but he's hitting 'em, and hitting 'em good, but not as good as he will hit 'em though, cause he's got the catarrh, and is stopped up in the head. When you're stopped up your 'lamps' ain't right," explained a downtrodden and clearly ailing Pete. But then he showed his characteristic swagger: "Wait until the sun gets hot and the catarrh leaves the old hoss. Then the pitchers will have to look out. Will I lead the league in hitting? Why not? Look out for me. . . . The old boy is still ready money, and worth one hundred cents on the dollar."[31]

Four days later, Pete was released by Louisville. Four days after that, he signed with Cincinnati. His first game with his new team was in Louisville against his old club. Wearing his Cincinnati uniform from the season before, Pete went 0 for 3.

A few weeks later on June 6, Benjamin Harrison became the first sitting US president to attend a major league game when he watched the Cincinnati versus Washington contest at Boundary Field, located just two miles from the White House. Cincinnati won the game in the tenth inning when it scored three runs. Harrison was not around to see the exciting finish, as he had left in the bottom of the sixth. Even more impressive than the distinguished guest was Pete's bunt for a hit in the fourth inning. Later in the month, Cincinnati played another extra-inning affair against Chicago, this one lasting 20 innings. The game was tied 7–7 when it was called due to darkness. Both pitchers, Mullane for Cincinnati and Ad Gumbert for Chicago, pitched complete games. Pete went a pedestrian 2 for 7 at the plate but was marvelous in the field, with two game-saving acrobatic catches that brought the spectators to their feet for "shingle splitting ovations."[32] The 20-inning marathon set the record for the longest game played. That record was equaled twice in 1905 but not exceeded until July 17, 1914, when New York and Pittsburgh engaged in a 21-inning duel, with New York prevailing 3–1.

Again, a change in scenery and the positive atmosphere of the Cincinnati clubhouse invigorated Pete, who returned to form at the plate. His fielding, however, caused consternation among his teammates and local sportswriters. Though still capable of awe-inducing plays, Pete had added a new trick to his defensive arsenal that was not having positive results: he had taken to stopping grounders with his feet and shins. This lack of defensive effort was growing tiresome, and Pete was moved from center field to right. On July 13 his unique defensive technique resulted in giving up a run in a 4–2 loss to Brooklyn. "Instead of going after it with his hands [Pete] tried to stop it with his number tens. The consequence was that he got tangled up and before he could get straightened out had kicked the single into a triple."[33] Despite Pete's "shinning" and "kicking" of balls in the outfield, manager Charles Comiskey defended him, saying, "There has been some complaint about fielder Pete Browning, I don't see where it comes in. I know he isn't the best fielder in the world, but I can get along with a little poor fielding, providing he keeps up his current batting lick."[34]

In addition to his standout performance at the plate, Pete possessed a level of cunning and smarts acquired from his years in baseball. In a game against Baltimore and Hall of Famer John McGraw, Pete was able to score a run by fooling McGraw, who was known for the dirty tricks he deployed in an effort to win at all costs. McGraw recognized that, with only one umpire on the field, the umpire's attention was often elsewhere, so McGraw used any method he could think of to stop runners from advancing. This included hooking his fingers inside the base runner's belt. Pete, aware of McGraw's tricks, loosened his belt upon arriving on base. On a hit into the outfield, Pete took off and left a stunned McGraw holding his belt as Pete, one hand holding up his pants, scored.[35]

Pitcher Ad Gumbert, who had a solid nine-year career, often told a tale of how a cunning Pete spoiled a no-hit game for him. With two outs in the ninth inning, Gumbert was one out away from pitching a no-hitter when Pete strolled up to the plate. "I didn't like Peter's looks, the murderous old slugger that he was, but I'll swear it was all on an accident," said Gumbert. "I didn't try to hit him so as to lose him and get a whack at the next one, but the ball slipped. It whizzed in with a load of speed and shelled Pete in the ribs." Pete groaned with fury and shook his bat at Gumbert before taking his base. The next batter had two strikes when he hit a weak grounder toward second. "Pete Browning, of course, [was] running down from first," continued Gumbert, "and just as the second baseman was dipping for the ball, Old Pete deliberately stuck his leg in front of the bounding globe, letting it rap him on the calf. Under the rules, Pete was out—man hit by batted ball—and that ended the game. But also under the rules, the batsman got a hit and thus I was robbed [of] a no-hit game." As he jogged off the field, Pete gave Gumbert a Cheshire cat grin and said, "I fixed ye. Get smart and soak me with the ball will ye? You and your no-hit game."[36]

On July 15 Pete was reportedly seriously sick at home. Two days later, he was cut by Cincinnati. Despite the public support from Comiskey, who was known as a taskmaster, he had grown tired of Pete's antics. Comiskey was loyal to his former players and teammates and signed Curt Welch from Baltimore to replace Pete. Welch had won four straight pennants in St. Louis, from 1885 to 1888, with Comiskey. Ironically, in replacing Pete with Welch, the team replaced one hard-drinking man with another. Whereas Pete had curtailed his excessive drinking over the past few years, Welch never tamed his habit. He was known to keep a case of beer behind the center-field fence to drink between innings. The *Trenton Times* called it "a bad swap as far as personal habits are concerned."[37]

Pete's release by Comiskey caught him completely off guard. He had recently complained about a pay cut he and many other players had been forced to take due to monies the NL owed to the AA as part of an agreement between the two leagues when the AA folded. Still, Pete was in shock when informed of his release, and he disappeared for a few weeks. His whereabouts were a regular topic of speculation in the papers until it was reported that he was recuperating at the hot springs in French Lick. His future on the diamond was uncertain. There were rumors that he would sign with Washington to finish out the season, then that he would sign with St. Louis, and finally that Cincinnati was interested in re-signing Pete to replace the recently released Welch. Cincinnati denied the report, claiming that it was interested in finding Pete only to pay him the money it owed him. A few days later, Pete's whereabouts were again unknown, leading to worry that he might be off on "another fishing excursion to Kansas City."[38] Two weeks later, he was spotted watching the game from the scorer's box in Cincinnati. A few days after that, he signed with Cincinnati for the third time in two seasons.

His first game back, Pete had his "lampteenies trimmed," as he laced three hits.[39] The following day, after tripling in his first at-bat, he was removed from the game due to an attack of vertigo—a sign of his deteriorating physical condition. Pete's recent switch to stopping ground balls with his feet and shins may have been an attempt to deal with the vertigo he experienced on a daily basis. The simple act of bending over to pick up a ball caused dizziness, so he avoided doing so.

Upon his return to Cincinnati, Pete played solidly but unspectacularly, highlighted by a tenth-inning walk-off homer off St. Louis ace Bob Caruthers on October 2. He hit .303 over the rest of the season and finished the year at .292—only the second time in his career his batting average was below .300 for the season. Much like the previous season, it is fair to assume that if he had spent the entire season in Cincinnati and had not been beset by injuries and ailments, his average would have been much higher. Cincinnati finished a respectable fifth in the league, the first time Pete ended the season on a team with a winning record since Louisville went 76–60 in 1887.

After the 1892 season, Pete's future seemed uncertain. "Very few cranks believe that he will be retained for '93's campaign," wrote the *Courier-Journal.* "Old Pete is one of the greatest of the in-and-outers who took part in the game. When the bell finally rings for his retirement, one of the greatest hitters who ever smote the leather will disappear."[40] On March 25, 1893, as teams were preparing for the upcoming season, Pete's retirement was announced. He complained about a cut in salaries and said he planned to purchase a billiards saloon on Jefferson Street in downtown Louisville, a few blocks from his home. The *Courier-Journal* trumpeted, "The Gladiator will no more knock the cover off the ball to the delight of the boys in the bleachers. He will no more make his great one-handed catches."[41] Three days later, the deal to purchase the saloon fell through, and Pete's future was once again uncertain. "Pete may be seen on the diamond again this year," speculated the *Courier-Journal.* "If he is, it is certain that the Gladiator will line them out and field as in the olden days."[42] Pete stayed in shape in case an opportunity arose, and he even played in a couple of indoor baseball games, which were becoming popular in Louisville.

With his limited education and little interest in other pursuits, Pete had few options. He may have been loud, boastful, and full of swagger and confidence, but at the end of the day, he was a man with few skills off the baseball diamond. His only other major talent—drinking—did not amount to a career. In modern times, given his charisma and popularity, he would have been a perfect candidate to become a TV sports personality, but unfortunately, that was not an option in the nineteenth century. Pete was genuinely passionate about baseball, or at least the batting part of it, but he found the business side of the game and the rules imposed on him tiresome. He loved the notoriety baseball gave him, but not much else.

The month of April came and went, and the 1893 baseball season started without Pete. He was still at home, impatiently waiting for another chance to prove that he could still "line 'em out." Despite this, Pete's confidence had not waned. "Line 'em out? I should say I can," he emphatically declared to a sportswriter from the *Cincinnati Enquirer* in May. "I led the Association in '82 and '85, the Brotherhood in '90, and was second in the League in '91, and can lead them dead easy this season. Dead cinch. Don't intend to retire from the diamond, as has been reported. Too young for that, you know. I'm good for twenty years yet. Be foolish to do that. They miss old Pete already. There's only one Gladiator you know." As Pete continued his conversation with the reporter, he made it clear where he would like to play:

> Don't know where I'm going, but would like to go to Brooklyn. . . . Don't want more money than I am worth but want good money just the same. I have got more confidence in myself than I ever had, and if I get in Brooklyn, I will come pretty near showing them that I am in it. I am practicing every day when the weather will allow me and am in better condition than I ever was. I am like a piece of steel. Feel it. No gloves there, eh? Well I should say not. Eye like an eagle. Can see my contract and advance coming now.[43]

Over the ensuing month, Pete would "adopt" visiting managers who were in town to play Louisville, staying close by their sides in the hope of being signed. When Louisville was away, he frequented the saloons where game scores were received—not to drink, only to get baseball updates. "He has been sober for over a year now and cannot understand himself why someone does not sign him," wrote the *Courier-Journal*. "Weeks ago, he was hopeful of being signed, but now takes a decidedly blue view of the outlook. Playing ball is as necessary to Browning's existence as corn is to hogs, and without that employment there is no telling what he will do."[44] Finally, on May 26, 1893, the hometown Colonels signed Pete. Ironically, he would be replacing Curt Welch, who had replaced Pete in Cincinnati the previous season and was being released for excessive drunkenness. Welch's final days with the club were a hazy mix of whiskey and late nights. The final straw came when he showed up at the ballpark drunk and then missed the next day's practice. "Welch has always been considered one of the best fielders in the country, but his love for whiskey has been his downfall," lamented the *Courier-Journal*.[45] Welch's hard living led to his untimely death in 1896 at the age of 34.

Pete's 1893 season was a repeat of much of his career: he had a highly productive year on an embarrassingly bad team. Even at the tail end of his career, Pete was still the best player on the team in all aspects of the game—playing sterling defense and hitting well over .300. His production at the plate was no doubt aided by one of the most revolutionary changes in baseball: the elimination of the pitching box and the creation of the pitching mound and pitching rubber, which increased the distance pitchers had to throw the ball to the modern-day 60 feet 6 inches. This change was a major boon to offense, with the league average jumping from .245 in 1892 to .280 in 1893. It also sparked a 39-point increase in OBP from .317 to .356. It was murder on pitchers' careers, however. Older pitchers who had already logged monstrous numbers of innings in the premodern days of limited pitching staffs found the increased pitching distance too much for their overworked arms. This led to an exodus of dead-armed over-30 pitchers from the league.

Amidst this change, Pete was getting high praise for both his offensive and defensive work, despite the poor play of the rest of the last-place Colonels. The *Courier-Journal* penned this tribute:

> Pete Browning has been hitting the ball hard and often since he signed with the Louisvilles, and the many defeats are not due to his playing. In Brooklyn one day last week he electrified the spectators by making a circus catch, the equal of which has not been seen on the Brooklyn grounds this season. It is very gratifying to the Gladiator's friends in this city that he has regained his old form. From the resorts Pete is playing the game of his life, and the local cranks do not seem surprised. They all hold Browning in the light of a man from whom anything may be expected, but who will surprise no one by failure to do anything brilliant. But the Gladiator reformed long ago, and his work this season seems to eclipse that of former years. If no bad luck befalls him, he may yet give the leaders a race for batting honors.[46]

Longtime friend and current Colonels captain Pfeffer remarked that he "would rather have Browning than half the young players of the country."[47] Pete's strong play continued throughout the summer. He hit his only home run of the season and the final of his career on June 8 against Bumpus Jones and Cincinnati. The highlight of the summer came on July 1, when he went 2 for 5 with a double and a triple and almost single-handedly sparked a ninth-inning rally against Baltimore. Despite the Colonels' eventual loss, yet another article raved about Pete's revitalized form, proclaiming, "Long live the Gladiator!"[48] Pete's hot batting included a multihit game off Denton True "Cy" Young on July 21. Young picked up his famous nickname from the fences his fastball destroyed, which looked like they had been hit by a cyclone.

Even with his stellar play at the plate, Pete had lost a step. He had once knocked doubles with astonishing regularity, using his speed to leg out extra-base hits. He finished in the top ten in doubles eight times, third or better five times, and led the league in 1890. Over the 1892 and 1893 seasons, however, they were a scarce commodity for him.

It was also becoming clear that his mastoiditis was causing greater pain and discomfort. On July 11 he missed a game with what was described as "violent pains in his head." The *Courier-Journal* detailed his struggles: "Several years ago Pete was slightly overcome by the heat and since that time he has suffered more or less on hot days with pains in his forehead."[49] Heat had long exacerbated Pete's mastoid issues, and playing the majority of his career in the steamy, summer days of Louisville proved challenging. His deteriorating condition helped hasten the end of his career, as it began to severely impact his performance on the field. Even as he struggled with his health, he was still capable of moments of greatness and regularly produced at a level beyond that of most players.

Pete missed four games due to vertigo before returning on July 15 with a 2-for-5 game. He closed out July hitting safely in 13 of 17 games and batting over .400. Three days into August, Louisville inexplicably gave Pete a ten-day notice that he was being released. No reason was given. Upon learning the news after that day's game, he donned his most expensive clothing, carefully adjusted the large diamond in his scarf, brushed several specks of dust from his patent leather shoes, and stormed out of the clubhouse in disgust. A reporter from the *Courier-Journal* caught up with him on the street and asked about his release. "You see," said a clearly irritated Pete, "I was just beginning to feel good. I have been sick but played anyway because they were short of men. Today I never felt better and was just in shape to line 'em out. Pfeffer ought to have told me of this. He knew it all the time and told me I wasn't going to get it. Biggest surprise on earth, but I can't help it."[50] Pete played his last game of the season on August 6, going hitless.

There was no logical reason for Pete's release. He was Louisville's leading hitter at .355 and one of its most popular players—one of the few attractions for fans. Perhaps his release was tied to his health and the assumption that Pete could no longer play. More likely, it was another poorly thought out move by the team's dysfunctional management, which was known for releasing and signing players on a whim and generally making poor decisions.

Shortly after his release, rumors that Pete would sign with Brooklyn or Philadelphia appeared in the sporting press, but they quickly evaporated, and so did news of Pete. When he was dropped from the team, he was dropped from the public's consciousness. He had always been a good source of quotes and anecdotes while he was playing, but following his release in 1893, he was forgotten. Pete wasn't mentioned in the Louisville papers until a few days before the end of the season, when the *Courier-Journal* ran an article on where the players from the 1883 Louisville team were a decade later. Wolf was the only player still with Louisville. Hecker was running a grocery store in Oil City, Pennsylvania. Joe Gerhardt was managing a team in Albany, New York. Leech Maskrey was an art teacher.

John Reccius was selling baseball supplies in Louisville. And Pete? He was said to be "mashing the pretty girls on Fourth Avenue after the matinees."[51]

It appeared that Pete's career was finally over, although Pete himself was not ready to call it quits. When asked about the 1894 season, he defiantly responded, "Well, I don't know. It looks like they think the old man has seen his best days, but he can fool many of them yet."[52]

Pete finally caught the attention of a team at the end of April 1894, but despite his bravado, it was not an NL team. He signed with Allentown, a minor league team in the Pennsylvania State League that was owned by Pete's longtime friend Al Johnson. It was managed by future Hall of Famer Mike "King" Kelly and featured several former major leaguers, including Jocko Milligan, George Wood, Henry Larkin, Joe Mulvey, and Sam Wise. The veteran lineup was referred to as the Ancient Nine and Kelly's Killers. Kelly was notorious for his hard-drinking lifestyle. When asked if he drank while playing, he famously answered, "It depends on the length of the game."[53] Kelly was a baseball innovator, trickster, villain, and showman who drank himself to an early death at age 36. Even with his current sobriety, Pete felt an affinity for Kelly.

Pete's tenure with Allentown was productive if uneventful. In 44 games against lesser competition, he hit a respectable .332 with 16 doubles, three triples, and two homers. The rest of the players did not match Pete's production, and Kelly was distraught over the team's miserable play. On the way home after another loss, he reportedly told the conductor he wanted the train to take a turn into the nearby Susquehanna River and end his misery. At the beginning of July, Pete was inexplicably released again. The *Washington Post* claimed it was "some sort of misunderstanding."[54] Pete clearly felt he had lived up to expectations and could have done even better if he had gotten some help from the rest of the lineup. "I would have led the league in long hits if it wasn't for poor Mike Kelly, who batted just before me," he explained. "Kel would go to first, and I would hit a corker that would be good for a three-bagger or homer, but Kel was so fat and puffy the best he could do was get around to third, and I would have to content myself with a double."[55] Pete later claimed Kelly explained his released by saying, "You're playing such good ball you're showing all the rest of us up."[56] As always, Pete was a fan favorite, and the Allentown fans circulated a petition to have him reinstated, to no avail.

Pete could not stay away from the game, and by the end of the month he had hooked up with a local team in Georgetown, Kentucky. He played first base and, for the first and only time in his career, served as captain. Pete briefly returned to the big leagues when he signed with St. Louis to fill in for outfielder Fred Ely, who had gone home to be with his sick wife. Pete appeared in two games when St. Louis played in Louisville. He wore his old gray Cincinnati uniform and went 1 for 3 and 0 for 4 but shined defensively, making a "fine catch in centerfield" and drawing praise from his St. Louis teammates.[57] As he walked off the field, the Gladiator's old swagger returned as he observed, "[I] thought it was a pretty good catch . . . considering [I] haven't touched a ball [for] six weeks."[58] The *Courier-Journal* wrote of his appearance, "His cheeks were tanned and lean, and he wore a very sad expression. The uniforms of the St. Louis team are of a very dark blue and the gray uniform in center made the wearer look like a stranger in a foreign land. . . . Those who looked closely, and remembered well, saw that Pietro Gladiator Browning, ex-champion batter of the world for several seasons, and until recently with Mike Kelly's Allentown aggregation was to play center field for St. Louis."[59]

After a two-game absence, Ely returned and Pete was released. Despite his stubborn belief that St. Louis was going to sign him permanently, Pete remained a man without a team. No teams showed any interest in him until the final day of the 1894 season, when the Brooklyn Bridegrooms, who were playing a season-ending doubleheader in Louisville, signed Pete to play in the final game. The hometown hero was cheered loudly every time he walked up to the plate. Pete did not disappoint, playing a solid game and going 2 for 2 with two singles, a walk, and a run scored.

As 1895 dawned, Pete's options were slim. Despite his usual overconfidence that he would be "lining 'em out" for some NL team next season, the two hits for Brooklyn proved to be his final major league hits, and the possibility of a return to MLB faded away.

13

After Baseball (1895–1899)

"I didn't tell you about the tale of one of Pete Browning's bats?" asked Honus Wagner. At the time, Wagner was a 23-year-old rookie with the Louisville Colonels at the outset of his legendary Hall of Fame career. He continued, "Pete used to come around to our boarding-house in Louisville and distribute fatherly tips on batting."[1] Wagner struck up a friendship with Pete and was invited to his house one afternoon to look over his massive collection of bats. Wagner was amazed, as each bat was labeled with the deeds it had accomplished. He was especially "stuck on one stick in the lot" with a label reading: "In '87, at St. Louis, Old Pete put a dent in the center field fence for a home run. Three were on the sacks, and it was the last inning, and that four-sack bingle of Pete's won the game."[2] The bat had a weight and feel that Wagner liked, so "Pete made me a present of it," he said. "It's been my mascot ever since."[3]

A few years later, in 1905, Wagner became the first player to endorse a bat when he signed a contract with the Hillerich Company. It is not hard to believe that his first encounter with the Louisville Slugger was when Pete gifted him one of his custom-made bats and spoke of its exploits. Wagner, like Pete, believed in the power of bats and thought no two were created alike. He said, "Bats are strange and moody things," and he understood why Pete "used to talk to his bats and credit them with human understanding."[4]

Over the years, visitors to Pete's basement shared their astonishment at his wall-to-wall collection of bats. George Dovey, owner of the Boston Doves (which later became the Atlanta Braves), visited Pete in Louisville in early 1890. He remembered Pete as being the most peculiar ballplayer he had ever dealt with, yet Dovey was awed by his passion for the game. After chatting about baseball in the kitchen for an hour, Dovey was invited down to the basement to see Pete's extensive collection. "The basement looked like a cave," recalled Dovey:

> From the ceiling hung more baseball bats than I have ever seen before or since. Not only this, but around in the corners of the room were the other bats standing against the wall. Browning knew the history of every one of those bats. . . . Going along the line he would tell the record of every bat in the lot. Some had made particularly long hits, while others had won games. Those in the corners were the ones he had discarded, and he would tell you that certain bats were only good to make fouls or pop flies.[5]

After his retirement, Pete, like the bats in his basement, began to collect dust. He tried to stay connected to the game any way he could, telling tales of his glory days to whoever would listen, visiting old friends and teammates who were still playing when they stopped in Louisville, and dispensing advice to the next generation of ballplayers in the city. Talking with the younger players made Pete feel needed and kept him involved in baseball, which was the only meaningful thing in his life. Since childhood, his skills on the diamond had defined who he was and given him a purpose. His drinking, eccentricities, and misbehavior were overlooked and tolerated, but after his career was over, he did not find the same acceptance.

After taking his final swings with Brooklyn in the last game of the 1894 season, Pete waited for opportunities to come along in 1895, but there were few. He could not resist the lure of the diamond, no matter where he had to play, so when no NL team came calling, he almost signed with the Western League's team in St. Paul, Minnesota, which was managed by Pete's former manager in Cincinnati, Hall of Famer Charles Comiskey. When asked about the negotiations, Pete said, "Commy knows what the old boy can do. There is plenty of good ball playing left in old Pete yet. You ought to have seen me in Allentown last season. Best in the business. Hit? Why I crippled three infielders up there in one game."[6] Despite regular correspondence between Pete and Comiskey, the deal fell through when Pete demanded more money. There were also rumors that he would join a proposed new league or return to Allentown, but neither happened. It seemed that Pete, the notorious homebody, was now willing to go anywhere to play baseball. The Augusta (Maine) Kennebecs of the New England League were mentioned as a possible landing spot, but the *Bangor Daily Whig & Courier* reported that manager Walter Burnham decided not to engage Pete when he found someone better to man his "left garden."[7] Pete's inability to get a job in the lowly New England League spoke to the widespread view of his declining but once unparalleled skills. The start of the 1895 season found Pete unsigned and at home.

On April 23, as the season was getting under way without him, Pete again planned to buy a saloon and billiards hall. He withdrew the purchase price of $1,500 from the bank and went to his brother Samuel's bar, where he displayed the large wad of cash to a group of men. Among them were Charles Ewing and Charles Rankin, two "well-known characters" in town who hoped to relieve Pete of his money.[8] The following night they went to Pete's house, which he shared with his mother and his sister Fannie, planning to rob him. Upon arriving at the house, they first tried to gain entrance by prying open the shutters on the lower windows. When that failed, they lashed together two step stools to reach an open bedroom window. Fannie awoke to the sight of the two men crawling through her window. She screamed, alerting two policemen in the area and scaring the would-be burglars, who fled back down their makeshift ladder. Despite the late hour, the commotion drew a crowd to the house to see what was happening. Rankin and Ewing were arrested a few hours later and connected to other robberies in the area. Even if they had gained entrance, the two burglars would have come up empty, as Pete and his money had spent the night at his brother's house. Pete, never one for modesty, opened a billiards hall at the corner of Thirteenth and Market Streets and named it The Gladiator.

A month into the season, rumors circulated that Louisville was looking to sign Pete, paving the way for a possible return to the big leagues. Those rumors proved unfounded, likely due to the opinion of Louisville manager John McCloskey, who steadfastly refused to sign Pete. The lack of interest from Louisville might have turned off other teams, which reasoned that if the cellar-dwelling Louisville club did not deem its own homegrown hero worth signing, there was probably no magic left in his bat. Pete's age surely factored into the dearth of interest, despite his proven value as a hitter. In May 1895, while watching Louisville struggle through another loss on the way to a last-place finish, Pete claimed McCloskey offered him a contract, but Pete found it insulting and turned it down, saying, "He didn't want to give me much. Must think I'm a Southern Leaguer or a commons." There is no evidence to prove or disprove Pete's claim, but either way, he was ready to play as soon as the right opportunity arose. "My cellar down home is half full of as good sticks as you will ever see—all oiled and rubbed," said Pete.[9] He publicly expressed an interest in playing for Boston, but that interest was not reciprocated.

Pete finally saw his first baseball action in June. Unfortunately, it was for an amateur team in Louisville. For the rest of the season he played with amateur teams in charity games and exhibitions. He made one appearance in a Louisville Colonels game at the end of September—a charity game between the regular team and reserves. Pete went hitless not because of poor play at the plate but because he was umpiring the game. He was long recognized for his honesty on the field, and a move to umpiring seemed logical.

Opportunities entering the 1896 season were even slimmer than the prior year. There were those who felt that no matter how well Pete could still hit a baseball, his reputation for excessive drinking, late nights, and fast company was reason enough to steer clear of him. Even so, Pete had not lost his confidence and believed he was still the premier hitter in the game. "Think I'll catch on?" a pugnacious Pete asked a crowd of adoring fans as he puffed on a cigar and recounted tales of his glory days. "Of course I will. They can't do without 'Pete.' They ain't been no hitting done since I quit the game. [Hugh] Duffy and [Jesse] Burkett can't hit. They line 'em out over second and short for singles. Why don't they break splinters off the fence?"[10]

"Old Pete is not meant for the minor league, if he can't play with the big ones, he will not play at all," Pete once declared. Yet it seemed that a year away from baseball was too much for the Gladiator, as he was making a concerted effort to find any team to play for, minor league or not, in 1896.[11] He knew the odds were stacked against him, and given his struggle to find a regular spot last season, he knew he had to prove that he was serious about playing again. To that end, he sold his saloon and began integrating himself back into the local baseball community. Even with this proactive approach, none of the NL teams showed an interest in Pete. He eventually signed with Columbus, Ohio, of the Southern League. Expectations were low, as Columbus manager Tom Loftus said he hoped only "to keep the Gladiator sober at least half the time."[12] Loftus should have been less worried about Pete's drinking (he was mostly sober at this point) and more concerned about his skills, as he had not played professional baseball in more than a year and had not played a full season since 1892.

An early-season exhibition game saw Columbus taking on the Colonels in Louisville. A crowd of 1,500 attended the game, and 1,000 of them were believed to be personal friends of Pete's. The fans were excited to see their hometown star and cheered wildly when he came to the plate. It was an unhappy homecoming for Pete, who struck out in the ninth inning with the bases loaded to end the game. The *Courier-Journal* compared his performance to the legend of Casey at the bat: "Alas! The mighty have fallen. The sneer is gone from Browning's lips, his teeth are clenched in hate. Like Casey he has struck out," lambasted the paper.[13]

Pete shook off the poor performance and started the regular season hitting cleanup like the Pete of old and playing center field. After the first week of the season, Pete was home in Louisville visiting friends and celebrating what he considered a successful start. Tom Brown, who had played with Pete for Louisville in 1892 and 1893, recalled the visit: "Pete had a cargo of Kentucky oolong concealed on his person," remembered Brown, "and went to the Buckingham Theater. . . . A burnt cork song and dance team were doing their turn when Pete entered the theater. One of the characters in the song and dance sketch was dubbed Pete by his partner. 'Say Old Pete what hab you been doin' der las' week,' he said? Pete Browning thought he was the Peter referred to, and, jumping from his seat, yelled, 'What's Old Pete been doing this week? Not a thing I guess. Only four hits every day last week, and two of those singles were for three sacks, and another was over the fence for a homer.'"[14] As Pete yelled at the stage, the theater crowd looked at the aging slugger with shocked embarrassment.

The high times would not last, as Columbus began to struggle. The team's roster, which was full of veterans, was heavily criticized. "Pete Browning is now enjoying his third time on earth," wrote the *Indianapolis Journal* on May 5. "Tom Morrissey is currently reputed to have played ball with Moses. [Joe] Cantillon, [Jim] Callopy, and [Bumpus] Jones have been in this class for the last decade. [Bobby] Wheelock is an old association player. [Peck] Sharp is an old-timer."[15] The same day, Columbus signed Tom Hernon to replace Pete in center field; Pete moved to right field and dropped to fifth in the batting order. He still had moments of greatness, including a 4-for-5 day with a double in a 9–3 win over Indianapolis on May 8, but for the most part, he was average at best. A stretch of hitless games led the *Kansas City World* to write, "Pete's lamps are very bum, and a Roentgen Ray would undoubtedly discern pachyderms, trinidads, plate glass, cobble stones, and everything else in his throwing arm. The first high ball hit to Pete caused him to stop and blink like an owl. He couldn't see it any more than a rabbit."[16] On May 22, as Columbus was struggling with a 7–19 record, the club announced the release of several veteran players, including Pete. He had been with the team for a little over a month. Pete could not stay away from baseball and was soon playing in charity and exhibition games in Louisville. In July he joined the Louisville All-Professionals, a traveling exhibition team composed of ex–big league players. At the end of the 1896 season, Pete defiantly declared that he would be back in the game next season.

Pete occasionally practiced with the Louisville team to stay in shape for a possible comeback, and rumors of potential opportunities circulated at the beginning of the 1897 season. It was thought he might end up with the Savannah, Georgia, club of the Southern League, but that door closed when the league suspended operations before the season started. He was strongly linked with rumors of a move to the Fort Wayne, Indiana, club of the Inter-State League, along with fellow Louisville resident Gus Weyhing, with Weyhing serving as team captain and Pete playing first base. Throughout his career, Pete had been reluctant to play outside of Louisville and preferred to play on teams with some connection to his network of hometown friends. At the end of January, negotiations hit a snag when Pete balked at the team's offer and refused to sign unless he got his asking price. Despite his age and declining skills, *Sporting Life* noted, "The old man has never lost confidence in his own abilities."[17] Pete claimed that if Fort Wayne didn't make an acceptable offer he would seek an appointment as an umpire from NL president Nick Young. After months of speculation about the pair joining Fort Wayne, it was announced days before the start of the season that Weyhing had been released and Pete had never signed. Even so, Pete's confidence never wavered. "Take a peep at them lampteenies," he declared. "No moss growing in them. Clear as a locomotive headlight and full of o' base hits. . . . The game ain't right without Petey, and before next season opens Petey'll have offers to turn down."[18]

In the opinion of many sportswriters, it was not Pete's declining ability to hit the ball that precluded him from finding a team to play for. Rather, he was ill-equipped to adapt to changes in the game. "More brains and less brawn," wrote the *Pittsburgh Press* in 1898, as it detailed baseball's adoption of a more thoughtful hit-and-run approach exemplified by John McGraw's Baltimore Orioles. "The fence-hitters like Pete Browning who pushed knots out of the fences with long home runs are more valuable as section hands or hod-carriers in these days of baseball," wrote the *Press*.[19] Pete had the ability to play this type of baseball, as he had long been recognized for his bat control, but it was his stubborn reluctance to adapt that left him unsigned.

Even without stepping onto the field in 1897, Pete was recognized for his defensive work and proved that he was still a fan favorite. During a game between Louisville and Pittsburgh, Pete, who was in attendance as a spectator, was standing near the right-field foul line and twice stopped balls headed his way. Each time the crowd in the bleachers erupted in cheers, delaying the next pitch, while Pete waved to the adoring fans and basked in his former glory.

Pete's hoped-for appointment as an NL umpire never materialized, despite his ongoing efforts to secure a spot. The reluctance to hire Pete as an umpire has never been explained, and it seems illogical, given his well-known honesty on the field, which was praised in 1887:

> Pete Browning may have his shortcomings as a ballplayer, but no one has ever questioned his honesty. He never resorts to trickery, and always admits the truth when he is declared either safe or out in a close play. Umpires know this. Whenever Pete claims that he was not touched by the baseman in a close play, it can safely be put down that Pete is right. He seldom makes a kick, but justice is generally on his side when he does. He won't tell lies about any play that comes up, no matter whether it be to his advantage or against it.[20]

One can only imagine that the over-the-top descriptions of Pete and his on-field and off-field exploits played a part in his inability to secure a spot as an umpire. The *Courier-Journal* wrote, "Pete Browning's application for a position on the League staff of umpires didn't create much of a stir at League headquarters. Your Uncle Nick just filed it, and it is liable to remain on the file until the crack of doom."[21] Some believed that Pete's hearing issues alone were enough to disqualify him as an umpire.

The *Daily Review* went so far as to call Pete's potential appointment as an umpire "a joke."[22] Despite those beliefs, Pete actually umpired some of the Colonels' home exhibition games in the preseason, working on Sundays using the new two-umpire system. Unfortunately for Pete, this did not lead to a regular position.

Pete never really left baseball. It was what he knew best, and it was the only thing he was truly good at. Without baseball, Pete was lost. He worked as an umpire, owned a saloon, sold cigars, ran unsuccessfully for councilman of Louisville's Eleventh Ward, and reportedly worked on an Ohio River steamer, all with little success. After his death, the *Washington Post* even claimed he had manufactured baseball bats, but this seems unlikely and is probably a recasting of his role in the development of the Louisville Slugger brand.

Pete identified himself solely as a baseball player and could never move beyond that. Years after his last professional swing, he still recounted the old stories to anyone who would listen, including his favorite claim: "Old Pete can still line 'em out." He said his legendary skills with the bat remained intact and talked of a comeback. Unfortunately, that comeback never materialized. Unlike other ex-players who went into managing or coaching, Pete didn't have the acumen for that. Just as Pete couldn't let go of baseball, baseball couldn't let go of him. His accomplishments were frequently recounted in newspapers across the land, and young hitters were often compared to him—all serving to grow his legend. In 1904 Hall of Famer Jake Beckley was reminiscing about what he called the "golden age of batting," from 1885 to 1891: "They say there were no batters in those times like [Napoleon] Lajoie and Wagner, but I think the sluggers of that generation were the genuine article. . . . The hits that Brouthers, O'Neill, and Browning made were the real thing. They fairly smoked as they sped along. . . . If they could be taken back in the game and as husky as they were then [they] would bat .850 easy."[23]

During the 1880s the identities and fortunes of Pete and Louisville were inextricably intertwined. Pete *was* Louisville baseball. He was the city's best player and, for better or worse, the face of the franchise. In typical Pete fashion, the city experienced its greatest success while the selfish slugger was plying his trade in the Players' League. His return to Louisville was brief and hollow. Peter never again found the individual success he first experienced in Louisville, and Louisville never shared the success it found without him when he returned.

In 1899 Louisville Colonels owner Barney Dreyfuss saw that the end was near. The NL was looking to cut teams, and many speculated that it might target the perennial cellar-dwelling Colonels. Dreyfuss, who had recently acquired full ownership of the Colonels, bought a controlling interest in the Pittsburgh Pirates. As part of the deal, he negotiated the transfer of 14 Louisville players, including the team's best—Honus Wagner, Fred Clarke, Tommy Leach, Deacon Phillippe, and Rube Waddell—to the Pirates. Colonels president Harry Pulliam also moved to the Pirates and became that team's president. Dreyfuss eventually bought out his partners in Pittsburgh, taking complete control of the team. The defection of 14 of Louisville's best players, as well as its decade of underperformance, made the Colonels an obvious choice to be dropped from the NL, ending Louisville's participation in Major League Baseball. Until the Montreal Expos relocated to Washington, DC, in 2004, Louisville was the last city to lose an MLB franchise and not replace it with another. Despite the limited success of the Eclipse-Colonels franchise in its 18-year history, of the 46 teams that played in the NL and the AA prior to 1900, only five—Boston, Chicago, Cincinnati, St. Louis, and Pittsburgh—lasted as long as or longer than Louisville. But as the nineteenth century ended, so did MLB in Louisville.

14

Final Days (1900–1905)

At 7:00 p.m. on August 28, 1905, Pete, who was a patient at the Louisville City Hospital, said he "had grown tired of the sight of white robed nurses . . . [and did] not like to hear the groans of the other patients [as] it makes [me] blue and homesick." So he got up and walked out of the hospital, located at the corner of Preston and Chestnut Streets. As the sun began to set, Pete, his head still wrapped in bandages from surgery two weeks prior to lance an abscess, headed down Jefferson Street and trudged the two miles to his mother's house, his "huge frame . . . wasted by disease, and [resembling] a spirit of the former Pete Browning." He was not missed at the hospital until his sister Fannie called to inform them that he had shown up at home. She asked that an ambulance be sent to retrieve him, as she was concerned about his health and safety. A police patrol wagon was dispatched to take Pete back to the hospital, and as he was helped into the wagon, he was overheard dejectedly murmuring, "I would have liked to have spent one night at home."[1]

Despite his imposing physical appearance and god-like strength on the diamond, Pete's health had always been an issue. And since he had last swung his mighty bat, Pete had floundered, unable to fill the void left by baseball. The years since his retirement were mostly quiet. His family's wealth and the money accrued from his playing days allowed him to live a comfortable life without worrying about finding a job. But he missed baseball and let it be known in 1900 that he was willing to sign with any team that would have him as a "reserve slugger," someone who could deliver a timely hit when needed while sitting on the bench the rest of the game.[2] There were no takers. In 1901 he expressed interest in playing for a new minor league team in Oklahoma City, but nothing ever came of it. Today, one could imagine Pete carving out a lengthy career as a designated hitter, like Edgar Martinez or David Ortiz.

Despite his brash exterior and outgoing personality, it was a sad, lonely time for Pete. He had never created much of a life for himself outside of baseball and outside of Louisville, where he still attended games and regaled fans with tales of his glory days. He never married, never had a family of his own, and never found meaningful employment besides baseball. And except for a few years in the early 1890s when he was playing in Cincinnati, Cleveland, and Pittsburgh, he lived his entire life in his childhood home with his mother.

The summer of 1905 was a rough time for Pete. In June he was in the news when he suffered a mental collapse. Pete had been "slightly off" and withdrawn for a few weeks, and he had taken to spending the whole day fishing by himself. He eventually decided that something was wrong and confined himself to bed. His worried family called a physician, who determined that Pete "showed unmistakable signs of insanity and . . . he might at any time become violent and hurt someone."[3] After a number of troubling episodes, he was officially declared mentally unsound on June 7 and remanded to the Central Kentucky Asylum at Lakeland for observation. His commitment to the asylum at Lakeland was largely due to a misunderstanding of mental health at the time, rather than an actual diagnosis of insanity. During the hearing to determine his mental state, it was revealed that Pete had never attempted suicide or exhibited violent behavior, had never had to be restrained, and had experienced no "fits"; his temperament in general and attitude toward his family were kindly. Only his inability to talk intelligently and brief periods of impaired lucidity indicated any kind of mental disorder. With an improved awareness of mental illness and a better understanding of the serious effects of his mastoid condition, his diagnosis likely would have been very different.

Some speculated that getting hit in the head by a pitch during his playing days was the reason for the "softening of his brain."[4] Pete had been struck in the head on May 9, 1896, by Indianapolis pitcher Wiley Davis while playing for Columbus of the Western League. The pitch staggered Pete, who made his way off the field and removed himself from the game. Local physician W. B. Clarke was behind the bench when Pete sat down, and he recalled the moment: "He came over in the shade, sitting on the grass, with his back against the grandstand, right in front of me," said

Clarke, "where he bathed his sore head the rest of the game. I heard him muttering and talking to a companion . . . I heard him say, 'That's the first time a pitcher ever got me on de block.'" Dr. Clarke believed Pete's health issues and death stemmed from this event. "The trouble that finally caused Pietro's death has been of long duration and I think it is perfectly reasonable to trace it to the incident described," explained Clarke.[5] This misdiagnosis by Clarke became part of Pete's lore, and it received even greater attention following the death of Ray Chapman in 1920. While playing for the Cleveland Indians, Chapman was struck in the head by a pitch thrown by Carl Mays and died 12 hours later. It was eventually determined that an abscess on the brain was the cause of Pete's symptoms, not a past beaning. When the abscess resolved a few weeks later, Pete's condition improved, and he was discharged and sent home under the care of his mother and sister.

With Pete's diagnosis of "insanity," he became the fourth player from the 1885–1887 Louisville squad to be declared insane and committed to Lakeland. The first was Reddy Mack, who was committed in 1900, followed by two of Pete's oldest and closest friends, Chicken Wolf and Phil Reccius. Wolf was committed in 1901 after it was observed that his "mind was awry." His issues started after he retired from baseball and was working for a local firefighting company as an engine driver. On March 8, 1901, Wolf's company was responding to a call, and he was driving the horse-drawn engine. When it rounded a corner, it found its path blocked by a small cart. Wolf was unable to stop the horses in time, and they plowed into the cart, snapping the harness attaching them to the engine. The frenzied horses continued to gallop forward, yanking Wolf out of his seat, dragging him along the street, and repeatedly slamming his head into the cobblestones. The result was a serious head injury from which he never fully recovered. This, combined with the tragic death of his son a short time later, led to severe depression and "serious attacks of melancholia," and he was eventually institutionalized.[6] Wolf stayed at Lakeland for the next two years before being released into the care of his mother in early 1903. His condition continued to deteriorate, and he was readmitted to Lakeland in early May 1903, where he died on May 17.

Reccius was committed to Lakeland in 1902 and died the following year. His problems were believed to stem from his playing days. In 1894, while playing with Spokane of the Northwestern League, Reccius was pitching to "a big, husky Frenchman" who hit a rocket back up the middle. Reccius was unable to react quickly enough and was struck above the left temple with a sickening thud. When the ball dropped at his feet, he instinctively picked it up and threw the runner out at first before toppling over, unconscious. The ball had broken off a piece of his skull, and surgeons were unable to remove it. It was thought that the bone fragment "weighed so heavily on his brain that he finally became violent" and was committed. He remained at the hospital until he was "declared out by Life's Great Umpire" on February 15, 1903.[7]

The years were kinder to some of Pete's other teammates. Alcohol abuse drastically shortened Toad Ramsey's career, but he eventually got relatively sober. He played his last major league game in 1890 after only six frustrating years, during which time he was among the game's best and worst pitchers. He bounced around the minors for a handful of years before playing his last game with the St. Joseph (Missouri) Saints of the Western Association. He returned to his hometown of Indianapolis, where he lived the remainder of his life. Ramsey worked as a bartender at his brother's bar and eventually married. He died on March 27, 1906, after a bout with pneumonia. His 114 career wins are the most by any pitcher who never played in the National League or the American League.

Despite the ugly end to his career—playing in back-to-back seasons on teams with 100 or more losses (the first player to do so)—fellow pitcher Guy Hecker had a decent life after baseball. After being released by Louisville following the disastrous 1889 season, he signed with the NL's Pittsburgh club as a player-manager. Because the best players in the country had defected to the Players' League, Hecker oversaw a talentless bunch who bumbled their way to a 23–113 record and a last-place finish. It was Hecker's last season in the majors. He spent the next two seasons playing with and managing minor league teams. Old teammate and nemesis Ramsey played two games for Hecker when he managed the appropriately named Jacksonville Lunatics of the Illinois-Iowa League in 1892. Ramsey went 0–2 in his two starts. Hecker returned to his home in Oil City, Pennsylvania, in 1893 and continued to manage local teams while working in the oil business. Even during his playing days, Hecker had always been a businessman, owning multiple stores over the years, and this continued once his baseball days were over. He and his wife eventually settled in Wooster, Ohio, and opened a grocery store. A car accident in 1931 seriously injured his right arm, which had been the bane of so many batters in the nineteenth century. He died on December 3, 1938, at age 82, due to intestinal nephritis.

Over 13 seasons, Pete's former teammate and longtime tormentor Tony Mullane compiled a 284–20 record. His 284 wins put him in fourth place among eligible players not in the Hall of Fame, behind Roger Clemens (354), Bobby Mathews (297), and Tommy John (288). Like Pete, the fact that Mullane's best seasons came in the AA impacted his chances for election into the Hall of Fame. His surly demeanor, overt racism, and sordid behavior were also big factors. After he retired as a player, Mullane worked for many years as an umpire. He joined the Chicago Police Department in 1903. In 1911 Mullane suffered a near-fatal brain abscess requiring surgery. He made a full recovery and continued to work as a police officer until his retirement in 1920. He died in 1944.

Though they were professional teammates for parts of only two seasons in Louisville (1892 and 1893), Fred Pfeffer and Pete had a long friendship dating back to their boyhood days playing ball on the commons. They played together for a couple of years on the powerhouse semipro Eclipse teams before Pfeffer signed with Troy, starting a 16-year career. Pfeffer was one of the last players to play barehanded. After retirement he became a successful saloon owner until the enactment of Prohibition in 1920, when he was forced to sell his bar for $1.50. He was 72 when he died of heart disease in 1932.

John Reccius's baseball career was relatively short, but he lived a long life, dying in 1930 at age 70. He was a key member of the semipro Eclipse teams in the late 1870s and early 1880s but played only two years in the major leagues. His career came to an end when his business interests occupied more and more of his time. He owned a doll store in downtown Louisville, where he discovered he had a knack for repairing some of the trickier elements that make dolls lifelike, such as their fluttering eyes. His store eventually became a "doll hospital" renowned for its ability to repair even the most worn-out or damaged doll. Even though he stopped playing at the professional level, Reccius remained heavily involved with baseball, managing and running many amateur and semipro teams in Louisville. He and Pete remained close their entire lives.

A few weeks after being released from Lakeland, Pete's condition worsened, and he was taken to City Hospital. The abscess that had caused his mental symptoms was determined to be long-standing in nature. Pete had an operation in June 1905 that found the mastoids filled with a "foreign growth" pressing on his brain.[8] Although the operation removed the growth, it returned a few days later. The *Baltimore Sun* somberly reported, "He has had a relapse and it is now feared he will die."[9] A second operation was planned, and during a presurgery exam, a small tumor was discovered in his breast. Both the abscess and the tumor were removed, and the surgery was deemed successful. Pete had been mostly absent from the national sporting news since his retirement in 1894, but now the seriousness of his condition dominated sports pages across the country.

He spent the next month at City Hospital until the night of August 28, when he escaped. Shortly after his return to the hospital, another growth was found on his neck. His condition deteriorated rapidly over the next few days. On September 10 at 2:15 p.m., surrounded by his mother Mary, sisters Florence and Fannie, and brother Charles, the Gladiator's lamps dimmed forever. He was 44. Fannie died two years later on March 16, 1907.

Even in death, Pete continued to confound and cause confusion. A picture from his 1887 Old Judge Cigarettes baseball card accompanied the *Courier-Journal*'s coverage of his death. The image was inadvertently reversed in the paper, forever immortalizing the right-handed Pete batting as a lefty.[10]

The official cause of Pete's death was given as asthenia, a catchall nineteenth-century term meaning general weakness and loss of body strength. The *Owensboro Messenger-Inquirer* was more blunt, writing that he had been done in by "old age and raw liquor."[11] It was true that his body had been ravaged by years of hard living and heavy drinking, and he likely had liver damage. The discovery of a tumor in his breast raises the possibility that he had cancer. It has also been suggested, without much evidence, that Pete died from general paresis due to late-stage syphilis. This neuropsychiatric disorder can result in a total mental breakdown (easily misdiagnosed in the nineteenth century as insanity). Both syphilis and gonorrhea were prevalent in Pete's time and were untreatable until the advent of penicillin decades later. Pete had an alleged fondness for the prostitutes who inhabited the brothels a few blocks from his home, so syphilis was a possibility, and his mental breakdown could have been caused by general paresis, but those two factors do not establish a definitive diagnosis. It is more likely that a combination of ailments led to the end of the Gladiator.

Pete's hospitalization and death put him in the headlines again when City Hospital and its superintendent Julius Vogt were accused of incompetence. They were charged with creating a hostile work environment for staff and poor conditions for patients, including operating tables that were "filthy," defective surgical instruments, abuse, and rotten food. Pete's family became part of the case against Vogt and the hospital when they claimed that conditions there were deplorable. His sister-in-law testified that when she visited Pete she found him unconscious, with his mouth hanging open, as "ants and flies . . . swarm[ed] over him," with no nurses around to help.[12] After testimony from many former patients and their families, as well as current and ex-staff, Vogt and the hospital were found not to be at fault, and the charges were dismissed.

A simple funeral service was held the day after Pete's death at his mother's home. The parlor was filled with friends and ex-teammates "who knew him when he first swung a bat and who saw him hit the ball on the nose in the day of his glory, as no player had done before."[13] A long line of visitors passed by the casket for one last look at the Gladiator. His powerful hands, which had wielded his Louisville Slugger so mightily and had frightened many a pitcher, were peacefully folded across his chest. Ex-teammates John Dyler, Isaac Van Burkalow, Tim Lehan, Tom McLaughlin, Charles Pfeiffer, and John Reccius served as pallbearers, and the funeral procession accompanied Pete to his final resting place at Cave Hill Cemetery. Pete's gravestone misspelled his first name "Lewis," and it remained that way until 1984, when the city of Louisville and Hillerich & Bradsby worked together to create a proper marker and monument for one of the city's all-time greats—one that spelled his name correctly and listed his baseball accomplishments.

Following Pete's death, papers across the country eulogized the slugger and remembered his greatness. The *Chicago Daily Tribune* hailed him as "one of the greatest ball players ever."[14] The *Washington Post* exalted his legend and mythologized his life:

> Pete Browning is dead, the mightiest slugger of the diamond, Old Pete. He is in Elysium with the other demigods and heroes, communing with Hercules and Spartacus, Theseus, and Coeur

de Lion, Achilles and Dunois, Castor and Pollux, and Graeme Claverhouse, and all the rest of them. And truly in his way he was a hero with the mightiest swing and the truest eye that a pitcher ever faced. . . . Pete was no Solomon, but he acted his part. He found his gift, and he cultivated it. In the history and tradition of the National Game he is an Immortal.[15]

15

Legacy

In death, Pete Browning is just as polarizing as he was in life. In the decades since his death, his legacy and accomplishments on the field, and his misbehavior and struggles off it, have been debated, with no clear conclusion. Was he one of the greatest hitters of the nineteenth century? Or was he a talented player who found success while playing in a lesser league? Was he an out-of-control drunk? Or was he a troubled man who battled health and addiction issues his whole life? Was he all these things? Adding to the debate is the question of why sportswriters have overlooked Pete so completely. There are no easy answers to who Pete was. He was an enigma who lived a life of contradictions. He was a man who somehow managed to play professional baseball at an incredibly high level despite a chronic health issue that impacted every facet of his life and should have made a career as a pro athlete nearly impossible.

At the heart of the debate surrounding Pete and his career is whether he belongs in the Hall of Fame (HOF). Enshrinement in the HOF is the highest honor in baseball, a way to recognize the best of the best. As of 2023, only 270 players have been inducted since the first election in 1936. No objective criteria exist for inclusion in the HOF (although there are rules that address how players become eligible). It can therefore be difficult for voters (members of the Baseball Writers' Association of America) to determine which players are deserving of the honor. It is even harder when that player last stepped onto the field more than 125 years ago. Many of the modern awards and benchmarks used to gauge the value of a player did not exist in the nineteenth century. There were no Most Valuable Player

(MVP) awards, no All-Star games, no Gold Gloves. There was only the record the players compiled on the field.

Individually, Pete achieved great success. He began his career by ranking in the top three in hitting for seven straight years, finishing first, second, third, first, second, second, and third from 1882 to 1888—a staggering run of consistency. Over his career he won three batting titles (1882, 1885, and 1890) and finished in the top three nine times, with three runner-up finishes. He was a whisker away from five career batting titles (and three consecutive titles), losing to teammate Guy Hecker by a single point in 1886 and posting career bests in almost every statistical category, including a .402 average, in 1887 but running up against the even better year enjoyed by Tip O'Neill. Although Pete was one of the most dominant and consistent players of his time, he is also one of the most overlooked.

In the 150-year history of professional baseball, only 27 players have won three or more batting titles, and only two of them played in the nineteenth century: Pete with three and Hall of Famer Dan Brouthers with five.[1] Among that group, 21 have been inducted into the HOF, three are either still active or not yet eligible (as of 2021), and only three—Bill Madlock, Pete Rose, and Pete Browning—are eligible but have not been inducted. Pete is one of only 20 players to hit .400 in a season, one of only five rookies to win a batting title, one of only five players to win a batting title at age 21 or younger, and one of only four players to win batting titles in multiple leagues. And he is the only player to do all that.

The lingering question is whether Pete is worthy of the HOF. At first glance, his numbers indicate that the answer is yes, but his short career (by baseball standards) is often held against him. He was unable to compile enough lifetime statistics to make his worthiness of HOF status an open-and-shut case. His decade-long run of greatness is similar to that of other players who are considered among the best of their time, but are they among the best of all time?

Baseball seems to value lengthy careers, and the voting sportswriters tend to favor very good players who had long careers. Except in special cases, such as Dizzy Dean, Ralph Kiner, Sandy Koufax, and Jackie Robinson, players who were great for just a short time do not receive much recognition. Pete's career was over in 1893 after 12 years (plus three games in 1894). But during that time he put together a monstrous career batting average of .341—the sixteenth highest career average and among the top five for righties, resting comfortably among a group that includes Hall of Famers Rogers Hornsby, Ed Delahanty, and Harry Heilmann and placing him above such legends as Lou Gehrig, Tony Gwynn, Stan Musial, Rod Carew, Honus Wagner, and Joe DiMaggio. He also added a .403 OBP, .869 OPS, and 163 OPS+. Yet he has been denied admittance to the HOF because, in the eyes of some, he did not play long enough to accumulate sufficient career statistics.

It is hard to evaluate and compare players from different generations due to the changes in the game. It is especially difficult when considering players from the premodern era (before the 1900s), when Pete played, with its bigger fields, poor equipment, and evolving rules. When asked how he determines a player's value, former Chicago Cubs and Washington Nationals manager Jim Riggleman said simply, "Compare players to their peers. What did the player do in his career compared to those he played with and against?"[2] When this metric is applied, Pete stands out as one of his era's greats. His career .341 batting average ranks fourth behind Ed Delahanty (.345), Billy Hamilton (.344), and Dan Brouthers and Dave Orr (both .342). All but Orr are in the HOF, and Orr's exclusion is attributable to his brief eight-year career. Pete's total of three batting titles in the nineteenth century is second only to Brouthers's five. His run of nine top-three finishes in ten years is unmatched in the era. Brouthers comes closest, with eight top-three finishes in eleven years. Among players of his generation, Pete's batting average was more than 80 points better than the league average. He was heads and tails better than most players of his era. So why has he not received a single vote for admittance to the HOF?

Even when Pete's numbers are compared across generations, his career statistics are still impressive. He is one of only four players ranking in the top 22 in batting average who are not in the HOF. The other three are "Shoeless" Joe Jackson, Lefty O'Doul, and Dave Orr. Jackson is not in the HOF due to his alleged involvement in the 1919 Black Sox gambling scandal, while the careers of Orr and O'Doul (who played eleven years but only seven full seasons) are considered too short. Pete's career OPS+ of 163 is tied for fourteenth with Hall of Famer Jimmie Foxx and Mark McGwire. McGwire's exclusion from the HOF is based on his association with steroids and has nothing to do with his numbers, which would appear to make him a shoo-in. Of the 13 players with better OPS+ statistics, all but three are in the HOF. One of the three is Mike Trout, who is still playing, and the other two are Jackson and Barry Bonds, who has also been linked to steroids.

In the modern era of statistical analysis, baseball writers are continually looking for better ways to compare players from different generations. Pete's lofty batting average, which is regularly cited as his most impressive feat, is often afforded less importance among HOF voters, who now rely on advanced metrics to determine a player's value. For many modern-day HOF voters, Pete's exclusion is largely due to a lack of familiarity with the man and his accomplishments.

While statistics are useful to measure the greatness of a player and his HOF worthiness, a player's contribution to the success of his team is harder to quantify. Should players on great teams with less individual success be valued more highly than players who achieved great individual success on teams that were only mediocre or worse? In Pete's case, he piled up flashy numbers during his career, but his teams were generally underachievers. How much of the blame can be laid at Pete's feet? Over the years, the Louisville players were chided for selfishness; they flaunted team rules and did their own thing, to the detriment of the team. Should the club's lack of success be held against Pete, or can it be attributed to a team-wide behavior problem, lack of leadership, and poor management?

Pete's numbers seem HOF worthy, but election to the HOF is about much more than numbers. Character and leadership are often considered, although there are many miserable bastards in the HOF. Leadership is one of the many qualities that can elevate a really good player to an HOF-caliber player, but it is hard to gauge a player's true work ethic and character. These qualities may be well known to a player's teammates, but they are difficult for outsiders to judge. Despite his rough exterior and heavy drinking, Pete was well liked, even when he sometimes rubbed his teammates the wrong way with his boisterous, braggadocious manner. Pete was remembered as "having one of the biggest hearts in the world and [being] one of the easiest going men," yet he was never named team captain.[3] He was never seen as a team leader in the mold of some of the game's legendary captains such as Gary Carter, Derek Jeter, and Tony Perez. While Pete's skills were held in high regard by his teammates, he did not inspire them with his leadership or his work ethic. His character is often questioned due to his heavy drinking, influencing HOF voters' perception of him.

One of the biggest negatives when assessing Pete's greatness is that, despite his individual heroics, he never led his team to a championship—or even close to one. It would be nice if every story ended with the hero hitting the game-winning home run to capture the championship, but Pete's is not one of those tales. He was a great player who never scaled the championship mountain. Should he have been able to inspire his team to greater heights? In a game like baseball, it is hard for one player to lead a team to greatness. It is not a sport like basketball, where one dominant player can lift his teammates and carry them to a championship. A baseball player can get a hit every time he comes up to bat, but if his teammates are not getting on base ahead of him or hitting behind him to drive him in, no number of hits by any one player will win games. Pete was a great player on some really bad teams. He was never surrounded by an abundance of talent in Louisville. Hecker is recognized as one of the best pitcher-hitter combinations of the nineteenth century; Tony Mullane was a special talent but played only one season in Louisville; Toad Ramsey was an elite pitcher, albeit for only a few short seasons; and Chicken Wolf had moments of greatness but was better remembered for his stability, durability, and leadership. All four fell short of the sustained greatness that would have helped propel Louisville to success. The Louisville roster during Pete's tenure usually featured a rotating lineup of serviceable players; it was overly reliant on one pitcher to shoulder the bulk of the work and one or two hitters to provide the offense. This, along with the club's ineffective management and the players' indifference to team rules, proved to be a failing combination.

For Pete, one of the biggest reasons for his exclusion from the HOF seems to be the little time he spent in the National League. His impressive numbers are often dismissed because he played most of his career in the American Association, a rogue league formed to compete with the NL. In the early years of the HOF, the AA was seen as the lesser league, and Pete's statistics are often viewed as being achieved against lesser competition, though this is far from true. While AA statistics are recognized as part of MLB history, players from the AA have often been perceived as second-class citizens who played in an inferior league. But this perception is wrong, tainted by the NL's long-held bias against the rogue circuit. Players regularly moved between the two leagues with no discernible difference in their production. A good player in one league could expect to finish in roughly the same position he had in the other league. In the one-year existence of the Players' League, which was by far the most talented of the three leagues at the time, Pete won the league batting title. The PL featured such established hitters as Jake Beckley, Dan Brouthers, Ed Delahanty, Hugh Duffy, King Kelly, Jim O'Rourke, and John Ward, yet only its champion batter has not been enshrined in the HOF. In Pete's two full seasons in the NL, which came at the end of his career, he finished third in batting in 1891 and finished just outside the top ten in the injury-plagued 1892 season.

Only four men who played more than three seasons in the AA's ten-year existence are in the HOF. Two of them, Charles Comiskey and Wilbert Robinson, are recognized more for their managerial and ownership skills, while Tommy McCarthy played longer and had his most productive years in the NL. Until Bid McPhee was inducted, no player who had won fame primarily in the AA had been welcomed into the HOF. Both McPhee and McCarthy were recognized for their defensive skills and put up offensive numbers that pale in comparison to Pete's (and both have questionable resumés in terms of HOF worthiness). The AA produced some of the best baseball and some of the best players of the decade. Pete was one of those players and should be recognized as such. Others who played the bulk of their careers in the AA have legitimate cases for enshrinement in the HOF as well, including Bob Caruthers, Guy Hecker, Tony Mullane, Tip O'Neill, and Harry Stovey. MLB has long recognized the AA's statistics as part of its history, and it is long past time to recognize the men who put up those numbers.

Unfortunately, when Pete retired, there was no HOF, which inducted its first class in 1936. As a result, Pete and many of his contemporaries have been overlooked. True baseball scholarship did not exist in the 1940s, when the HOF first started evaluating nineteenth-century players. It appears that many inductees who played in the nineteenth century were elected based on personal preferences rather than statistical records, as players with far superior achievements and statistics have been excluded. In addition, many of the early record books did not list the yearly leaders for defunct leagues, so Pete's three batting titles and career batting average did not become common knowledge until later. The general perception of Pete was that of a heavy hitter in a baseball backwater who was known for his excessive drinking, frequent absences, bad fielding, and link to the Louisville Slugger.

The first group of HOF honorees who played entirely or primarily in the nineteenth century were inducted in 1939.[4] In response to criticism about the lack of nineteenth-century inductees, a Hall of Fame Committee (Veterans Committee) was formed to identify potential honorees, and six were chosen for induction. Since then, only 35 other nineteenth-century players (plus 16 nonplayers) have been inducted. Seventeen of those selections came in 1945 and 1946, when the Veterans Committee made an effort to bring players from the nineteenth century to the attention of voters, particularly younger sportswriters who might be reluctant to vote for players about whom they had limited firsthand knowledge.

Famed baseball writer Bill James cites the impact the lack of baseball scholarship had on early HOF selections: "We should not judge the Old-Timers Committee without remembering, again, that the world of baseball research, as we know it now, did not exist at the time. Without even a good encyclopedia to refer to, it was a lot harder to put together a file of information on twenty or thirty candidates." But, at the same time, this does not excuse the selection of players who were not the "greatest of the great." According to James, "They could have done a lot better job if they had taken their position more seriously. It's called research. It's called homework." He uses the example of Jim O'Rourke, elected to the HOF in 1945 by the Veterans Committee, as an example of the flawed approach to evaluating nineteenth-century talent. James does not question O'Rourke's credentials, although he finds them borderline at best, but he asks why players with equivalent or superior credentials such as Jake Beckley, Billy Hamilton, George Van Haltren, Sam Thompson, and Pete had to wait another twenty or thirty years to be selected, if then. "There's no answer," explains James. "It just happened. They focused on O'Rourke almost at random because they hadn't done their homework."[5]

One of the first studies to recognize the impact and value of nineteenth-century batters was done in 1972 by acclaimed historian Eugene Murdock.[6] Murdock used seven "power categories"—runs, doubles, triples, home runs, RBIs, slugging average, and batting average—to determine a player's true impact. He used a per-game average of the power categories so players with shorter careers were on an equal footing with those who had much longer careers. He ranked the top 12 players in each category and assigned points (the player finishing first received 12 points, the player placing second 11 points, and so on). Then he totaled the points and compiled a final list. Murdock's list seemed to accurately identify the top players, as three of his top five players (Dan Brouthers, Sam Thompson, and Ed Delahanty) are in the HOF. Pete and Harry Stovey were the two players on the list but excluded from the HOF. This type of analysis has grown in scope and depth over time. In 2009 Pete was named the first winner of an honor bestowed by the Society for American Baseball Research (SABR): Overlooked 19th Century Baseball Legend, which recognizes a player, manager, executive, or other baseball personality from that era not yet inducted into the HOF. Some argue that there are already enough nineteenth-century players in the HOF, so why evaluate any more? The answer is that the HOF is supposed to represent the best players of all time, so all the best players should be enshrined.

There is no simple explanation of why Pete has been snubbed by HOF voters. Mostly, there seems to be a general lack of knowledge of Pete and his career. But as baseball scholarship has improved, so has the understanding of Pete's accomplishments. Still, as Pete's era recedes further into the past, interest in him and his contemporaries seems to diminish.

When asked about the criteria he uses when evaluating HOF credentials, sportswriter and HOF voter Jaime Aron said, "I'm a believer in evaluating how a player was valued in his era."[7] Pete was highly valued in his era. He was remembered as "the greatest natural hitter of his day," and his heroics on the field made him a fan favorite.[8] "He did not have a head for the game like Comiskey, or Ewing, or Ward," wrote the *Washington Post,* "but he was a greater popular favorite than any of them, and the bleachers idolized him as they did no other player the game has produced. It was an inspiration—the greetings he got when he came to bat in a pinch, when a hit would win the game; and when in his prime he rarely disappointed the expectative."[9] Much of the perception of Pete has been clouded by time and the advanced metrics now used to better understand a player's value. But back in the day, sportswriters viewed Pete as one of the elite players and one of the era's most dominant and feared hitters. Only with the passage of time has that opinion faded. Why should the opinion of those who actually saw Pete play be less relevant than the opinion of those who did not?

Aron asks, "A decade later, were people still saying, wow, we sure miss that sweet-swingin' Pete Browning, or did the game go on without people missing him much?"[10] Pete was very much remembered and missed a decade after his retirement. Five years after his death and more than 15 years since he last stepped on a major league field, a headline syndicated across the country roundly declared, "Browning and Delahanty Greatest Hitters Baseball Has Ever Known."[11] During his career, Pete carved out a reputation that, though sometimes overlooked, will never fade. "It is the greatest sport in the world, our Olympic game, and he that is a champion in it is a hero," mythologized the *Washington Post* upon his death. "In the years to come, long after Pete Browning shall have supped with the politics worms that devoured old Polonius, patrons of the game will relate traditions of the mighty gladiator and mournfully regret that there are no such sluggers nowadays."[12] Unfortunately for Pete, more than 100 years have passed, and he has been largely forgotten.

Pete's legacy and his place in the history of baseball are complicated. Though not considered a progressive innovator when it comes to the evolution of the game, Pete must be remembered for his role in the development of the Louisville Slugger and the modern bat. His meticulous attention to his bats, the all-important tools of his trade, helped other players recognize their importance. Bats evolved into highly specialized tools, crafted and designed for the unique needs of each individual player.

Teammate Lave Cross also advanced the notion that Pete inadvertently inspired the hit-and-run. "He was hard of hearing and one day couldn't hear the coach after getting to first on a hit and started for second on the first ball pitched," explained Cross. "He ran like a wildcat and got to third on a single. Pete would not have got past second had he not misunderstood the signals or if he would have heard the coaches. As it was . . . he got to third safely and would have been on the way home if he hadn't been held by the man coaching third. That play of Browning's suggested the hit-and-run game. Hugh Jennings heard of it, and the system was introduced in Baltimore and worked with great success."[13]

Pete's drinking and habitual disregard for the rules are regular points of discussion, as is his endless stream of unconventional and quirky behavior. He was not as overtly rebellious as Dock Ellis, who pitched a no-hitter while on LSD, or as defiant as Curt Flood, whose stubborn opposition to the reserve clause helped change the game. Pete's behavior was more akin to the off-the-wall eccentricities and antics of Detroit Tigers pitcher Mark "The Bird" Fidrych, who was known to talk to the ball, manicure the mound, and throw balls back if he believed they still had hits in them. Pete's outlandish life and unconventional approach to the game paved the way for the rebels and rule breakers who followed. He was also a uniquely talented individual who hit a baseball better than almost everyone in the early years of the game and whose skills separated him from most other players of his generation. His decade of hitting excellence ranks him among the all-time best.

Pete is often defined by his era, a time of rule changes and advances in the game. He, in turn, helped define that era. In 1903 Pete commented on the state of the game and compared it to his generation: "There ain't three men in the country today that can play ball like we used to. . . . There ain't no stick work, and the game ain't a bit heady. Why if nine of the old boys, as they was in their prime, would go to bat now, and one of these modern teams was in the field, they wouldn't get us out in a week." Then, in his own unique way, he addressed his own legacy: "Mind, I ain't sayin' that old Pete was out of sight, but there ain't nobody in the country that knows anymore about the game than I do."[14]

The perception of Pete's life and career has often been guided by the adage, when forced to choose between the truth and the legend, choose the legend. All legends involve myths, and myths are, at best, half-truths. There is a fine line between fact and fiction. Pete straddled that line his entire life. He is a contradiction and an enigma. He is a generational hitter whose skills have long been overlooked. He is the champion batter of the American Association. He is the Prince of Bourbon. He is the Old Warhorse and the Gladiator. He is the Louisville Slugger. He is immortal. He is a legend. He is all those things. He is Pete Browning.

Acknowledgments

Baseball is truly a team game. It takes a full roster of players working together to be successful. All their contributions, both big and small, determine the outcome of the game. This book is no different. Providing clutch contributions and always coming through with key pinch hits when I had questions were sportswriters and Hall of Fame voters Cormac Gordan and Jaime Aron, author David Nemec, writer Tim Sullivan, former major league manager Jim Riggleman, official Major League Baseball historian John Thorn, MLB Network researcher Jessica Brand, Peter Elwell from the Cleveland Public Library, Cassidy Lent and John Horne from the Baseball Hall of Fame, Bailey Mazik from the Louisville Slugger Museum, Amy Purcell from the University of Louisville Archives, Dr. Richard Barnstein, and the Society for American Baseball Research.

The backbone of a good team is its pitching staff, and Ashley Runyon and her team at the University Press of Kentucky—Margaret Kelly, Jackie Wilson, David Cobb, and Linda Lotz—were that backbone for me. They were there to guide this project from start to finish.

Every team has heavy hitters in the lineup, and this project featured many. Without their contributions, this book would not be in your hands now. Its genesis goes back to my years in graduate school in New York. I often spent summer evenings at my good friend Ben Shove's place, where we whiled away the time drinking many beers and listening to the Grateful Dead, Phish, moe., and Strangefolk as we watched Yankees games on mute. Ben was a die-hard Yankees fan (for those keeping score, I'm an Orioles fan), and the only thing he requested was that we turn the volume back on when the Yankees won so he could hear legendary announcer John Sterling utter his famous game-closing proclamation: "Ballgame over! Yankees win! Theeeeeee Yankees win." In the summer of 2000, those words were heard a lot. During the game Ben and I usually engaged in deep, endless debates about Hall of Fame–worthy ballplayers, often checking the newly launched Baseball-Reference.com website to back up our arguments. Thus began a lifetime of debate about the Hall of Fame worthiness of countless MLB and NFL players—a debate that still rages to this day.

Similarly, I have engaged in countless sports debates (and many discussions of the *Rocky* movies) with Rich Bauer since our college days. Over the years, Rich has become my go-to person for all baseball-related questions.

Thank you to Caleb Stine for all the conversations about music, creating art, and the process of storytelling. They have provided more inspiration than you know.

As always, I need to thank the legendary Email Group, Doug Martin, John Skozilas, and Paul Skozilas. The endless dialogue provides the best feedback, ideas, and criticism. And thank you for Camp Smart. We must never forget Camp Smart.

I must thank my all-stars, my wife Melissa and daughter Ella. Melissa made all this happen. This book was born from an idea she had while we were drinking beers at the Bluegrass Brewing Company after visiting the Louisville Slugger Museum. Then she listened patiently as I talked endlessly about this project. She provided constant feedback and ideas and read early drafts of the book. Thank you, Ella, for making me look at the world in a different way.

Finally, thank you to my mom, who was always my biggest fan. You are loved and missed every day.

Notes

Introduction

1. "As to Peter Browning," *Louisville Courier-Journal,* May 10, 1887, 2.
2. "Stories about Pete Browning," *Louisville Courier-Journal,* June 12, 1905, 6.
3. "Pete Browning a Noted Character," *Chicago Daily Tribune,* June 11, 1905, 9.
4. "Base Ball Gossip," *Cincinnati Enquirer,* July 12, 1891, 10.
5. "Pete Browning Slugger," *Washington Post,* September 12, 1905, 8.
6. "Diamond Jottings," *Atlanta Constitution,* March 1, 1885, 13.
7. A. H. Tarvin Papers, 1838–1949, National Baseball Hall of Fame, Cooperstown, NY.
8. "When Pete Browning Was Defender of Aristocracy," *Butte (MT) Miner,* March 15, 1908, 16.
9. "Stories of Old Pete Browning," *Louisville Courier-Journal,* October 15, 1905, 31.
10. "When Pete Browning Was Defender of Aristocracy," 16.
11. "Base Ball Notes," *Washington Evening Star,* April 25, 1901, 9.
12. "Won by the Umpire," *Louisville Courier-Journal,* August 11, 1889, 4.
13. "Stories about Pete Browning," 6.
14. "Notes on the Games," *Louisville Courier-Journal,* July 23, 1888, 2.
15. "Notes on the Games," *Louisville Courier-Journal,* May 27, 1885, 6.
16. "Pietro Browning and His Average—Other Matters," *Cincinnati Enquirer,* October 18, 1891, 2.
17. "Base-ball Notes," *Cincinnati Enquirer,* February 9, 1890, 16.
18. "Stories about Pete Browning," 6.
19. Jack Boyle, "Delahanty and Pete Browning Greatest," *Chicago Inter-Ocean,* December 2, 1910, 4.
20. "Plenty of Criticism," *Louisville Courier-Journal,* July 8, 1888, 7.
21. "How Pete Browning Got Four Hits but Forgot Score of the Game," *Louisville Courier-Journal,* January 29, 1907, 6.
22. Boyle, "Delahanty and Pete Browning Greatest," 4.

23. "Sam Trott Talks of Kilroy, Bennett, Nava, Latham, and Other Baseball Heroes of the Romantic Past," *Baltimore Sun*, September 16, 1906, 12.

24. "Some Lively Baseball Gossip," *Louisville Courier-Journal*, April 19, 1908, 38.

25. "Outfielder Pete Browning," *St. Louis Sporting News*, April 13, 1889, 1.

26. "Notes," *Louisville Courier-Journal*, August 24, 1891, 6.

27. "When Pete Browning Was Defender of Aristocracy," 16.

28. "Base Ball Gossip," 10.

29. "Some Lively Baseball Gossip," 38.

30. "Line up of the New Colonels," *Louisville Courier-Journal*, January 10, 1909, 30.

31. "Browning," *Cincinnati Enquirer*, July 2, 1891, 2.

32. "As to Peter Browning," 2.

1. Childhood (1861–1876)

1. "Baseball News," *Louisville Courier-Journal*, September 20, 1891, 13.

2. Ibid.

3. "Their Nicknames," *Louisville Courier-Journal*, August 17, 1888, 6.

4. Jeffrey Lee Puckett, "Is Louisville the North or the South? Let's Decide This Once and for All," *Louisville Courier-Journal*, August 31, 2017, https: //www .courier-journal.com/story/news/local/2017/08/31/louisville-north-south-debate /602066001/.

5. Ricardo Ferreira Bento and Anna Carolina de Oliveira Fonseca, "A Brief History of Mastoidectomy," *International Archives of Otorhinolaryngology* 17, no. 2 (2013): 168–78.

6. "Stories about Pete Browning," *Louisville Courier-Journal*, June 12, 1905, 6.

7. "Notes on the Game," *Louisville Courier-Journal*, May 27, 1885, 6.

8. "Notes," *Louisville Courier-Journal*, August 11, 1884, 8.

9. "For the Baseball Fans," *Washington Post*, April 2, 1896, 8.

10. "Notes of the Game," *Louisville Courier-Journal*, September 14, 1887, 3.

11. "Stories about Pete Browning," 6.

12. "Pete Browning Dead," *Philadelphia Sporting Life*, September 16, 1905, 3.

13. "Browning Can Write," *Louisville Courier-Journal*, June 20, 1886, 4.

14. "Some Lively Baseball Gossip," *Louisville Courier-Journal*, April 19, 1908, 38.

15. "Base Ball Gossip," *Cincinnati Enquirer*, July 12, 1891, 10.

16. "Sam Trott Talks of Kilroy, Bennett, Nava, Latham, and Other Baseball Heroes of the Romantic Past," *Baltimore Sun*, September 16, 1906, 12.

17. "Called Out," *Louisville Courier-Journal*, September 11, 1905, 5.

18. "How They Spend Their Time," *Louisville Courier-Journal*, January 13, 1889, 13.

19. "Base Ball," *Louisville Courier-Journal*, June 21, 1891, 13.

20. "As to Pete Browning," *Louisville Courier-Journal*, May 10, 1887, 2.

21. "Notes of the Game," *Louisville Courier-Journal*, August 20, 1887, 6.

22. "Base Ball Notes," *Louisville Courier-Journal*, April 4, 1886, 8.

23. "Jimmy Wolf in Town," *Louisville Courier-Journal*, June 21, 1892, 8.

24. "Browning's Notable Regret," *Louisville Courier-Journal*, February 18, 1891, 7.

25. Chris Silva, "The Fascinating History of the Game," Post Game, July 12, 2011, http://www.thepostgame.com/blog/throwback/201107/fascinating-history-baseball-glove.

26. "Base Ball—All about the Game," *Louisville Courier-Journal*, September 20, 1866, 2.

27. "A Match of Base Ball," *Louisville Courier-Journal*, July 15, 1859, 3.

28. *Louisville Courier-Journal*, July 18, 1867, 2.

29. George B. Kirsch, *Baseball in Blue and Gray* (Princeton, NJ: Princeton University Press, 2003), 121.

30. "Base Ball," *Louisville Courier-Journal*, May 21, 1865, 1.

31. "Base-Ball," *Louisville Courier-Journal*, April 4, 1866, 3.

32. "New Base-Ball Club," *Louisville Courier-Journal*, August 28, 1866, 1.

33. "Base Ball Clubs and Their Abuses," *Louisville Courier-Journal*, October 1, 1865, 2.

34. "Base Ball—All about the Game," 2.

35. "Base Ball Clubs and Their Abuses," 2.

2. Amateur Days (1877–1881)

1. "Base Ball," *Louisville Courier-Journal*, April 13, 1877, 1.

2. "Base Ball," *Louisville Courier-Journal*, April 14, 1877, 4.

3. "General Notes," *Louisville Courier-Journal*, July 26, 1877, 2.

4. "General Notes," *Louisville Courier-Journal*, July 28, 1877, 4.

5. "Base Ball," *Louisville Courier-Journal*, May 21, 1865, 1.

6. "Sporting Gossip," *Chicago Inter-Ocean*, January 15, 1891, 6.

7. Phillip Von Borries, *American Gladiator* (St. Petersburg, FL: Booklocker, 2007), 17.

8. Bill James, *The New Bill James Historical Baseball Abstract* (New York: Free Press, 2003), 748.

9. "Plenty of Criticism," *Louisville Courier-Journal*, July 8, 1888, 7.

10. "Baseball Gossip," *Washington Post*, February 14, 1904, B2.

11. "Called Out," *Louisville Courier-Journal*, September 11, 1905, 5.

12. "Stories about Pete Browning," *Louisville Courier-Journal*, June 12, 1905, 6.

13. "Had Mania for Bats," *Washington Post*, December 17, 1911, 19.

14. "Notes of the Game," *Louisville Courier-Journal*, July 27, 1887, 3.

15. "Notes and Comments," *Louisville Courier-Journal*, August 9, 1885, 5.

16. "Is Insane," *Louisville Courier-Journal*, June 8, 1905, 2.

17. "Short Baseball Stories," *Louisville Courier-Journal*, August 6, 1899, 7.

18. Ibid.

19. "Base Ball Gossip," *Cincinnati Enquirer*, July 11, 1891, 2.

20. Von Borries, *American Gladiator*, 17.

21. "Short Baseball Stories," 7.

22. "Baseball Notes," *Washington Post*, July 26, 1899, 8.

23. "Base Ball Gossip," *Cincinnati Enquirer*, July 7, 1891, 2.

24. "More about Scoring," *Philadelphia Sporting Life,* February 10, 1886, 2.

25. John Thorn, ed., *Total Baseball,* 8th ed. (Sports Media Publishing, 2004), 2415–17.

26. William A. Cook, *The Louisville Grays Scandal of 1877: The Taint of Gambling at the Dawn of the National League* (Jefferson, NC: McFarland, 2005), 116.

27. Haldeman may have appeared in other games for the Grays during the season. His father believed playing baseball was not an appropriate occupation for a gentleman, so Haldeman tried to keep his playing a secret. This seems to be confirmed by out-of-town box scores, which listed Haldeman as a player, while the *Courier-Journal* omitted any mention of him (Haldeman would have written those articles himself). He may have played for Cincinnati and St. Louis during the 1877 season as well.

28. Jim McLennan, "Baseball's Greatest Scandals, #7: The Louisville Grays," AZ Snakepit, May 24, 2011, https://www.azsnakepit.com/2011/5/24/2131205/baseballs-greatest-scandals-9-the-louisville-greys.

29. These lifetime suspensions were the second in baseball history. The season before, Louisville's George Bechtel became the first player suspended for life for intentionally losing games for money.

30. "No Base Ball in Louisville This Season," *Louisville Courier-Journal,* March 8, 1878, 4.

31. "Pete Browning Laid Off," *Louisville Courier-Journal,* June 27, 1886, 7.

32. "Baseball Game of Olden Days," *Louisville Courier-Journal,* February 18, 1908, 6.

33. Ibid.

34. "Baseball," *New York Clipper,* June 18, 1881, 204.

35. "Local Sports," *Louisville Courier-Journal,* July 17, 1881, 8.

36. "Another Chicago Club," *Louisville Courier-Journal,* September 12, 1881, 8.

37. "A Drawn Game," *Louisville Courier-Journal,* June 27, 1881, 2.

38. "Liners," *Louisville Courier-Journal,* June 27, 1881, 2.

39. "Browning's Last Call," *Louisville Courier-Journal,* May 23, 1881, 3.

40. Arthur R. Ahrens, "Fred Pfeffer, Stonewall Second Baseman," *SABR Research Journal,* http://research.sabr.org/journals/fred-pfeffer (accessed May 18, 2021).

41. "A Disabled Club," *Louisville Courier-Journal,* August 22, 1881, 8.

42. "A Brilliant Opening," *Louisville Courier-Journal,* May 2, 1884, 8.

43. Hugh S. Fullerton, "Color Line in Base Ball," *New York Age,* January 11, 1919, 6.

44. This story has many variations, with Pete asking what league, what position, what nine, or what team Garfield played for.

45. "Did Not Know There Had Been War," *Chicago Inter-Ocean,* January 8, 1899, 10.

46. "Stories about Pete Browning," 6.

47. Edward Achon, *The Summer of Beer and Whiskey: How Brewers, Barkeeps, Rowdies, Immigrants, and a Wild Pennant Fight Made Baseball America's Game* (New York: Public Affairs Books, 2013), 127.

48. "Complimenting the Eclipse," *Louisville Courier-Journal,* November 20, 1881, 10.

49. "Conquering Heroes," *Louisville Courier-Journal*, November 22, 1881, 6.
50. Ibid.
51. Ibid.

3. First Pro Season (1882)

1. "Local Base-Ball Affairs," *Louisville Courier-Journal*, August 28, 1881, 5.
2. "A New Association," *Cincinnati Enquirer*, September 12, 1881, 2.
3. "The New Base Ball Movement," *Philadelphia Times*, September 12, 1881, 3.
4. "Diamond Dust," *Louisville Courier-Journal*, September 12, 1881, 8.
5. "The Pittsburgh Meeting," *New York Clipper*, October 22, 1881, 504.
6. "The New Association," *New York Clipper*, October 29, 1881, 515.
7. Jeremy K. Hodges and Bill Nowlin, eds., *Base Ball's 19th Century Winter Meetings, 1857–1900* (Phoenix: Society for American Baseball Research, 2018), 370.
8. "Notes," *Louisville Courier-Journal*, June 20, 1883, 6.
9. *Louisville Commercial*, June 11, 1882.
10. A. H. Tarvin Papers, National Baseball Hall of Fame, Cooperstown, NY.
11. "Detroit's Derby," *St. Louis Globe Democrat*, April 14, 1882, 8.
12. "Base Ball Notes," *St. Louis Globe Democrat*, April 14, 1882, 5.
13. Mike Roer, *Orator O'Rourke: The Life of a Baseball Radical* (Jefferson, NC: McFarland, 2005), 99.
14. "Diamond Dust," *St. Louis Globe Democrat*, May 27, 1882, 9.
15. The terms "captain" and "manager" are used interchangeably. In early baseball, many teams had players who were "manager-captains," with the off-field responsibilities of managers and the on-field responsibilities of captains. Teams with nonplaying managers had a player who served as captain.
16. "Conquering Heroes," *Louisville Courier-Journal*, November 22, 1881, 6.
17. "Timely Sporting Topics of the Day," *Louisville Courier-Journal*, October 20, 1899, 6.
18. "Sam Barkley," *St. Louis Sporting News*, May 10, 1886, 5.
19. "Diamond Dust," *Saint Paul Globe*, August 22, 1895, 5.
20. "Terrible Tony," *Decatur (IL) Herald*, May 26, 1893, 6.
21. "From Cincinnati," *Philadelphia Sporting Life*, June 15, 1887, 2.
22. "Mullane Again," *Philadelphia Sporting Life*, April 9, 1884, 4.
23. "Chicago vs Eclipse," *New York Clipper*, December 24, 1881, 658.
24. "Base Ball," *New York Clipper*, March 11, 1882, 844.
25. "Base Ball," *Louisville Courier-Journal*, April 20, 1882, 2.
26. "A Talk with Hecker," *Louisville Courier-Journal*, May 15, 1887, 7.
27. "Base Ball," *Louisville Courier-Journal*, June 29, 1884, 5.
28. Guy Mcl. Smith, "Deeds of Hecker, Browning, Ramsey Are Recalled," *Louisville Courier-Journal*, September 24, 1933, 34.
29. "Base Ball," *Louisville Courier-Journal*, April 20, 1882, 2.
30. "Sporting Matters," *Detroit Free Press*, April 18, 1882, 1.
31. "Base Ball," *Louisville Courier-Journal*, April 20, 1882, 2.

32. "Sporting Notes," *Cincinnati Enquirer,* March 15, 1882, 5.
33. "Base-Ball," *Louisville Courier-Journal,* March 5, 1882, 10.
34. "Base Ball," *Louisville Courier-Journal,* April 22, 1882, 3.
35. "Sporting," *Buffalo Commercial,* October 18, 1882, 3.
36. "NL-AA Conflict and Expelled Players," *Cincinnati Commercial Tribune,* May 12, 1882, https://protoball.org/Clipping: NL-AA_conflict_and_expelled_players (accessed December 2, 2020).
37. "Base Ball," *Louisville Courier-Journal,* April 23, 1882, 14.
38. "Eclipse Fifteen, Browns Three," *Louisville Courier-Journal,* April 24, 1882, 8.
39. "Sunday's Game," *Louisville Courier-Journal,* April 25, 1882, 6.
40. "Liners," *Louisville Courier-Journal,* April 30, 1882, 8.
41. "Tips," *St. Louis Globe Democrat,* May 2, 1882, 7.
42. "On Top Again," *Louisville Courier-Journal,* May 6, 1882, 11; "The Browns at Louisville," *St. Louis Globe Democrat,* May 6, 1882, 3.
43. "Notes of the Game," *Louisville Courier-Journal,* June 5, 1882, 8.
44. "Poor Baltimore," *Louisville Courier-Journal,* June 19, 1882, 8.
45. "Louisville Does the Baby Act," *Cincinnati Enquirer,* June 30, 1882, 5.
46. "The Proper Caper," *Louisville Courier-Journal,* June 9, 1882, 8.
47. "Beaten by the Baltimores," *Louisville Courier-Journal,* July 19, 1882, 6.
48. "A Great Victory," *Louisville Courier-Journal,* September 12, 1882, 6.
49. *Pittsburgh Times,* September 20, 1882.
50. "Notes," *Cincinnati Enquirer,* July 10, 1882, 8.
51. "Hope for the Athletic Yet," *Philadelphia Times,* August 13, 1882, 2.
52. "Notes," *Louisville Courier-Journal,* August 13, 1882, 2.
53. "Browning's Conduct," *Louisville Courier-Journal,* August 14, 1882, 3.
54. Stuart Cameron, "Today's Sport Parade," *Middlesboro (KY) Daily News,* January 22, 1935, 4.
55. "Sporting," *Buffalo Commercial,* October 18, 1882, 3.
56. Bill James, *The New Bill James Historical Baseball Abstract* (New York: Free Press, 2003), 273–74.
57. "The Base-Ball Champions," *New York Times,* October 9, 1882, 5.
58. "To-Day's Game," *Louisville Courier-Journal,* September 2, 1882, 2.
59. "Notes," *Cincinnati Enquirer,* September 3, 1882, 2.

4. Battles with the Bottle (1883)

1. "For the Base Ball Fans," *Washington Post,* October 27, 1896, 8.
2. "The Cincinnatis Down South," *Cincinnati Enquirer,* February 11, 1883, 12.
3. Two home runs was the individual league average for the season.
4. O. P. Caylor, "Before Taking," *Louisville Courier-Journal,* July 11, 1883, 6.
5. "Notes," *Louisville Courier-Journal,* May 20, 1883, 5.
6. "Notes," *Louisville Courier-Journal,* July 8, 1883, 4.
7. "Notes," *Louisville Courier-Journal,* July 9, 1883, 8.
8. "The News," *Louisville Courier-Journal,* July 15, 1883, 3.

9. David Nemec, *Major League Baseball Profiles, 1871–1900*, vol. 2, *The Hall of Famers and Memorable Personalities Who Shaped the Game* (Lincoln: University of Nebraska Press, 2011), 281.

10. "A Base-Baller's Fastest Run," *Louisville Courier-Journal*, July 16, 1883, 8.

11. "The Eclipse Cripples, as Seen by St. Louis," *Louisville Courier-Journal*, July 24, 1883, 2.

12. Ibid.

13. "The News," *Louisville Courier-Journal*, July 25, 1883, 1.

14. "Notes," *Louisville Courier-Journal*, July 20, 1883, 8.

15. Ibid.

16. "The News," *Louisville Courier-Journal*, July 23, 1883, 1.

17. "Joe Gerhardt, the Eclipse Club Captain, Stricken with Partial Paralysis," *Louisville Courier-Journal*, July 27, 1883, 6.

18. "The St. Louis Ball-Tossers Gradually but Surely Gaining," *St. Louis Globe Democrat*, May 25, 1883, 6.

19. Edward Achon, *The Summer of Beer and Whiskey: How Brewers, Barkeeps, Rowdies, Immigrants, and a Wild Pennant Fight Made Baseball America's Game* (New York: Public Affairs Books, 2013), 132.

20. "Notes," *Louisville Courier-Journal*, July 31, 1883, 8.

21. "The National Game," *Pittsburgh Press*, July 17, 1891, 5.

22. Achon, *Summer of Beer and Whiskey*, 115.

23. "The National Game," 5.

24. "Joe Gerhardt," *Louisville Courier-Journal*, July 27, 1883, 6.

25. "Nearing the Goal," *Cincinnati Enquirer*, August 9, 1883, 2.

26. "Base Ball," *Louisville Courier-Journal*, September 12, 1883, 2.

27. Ibid.

28. "Next Year's Nine," *Louisville Courier-Journal*, September 14, 1883, 6.

29. "Notes," *Louisville Courier-Journal*, September 28, 1883, 8.

30. Achon, *Summer of Beer and Whiskey*, 247.

31. Quoted in Bob Bailey, "Guy Hecker," Society of American Baseball Research, https://sabr.org/bioproj/person/guy-hecker/.

5. The Louisville Slugger (1884)

1. Ash remained the wood of choice for making baseball bats for the next 100 years, until Hillerich & Bradsby and other companies switched to maple. The change was due to several reasons, including a beetle infestation that destroyed many ash trees and the discovery that maple is a harder, more durable wood that does not dent or flake.

2. Bob Hill, *Crack of the Bat: The Louisville Slugger Story* (Champaign, IL: Sports Publishing, 2000), 27.

3. Guy Butler, "Bat Factory Turns out Real War Clubs," *Miami News*, May 17, 1944, 2-B.

4. Frank Klein, "Trying Something New Created a Business," *Tampa Tribune,* November 10, 1968, 82.

5. "Pete Browning Bats Arrived Yesterday and Are Distributed," *Pittsburgh Press,* April 26, 1891, 6.

6. "Base Hits," *Pittsburgh Press,* May 17, 1891, 6.

7. "Williams Jump Was Foolish," *St. Louis Republic,* April 1, 1901.

8. Bill Spargo, "The Bats of Great Players," *Butte (MT) Daily Post,* September 2, 1909, 7.

9. Cy Peterman, "Baseball Bat Business Began as a Friend's Favor," *Philadelphia Inquirer,* April 22, 1940, 19.

10. "Louisville Gets Even with Indianapolis Team and Defeats It Eight to One," *Louisville Courier-Journal,* May 11, 1884, 7.

11. Guy Mcl. Smith, "Deeds of Hecker, Browning, Ramsey Are Recalled," *Louisville Courier-Journal,* September 24, 1933, 34.

12. "The Story of the Story of Browning's Bat," *Baseball History Daily,* August 12, 2019, https://baseballhistorydaily.com/2019/08/12/the-story-of-the-story-of-brownings-bat/.

13. "Where Famous Sluggers Get Perfect Clubs," *Louisville Courier-Journal,* June 17, 1924, 40.

14. Leslie Lieber, "Where Home Runs Come From," *Baltimore Sun,* October 5, 1974, 18.

15. "The Best Outfield," *Cincinnati Enquirer,* August 13, 1891, 2.

16. "Hillerich & Bradsby to Entertain National Baseball Delegates," *Louisville Courier-Journal,* December 5, 1922, 9.

17. "From Butter Churns to Bats," https://www.sluggermuseum.com/about-us/our-history (accessed November 16, 2022).

18. "Pete Browning a Noted Character," *Chicago Tribune,* June 11, 1905, 9.

19. "Pete Browning Bats Arrived Yesterday and Are Distributed," 6.

20. "Stories about Pete Browning," *Louisville Courier-Journal,* June 12, 1905, 6.

21. "Tip O'Neill and Pete Browning's Bat," *Cincinnati Enquirer,* March 25, 1892, 2.

22. "Base Ball Gossip," *Cincinnati Enquirer,* July 8, 1891, 2.

23. "Base Ball Gossip," *Cincinnati Enquirer,* July 12, 1891, 10.

24. "Baseball Bat Industry Brings Fame to City," *Louisville Courier-Journal,* June 17, 1924, 40.

25. "Had a Mania for Bats," *Washington Post,* December 17, 1911, 19.

26. "Famous Bats and Batsmen," *Washington Post,* July 21, 1907, MS3.

27. "Are Cranks on Bats," *Washington Post,* November 21, 1909, S3.

28. "Had a Mania for Bats," 19.

29. Richard Bak, "Ty Cobb Drove Pitchers Batty with His Custom Louisville Sluggers," Vintage Detroit, October 19, 2011, https: //www.vintagedetroit.com/blog/2011/10/19/ty-cobb-drove-pitchers-batty-with-his-custom-louisville-sluggers/.

30. *Louisville Commercial,* January 20, 1884, quoted in Bob Bailey, David Ball, and Bob McConnell, "The American Association History Project," https://sabr.org/research/article/the-american-association-history-project/ (accessed October 4, 2020).

31. "A Brilliant Opening," *Louisville Courier-Journal,* May 2, 1884, 8.
32. "Notes," *Louisville Courier-Journal,* May 26, 1884, 5.
33. "Notes," *Louisville Courier-Journal,* July 5, 1884, 6.
34. "Notes," *Cincinnati Enquirer,* August 14, 1884, 2.
35. "Notes," *Louisville Courier-Journal,* September 13, 1884, 5.
36. "The Louisville Club Makes the Washingtons a Present of Yesterday's Game," *Louisville Courier-Journal,* June 29, 1884, 5.
37. "Notes," *Louisville Courier-Journal,* September 8, 1884, 2.
38. "Nearly a Defeat," *Louisville Courier-Journal,* September 13, 1884, 5.
39. "A Game of Chance," *Louisville Courier-Journal,* September 12, 1884, 5.
40. "The Louisvilles Lose a Game to Brooklyn," *Louisville Courier-Journal,* September 19, 1884, 6.
41. "Browning's Brilliant Playing in Center Field," *Louisville Courier-Journal,* September 10, 1884, 5.
42. "Notes," *Louisville Courier-Journal,* September 12, 1884, 5.
43. The possessive (World's Series) would later be dropped. The 1903 World Series is considered the first modern one.

6. A Hitter of the Old Style (1885)

1. "Baseball Gossip," *Brooklyn Citizen,* July 19, 1891, 3.
2. "Baseball," *Louisville Courier-Journal,* November 8, 1891, 17.
3. "Is Insane," *Louisville Courier-Journal,* June 8, 1905, 2.
4. "Baseball Gossip," *Cincinnati Enquirer,* April 12, 1896, 2.
5. "Baseball," *Louisville Courier-Journal,* November 8, 1891, 17.
6. "Breaking in the Colts," *Washington Post,* August 14, 1896, 8.
7. "Pete Browning and His Lamps," *Buffalo Enquirer,* July 29, 1897, 8.
8. W. A. Phelon, "Little Tales about Baseball: Two Noble Sleepers," *Buffalo News,* June 10, 1911, 8.
9. "Ehret Shows up in Good Form," *Louisville Courier-Journal,* April 13, 1898, 6.
10. "Diamond Dust," *St. Louis Post-Dispatch,* July 1, 1885, 7.
11. "Local Base Ball News," *Louisville Courier-Journal,* January 11, 1885, 8.
12. "Base Ball Notes," *Louisville Courier-Journal,* January 25, 1885, 5.
13. "The Sporting World," *Louisville Courier-Journal,* February 1, 1885, 12.
14. *Louisville Commercial,* February 1, 1885, quoted in Bob Bailey, David Ball, and Bob McConnell, "The American Association History Project," https://sabr.org/research/article/the-american-association-history-project/ (accessed October 4, 2020).
15. "Were They Drunk?" *Louisville Courier-Journal,* June 14, 1885, 4.
16. "Notes from the Field," *Louisville Courier-Journal,* May 19, 1885, 6.
17. *Louisville Commercial,* January 20, 1884, quoted in Bailey, Ball, and McConnell, "American Association History Project."
18. "Threads from the Ball," *Louisville Courier-Journal,* May 22, 1885, 6.
19. "The Release of Baker," *Louisville Courier-Journal,* July 30, 1885, 3.
20. "Base-Ball Notes," *Louisville Courier-Journal,* May 3, 1885, 4.

21. "Threads from the Ball," *Louisville Courier-Journal,* May 20, 1885, 6.

22. "Notes on the Game," *Louisville Courier-Journal,* May 25, 1885, 8.

23. "Sullivan the Hitter," *Louisville Courier-Journal,* May 28, 1885, 6.

24. "The Catcher Struck Him in the Face," *Baseball History Daily,* December 23, 2020, https://baseballhistorydaily.com/2020/12/23/the-catcher-struck-him-in-the-face/.

25. "Field Notes and Comments," *Louisville Courier-Journal,* June 28, 1885, 6.

26. "Notes and Comments," *Louisville Courier-Journal,* August 16, 1885, 7.

27. "Roger Maris Proves the Old-Timers Weren't so Bad," *Baltimore Sun,* May 20, 1962, WM9.

28. Ibid.

29. Daniel Russell, "Physics and Acoustics of Baseball & Softball Bats," Graduate Program in Acoustics, Pennsylvania State University, October 6, 2003, https://www.acs.psu.edu/drussell/bats/batw8.html.

30. "John Reilly Talks about Pietro Browning's Peculiarities," *Cincinnati Enquirer,* February 24, 1889, 13.

31. "Baseball," *Dayton (OH) Herald,* May 14, 1887, 8.

32. "Base Ball Gossip," *Cincinnati Enquirer,* July 12, 1891, 10.

33. "Some Lively Baseball Gossip," *Louisville Courier-Journal,* April 19, 1908, 38.

34. "Pete Browning and His Lamps," 8.

35. "Notes from the Diamond," *Louisville Courier-Journal,* August 6, 1885, 6.

7. The Dude (1886)

1. "Pete Browning in Tears," *Louisville Courier-Journal,* February 12, 1886, 6.

2. *Louisville Commercial,* February 12, 1886, quoted in Bob Bailey, David Ball, and Bob McConnell, "The American Association History Project," https://sabr.org/research/article/the-american-association-history-project/ (accessed October 4, 2020).

3. "A Patriotic Louisville Judge," *Philadelphia Sporting Life,* February 24, 1886, 1.

4. "Baseball," *Nashville Banner,* April 12, 1886, 3.

5. "Still Attracting Attention—A Warning for Browning," *Louisville Courier-Journal,* January 24, 1886, 10.

6. "Notes and Comments," *Philadelphia Sporting Life,* March 3, 1886, 3.

7. "The Louisvilles," *Louisville Courier-Journal,* April 18, 1886, 10.

8. "Baseball Gossip," *Lincoln (NE) Evening Call,* August 4, 1888, 2.

9. "The Louisvilles," 10.

10. "Notes and Comments," *Philadelphia Sporting Life,* November 18, 1885, 3.

11. "Pete Browning's Big Drunk," *Louisville Courier-Journal,* April 10, 1886, 6.

12. Ibid.

13. "The Lousivilles," 10.

14. Hugh S. Fullerton, "Southpaws Are Very Eccentric," *Buffalo Courier,* January 21, 1906, 33.

15. "The Lousivilles," 10.

16. Ibid.

17. Fullerton, "Southpaws Are Very Eccentric," 33.
18. A. H. Tarvin Papers, National Baseball Hall of Fame, Cooperstown, NY.
19. Guy Mcl. Smith, "Deeds of Hecker, Browning, Ramsey Are Recalled," *Louisville Courier-Journal,* September 24, 1933, 34.
20. "Amos Cross' Peculiarities," *Louisville Courier-Journal,* July 19, 1888, 6.
21. "Estimate of Chances," *Louisville Courier-Journal,* April 17, 1886, 6.
22. "The Right Idea," *Louisville Courier-Journal,* April 4, 1886, 8.
23. "A Drunken Player," *Louisville Courier-Journal,* March 18, 1886, 6.
24. "From St. Louis," *Philadelphia Sporting Life,* November 24, 1886, 2.
25. "Notes and Comments," *Louisville Courier-Journal,* May 21, 1886, 3.
26. "Bunched Their Hits," *Louisville Courier-Journal,* June 14, 1886, 8.
27. "Louisville Defeated in Exciting Eleven-Inning Contest with the Pittsburghs," *Louisville Courier-Journal,* June 27, 1886, 7; "Pete Browning Laid Off," *Louisville Courier-Journal,* June 27, 1886, 7.
28. "Notes and Comments," *Louisville Courier-Journal,* July 2, 1886, 6.
29. "Pete Browning Laid Off," 7.
30. "Ramsey a Disturbing Element," *Louisville Courier-Journal,* May 21, 1886, 3.
31. "That Awful Fish Fry," *Cincinnati Enquirer,* July 5, 1886, 2.
32. "Louisville Lushers," *Louisville Courier-Journal,* July 4, 1886, 8.
33. Ibid.
34. "Turn About," *Louisville Courier-Journal,* July 6, 1886, 6.
35. "Going to Thunder," *St. Louis Sporting News,* July 9, 1886, 1.
36. R. W. L., "Pete Browning at the Springs," *St. Louis Sporting News,* August 2, 1886, 1.
37. "Notes and Comments," *Louisville Courier-Journal,* July 4, 1886, 8.
38. "Notes and Comments," *Louisville Courier-Journal,* July 11, 1886, 5.
39. "Notes and Comments," *Louisville Courier-Journal,* August 7, 1886, 6.
40. "Half a Hundred," *Louisville Courier-Journal,* August 9, 1886, 3.
41. "Notes and Comments," *Louisville Courier-Journal,* August 10, 1886, 6.
42. "Notes and Comments," *Louisville Courier-Journal,* June 2, 1886, 6.
43. "Notes and Comments," *Louisville Courier-Journal,* August 11, 1886, 6.
44. "Notes and Comments," *Louisville Courier-Journal,* September 27, 1886, 2.
45. "The Louisville Players," *St. Louis Sporting News,* October 25, 1886, 1.
46. "Caught on the Fly," *St. Louis Sporting News,* November 13, 1886, 5.
47. "Caught on the Fly," *St. Louis Sporting News,* October 11, 1886, 5.
48. "President Phelps," *Louisville Courier-Journal,* September 21, 1886, 2.
49. "Ahead on the Series," *Louisville Courier-Journal,* September 6, 1888, 2.
50. "Base Ball Matters," *Louisville Courier-Journal,* October 31, 1886, 10.
51. "Caught on the Fly," *St. Louis Sporting News,* October 18, 1886, 5.

8. The Gladiator (1887)

1. "An Awful Shame," *Louisville Courier-Journal,* November 6, 1886, 6.
2. "Base Ball Gossip," *Cincinnati Enquirer,* July 12, 1891, 10.
3. "An Awful Shame," 6.

4. "Mastoiditis," Columbia University Department of Otolaryngology, Head and Neck Surgery, https://www.entcolumbia.org/staywell/mastoiditis (accessed December 15, 2022).

5. "George M'Ginnis on Pete Browning," *Philadelphia Sporting Life,* March 23, 1887, 3.

6. "Browning Makes His Debut," *Philadelphia Sporting Life,* March 16, 1887, 6.

7. O. P. Caylor, "Caylor's Comment," *Philadelphia Sporting Life,* October 12, 1887, 5.

8. "Notes," *Louisville Courier-Journal,* March 28, 1887, 3.

9. "Browning Makes His Debut," 6.

10. "From St. Louis," *Philadelphia Sporting Life,* January 19, 1887, 2.

11. "Kelly and Hecker," *Louisville Courier-Journal,* May 6, 1887, 6.

12. "Louisvilles, 6; Mets, 2," *St. Louis Globe Democrat,* July 13, 1887, 8.

13. "Browning's Costly Drunk," *Louisville Courier-Journal,* July 13, 1887, 5.

14. Ibid.

15. "Notes of the Game," *Louisville Courier-Journal,* August 21, 1887, 5.

16. "Refereeing and Umpiring," *Washington Post,* October 9, 1910, 3.

17. "In and About," *Louisville Courier-Journal,* May 26, 1887, 4.

18. "Notes of the Game," *Louisville Courier-Journal,* June 22, 1887, 3.

19. "The Louisvilles Losing Games with Exasperating Regularity," *Louisville Courier-Journal,* June 10, 1887, 2.

20. "Base Ball Notes," *Louisville Courier-Journal,* May 17, 1887, 6.

21. "Kelly and Hecker," 6.

22. "In Second Place," *Louisville Courier-Journal,* August 7, 1887, 5.

23. "The Annual Tumble," *Louisville Courier-Journal,* August 25, 1887, 3.

24. "The Gladiator Drunk," *Louisville Courier-Journal,* August 25, 1887, 3.

25. "Will the Louisvilles Be Sold," *Louisville Courier-Journal,* August 10, 1887, 3.

26. "Notes from the Green Field," *Louisville Courier-Journal,* June 5, 1887, 8.

27. "Three from Brooklyn," *Louisville Courier-Journal,* August 29, 1887, 2.

28. "Notes of the Game," *Louisville Courier-Journal,* August 7, 1887, 5.

29. "Around the Bases," *Chicago Tribune,* July 28, 1887, 3.

30. "Notes of the Game," *Louisville Courier-Journal,* August 29, 1887, 2.

31. "Notes of the Game," *Louisville Courier-Journal,* September 14, 1887, 3.

32. "Notes of the Game," *Louisville Courier-Journal,* July 30, 1887, 3.

33. "Notes of the Game," *Louisville Courier-Journal,* October 10, 1887, 3.

34. "A Lively Imagination," *Louisville Courier-Journal,* October 17, 1887, 2.

35. "Diamond Dust," *St. Louis Globe Democrat,* October 18, 1887, 8.

36. "Sporting News," *Pittsburgh Dispatch,* March 24, 1890, 7.

37. "They Are Well-Known," *St. Louis Post-Dispatch,* November 19, 1888, 5.

38. "The Gladiator Enters Politics," *Philadelphia Sporting Life,* November 30, 1887, 3.

39. *Louisville Commercial,* October 9, 1887, quoted in Bob Bailey, David Ball, and Bob McConnell, "The American Association History Project," https://sabr.org/research/article/the-american-association-history-project/ (accessed October 4, 2020).

9. Gutter Fishing (1888)

1. "Sporting Procedures," *Kansas City Star,* June 21, 1888, 2.
2. "Pete Browning's Fall," *Louisville Courier-Journal,* June 22, 1888, 4.
3. Quoted in Richard Schenin, *Field of Screams* (New York: W. W. Norton, 1994), 49–50.
4. "Paragraphs about the Louisvilles," *Louisville Courier-Journal,* January 6, 1889, 16.
5. "Sporting Procedures," 2.
6. "Gossip of the Day," *Louisville Courier-Journal,* November 1, 1887, 6.
7. John Barleycorn is the personification of the barley crop and the alcoholic beverages made from it.
8. "Browning Makes His Reappearance, and Hits Hard but Catches No Flies," *Louisville Courier-Journal,* June 24, 1888, 14.
9. "Gossip of the Day," *Louisville Courier-Journal,* March 1, 1888, 6.
10. "Chamberlain and Browning Still Obstinate," *Louisville Courier-Journal,* March 25, 1888, 16.
11. Ibid.
12. "They Want More Money," *Louisville Courier-Journal,* March 24, 1888, 6.
13. Chamberlain was dubbed Ice Box for the ice water that was said to flow through his veins.
14. "They Want More Money," 6.
15. "Manager Kelly's Rules," *Louisville Courier-Journal,* April 2, 1888, 2.
16. "Notes of the Diamond," *Louisville Courier-Journal,* April 8, 1888, 14.
17. "All Sign the Pledge," *Louisville Courier-Journal,* April 17, 1888, 6.
18. "Notes of the Game," *Louisville Courier-Journal,* April 29, 1888, 4.
19. "The Diamond," *Louisville Courier-Journal,* May 6, 1888, 11.
20. "Grand Stand Chat," *St. Louis Globe Democrat,* May 28, 1888, 8.
21. "Base Ball Notes," *Philadelphia Times,* May 20, 1888, 16.
22. The months in which Pete hit below .300 were September 1883, August 1884, April 1886, June 1886, and July 1886.
23. "Base Ball Notes," 16.
24. "The President's Loss," *Louisville Courier-Journal,* May 23, 1888, 2.
25. "The National Game," *Pine Grove (PA) Press Herald,* May 18, 1888, 1.
26. "Aroused from Their Lethargy," *Louisville Courier-Journal,* May 29, 1888, 2.
27. "They Have Braced Up," *Louisville Courier-Journal,* June 2, 1888, 5.
28. "General Sporting News," *Baltimore Sun,* June 1, 1888, 5.
29. A. H. Tarvin, "Didn't Know Base Hit from Bass Viol but Davidson Saved Baseball Here," *Louisville Courier-Journal,* November 7, 1943, 6.
30. A. H. Tarvin, "History of Baseball in Louisville" (unpublished manuscript), 25.
31. Ibid., 24.
32. "Sounds More Natural," *Louisville Courier-Journal,* June 11, 1888, 6.
33. "Browning Makes His Debut," *Philadelphia Sporting Life,* March 16, 1887, 6.
34. "Plenty of Criticism," *Louisville Courier-Journal,* July 8, 1888, 7.
35. "Criticizing Louisville," *Louisville Courier-Journal,* July 3, 1888, 6.

36. "Grand Stand Chat," *St. Louis Globe Democrat,* June 29, 1888, 8.
37. *Louisville Courier-Journal,* July 10, 1888, 4.
38. "Captured the Series," *Louisville Courier-Journal,* July 11, 1888, 6.
39. "Base Ball Briefs," *Pittsburgh Press,* July 28, 1888, 5.
40. "The Gladiator Is Sick," *Louisville Courier-Journal,* July 22, 1888, 2.
41. "The Tall Centerfielder," *Louisville Courier-Journal,* August 19, 1888, 9.
42. "The Gladiator Left at Home," *Louisville Courier-Journal,* August 22, 1888, 6.
43. "Grand Stand Chat," *Louisville Courier-Journal,* August 24, 1888, 8.
44. "Big Pete's Challenge," *Louisville Courier-Journal,* August 25, 1888, 6.
45. Ibid.
46. "Diamond Dust," *St. Louis Globe Democrat,* September 5, 1888, 8.
47. "Grand Stand Chat," *St. Louis Post-Dispatch,* September 12, 1888, 8.
48. "Notes," *Louisville Courier-Journal,* September 20, 1888, 7.
49. "One Game Apiece," *Louisville Courier-Journal,* September 24, 1888, 3.
50. Peter Levine, "Business, Missionary Motives behind 1888–89 World Tour," *SABR Research Journals* archive, http://research.sabr.org/journals/business-missionary-motives-behind-1888-89-world-tour (accessed February 20, 2021).
51. "Browning's Resolution," *Louisville Courier-Journal,* December 31, 1888, 6.

10. The Worst Team in Baseball (1889)

1. "Notes," *Louisville Courier-Journal,* January 6, 1889, 11.
2. "Lewis Rogers and Tom," *Louisville Courier-Journal,* December 24, 1888, 8.
3. "The Base-Ball Kingdom," *Louisville Courier-Journal,* April 2, 1889, 3.
4. "Base Ball Cranks Happy," *Omaha Daily Bee,* February 27, 1898, 20.
5. "The Base-Ball Kingdom," 3.
6. "Sports with the Ball," *Louisville Courier-Journal,* January 6, 1889, 11.
7. A. H. Tarvin, "Didn't Know Base Hit from Bass Viol but Davidson Saved Baseball Here," *Louisville Courier-Journal,* November 7, 1943, 6.
8. "A Tragic Tale," *Louisville Courier-Journal,* May 9, 1889, 6.
9. "Notes," *Louisville Courier-Journal,* August 15, 1888, 6.
10. "Notes," *Louisville Courier-Journal,* June 5, 1889, 5.
11. "Very Funny Stories," *St. Louis Sporting News,* June 29, 1889, 1.
12. "Notes," *Louisville Courier-Journal,* May 3, 1889, 6.
13. "The Shake Up," *Louisville Courier-Journal,* May 8, 1889, 3.
14. "About Our Wandering Heroes," *Louisville Courier-Journal,* June 3, 1889, 8.
15. "Lost Again," *Louisville Courier-Journal,* June 5, 1889, 5.
16. *Louisville Commercial,* June 6, 1889, quoted in Bob Bailey, David Ball, and Bob McConnell, "The American Association History Project," https://sabr.org/research/article/the-american-association-history-project/ (accessed October 4, 2020).
17. Only four players—John Reilly, Bob Meusel, Babe Herman, and Adrian Beltre—have hit for the cycle three times.
18. "In a New Role," *Louisville Courier-Journal,* June 15, 1889, 6.

19. Due to a mistake in a newspaper in 1887, Fisher's first name was listed as Charles. It would remain so until 2023, when Justin McKinney, doing research for SABR, discovered the mistake and corrected Fisher's name to Walter.
20. "Notes," *Louisville Courier-Journal,* June 22, 1889, 6.
21. "In Debt to Davidson," *Louisville Courier-Journal,* June 22, 1889, 6.
22. "Adjusting the Fines," *Louisville Courier-Journal,* July 6, 1889, 6.
23. "Check on a Sand Bank," *Louisville Courier-Journal,* July 10, 1889, 6.
24. "Notes," *Louisville Courier-Journal,* August 4, 1889, 4.
25. "Sport on the Diamond," *Louisville Courier-Journal,* August 18, 1889, 14.
26. "Notes," *Louisville Courier-Journal,* September 6, 1889, 6.
27. "Other Chat of the Diamond," *Louisville Courier-Journal,* January 6, 1908, 6.
28. "A Good Start," *Louisville Courier-Journal,* October 23, 1889, 6.

11. The Brotherhood War (1890)

1. "The Gladiator," *Cincinnati Enquirer,* January 29, 1890, 2.
2. Ibid.
3. "For Amateur Base Ball," *Chicago Tribune,* January 21, 1890, 6.
4. "Browning Makes Neat Retort," *Washington Post,* July 23, 1905, S2.
5. "The Gladiator," 2.
6. "A Talk with Browning," *Cleveland Plain Dealer,* January 27, 1890, 7.
7. "Big Strike Imminent," *St. Louis Sporting News,* June 22, 1889, 1.
8. Harold Seymour, *Baseball: The Early Years* (Oxford: Oxford University Press, 1960), 129.
9. "The Base Ball Brotherhood," *Louisville Courier-Journal,* October 30, 1889, 3.
10. "Backing the Brotherhood," *Chicago Inter-Ocean,* October 30, 1889, 2.
11. Among those rookies were three future Hall of Famers: Jesse Burkett, Kid Nichols, and Cy Young.
12. "And So Does Pete Browning," *Buffalo Sunday Truth,* July 27, 1890, 12.
13. Ibid.
14. "Pete Browning's Latest," *Louisville Courier-Journal,* April 7, 1890, 10.
15. "Notes," *Baltimore Sun,* April 8, 1890, 4.
16. "Baseball Notes," *Pittsburgh Dispatch,* July 14, 1890.
17. "Held Down by Barston," *Chicago Tribune,* June 5, 1890, 6.
18. "Baseball Notes," *Cleveland Plain Dealer,* June 16, 1890, 7.
19. "Baseball Notes," *Pittsburgh Dispatch,* July 14, 1890.
20. Pasquale Cassano, Giorgio Ciprandi, and Desiderio Passali, "Acute Mastoiditis in Children," *Acta Biomedica Journal,* February 2020, https://www.ncbi.nlm.nih.gov/pmc/articles/PMC7947742/.
21. "Story about Old Pete Browning," *Sandusky (OH) Star,* November 14, 1898, 4.
22. Ibid.
23. "Sporting Notes," *Chicago Inter-Ocean,* June 15, 1890, 2.
24. "Still Going Pennant Wards," *Louisville Courier-Journal,* July 27, 1890, 17.
25. "Giants Win the Last," *New York World,* July 17, 1890, 7.

26. "Notes," *Louisville Courier-Journal,* July 14, 1890, 5.
27. "The Latest News," *St. Louis Sporting News,* May 10, 1890, 1.
28. "Still Going Pennant Wards," 17.
29. "Goodbye Players' League," *St. Louis Sporting News,* November 22, 1890, 4.
30. Ibid.
31. "Pete Browning in Town," *Louisville Courier-Journal,* October 20, 1890, 2.
32. The other three are Dan Brouthers (NL, 1882, 1883, 1889, 1892; AA, 1891), D. J. LeMahieu (NL, 2016; AL, 2020), and Luis Arraez (AL, 2022; NL, 2023). Brouthers is almost always overlooked (perhaps because his AA title came in the league's last year of existence). Ed Delahanty is often credited as winning titles in two leagues, but his 1902 AL title is disputed.
33. "Pete Browning in Town," 2.
34. "Odds and Ends of Ball," *Chicago Inter-Ocean,* November 7, 1890, 3.

12. Final Seasons (1891–1894)

1. "Base Ball Comment," *Philadelphia Inquirer,* March 22, 1891, 3.
2. "Galvin Talks Business," *Pittsburgh Press,* March 22, 1891, 6.
3. "This Day in History—March 19," *Owensboro (KY) Messenger,* March 19, 1891, 2.
4. "Sporting," *Pittsburgh Press,* March 31, 1891, 5.
5. "Browning in Hard Luck," *Pittsburgh Daily Post,* May 6, 1891, 6.
6. "One Run and No Errors," *Chicago Tribune,* May 6, 1891, 5.
7. "General Sporting Notes," *Pittsburgh Press,* May 20, 1891, 5.
8. "Base Ball Notes," *Cleveland Plain Dealer,* April 21, 1891, 4.
9. David Nemec, *The Official Rules of Baseball Illustrated: An Irreverent Look at the Rules of Baseball and How They Came to Be What They Are Today* (Guilford, CT: Lyons, 2020).
10. "Browning Explains Again," *Baltimore Sun,* July 8, 1891, 6.
11. "Base Ball," *Louisville Courier-Journal,* May 31, 1891, 13.
12. "Booked or Released," *Pittsburgh Press,* May 13, 1891, 6.
13. "Peter Wanted a Release," *Pittsburgh Press,* June 28, 1891, 6.
14. "Local Base Ball Gossip," *Pittsburgh Daily Post,* June 29, 1891, 6.
15. "Old Pete Liked the City," *Pittsburgh Dispatch,* July 1, 1891, 6.
16. "Base Ball Gossip," *Cincinnati Enquirer,* July 2, 1891, 2.
17. "Browning," *Cincinnati Enquirer,* July 2, 1891, 2.
18. "They Are Gone," *Louisville Courier-Journal,* August 24, 1891, 6.
19. "Base Ball Gossip," *Cincinnati Enquirer,* July 11, 1891, 2.
20. "Base Ball Gossip," *Cincinnati Enquirer,* July 15, 1891, 2.
21. "Base Ball Gossip," *Cincinnati Enquirer,* July 11, 1891, 2.
22. "Echoes of the Battle," *Chicago Inter-Ocean,* June 5, 1891, 3.
23. Quoted in Jimmy Keenan, "Cupid Childs," SABR, https://sabr.org/bioproj/person/cupid-childs/ (accessed June 18, 2021).

24. "Fast and Furious," *Cincinnati Enquirer,* August 19, 1891, 2.
25. "Base-Ball Gossip," *Cincinnati Enquirer,* August 20, 1891, 2.
26. "Base-Ball Gossip," *Cincinnati Enquirer,* July 11, 1891, 2.
27. "Base-Ball Gossip," *Cincinnati Enquirer,* August 28, 1891, 2.
28. Gleason would later gain fame as manager of the 1919 Chicago "Black Sox."
29. "Pietro Browning and His Average—Other Matters," *Cincinnati Enquirer,* October 18, 1891, 2.
30. "Didn't Get Him," *Cincinnati Enquirer,* November 26, 1891, 2.
31. "Base-Ball Gossip," *Cincinnati Enquirer,* May 14, 1892, 2.
32. "Smashed," *Cincinnati Enquirer,* July 1, 1892, 2.
33. "Base-Ball Gossip," *Cincinnati Enquirer,* July 13, 1892, 2.
34. "Base-Ball Gossip," *Cincinnati Enquirer,* July 14, 1892, 2.
35. The facts of this story, like many in Pete's life, have been misconstrued over time. It is often reported that McGraw was playing third at the time this happened, but McGraw did not make the switch to third base full time until 1894. When Pete played against McGraw, he was still playing second base and shortstop.
36. "Pete Browning Spoiled It," *Courtland (KS) Journal,* September 22, 1911, 5.
37. "Chat of Diamond," *Trenton (NJ) Times,* July 21, 1892, 8.
38. "Base-Ball Gossip," *Cincinnati Enquirer,* August 17, 1892, 2.
39. "Bad Fielding," *Cincinnati Enquirer,* September 3, 1892, 2.
40. "Base Ball," *Louisville Courier-Journal,* October 23, 1892, 9.
41. "Good-bye to the Gladiator," *Louisville Courier-Journal,* March 25, 1893, 8.
42. "Stratton for Gumbert," *Louisville Courier-Journal,* March 28, 1893, 2.
43. "The Gladiator," *Cincinnati Enquirer,* May 1, 1893, 2.
44. "The Green Diamond," *Louisville Courier-Journal,* May 14, 1893, 9.
45. "Local Ball Gossip," *Louisville Courier-Journal,* May 26, 1893, 5.
46. "Base Ball Is Sick," *Louisville Courier-Journal,* June 4, 1893, 5.
47. "Gossip of the Game," *Louisville Courier-Journal,* May 28, 1893, 3.
48. "Gossip of the Game," *Louisville Courier-Journal,* July 2, 1893, 4.
49. "Notes of the Field," *Louisville Courier-Journal,* July 12, 1893, 6.
50. "Three Men Released," *Louisville Courier-Journal,* August 4, 1893, 5.
51. "Will Louisville Go Higher," *Louisville Courier-Journal,* September 24, 1893, 4.
52. "Personal and Pertinent," *Philadelphia Sporting Life,* January 27, 1894, 3.
53. David Nemec, *The Beer and Whiskey League: The Illustrated History of the American Association—Baseball's Renegade Major League* (Guilford, CT: Lyons, 2004), 213.
54. "Baseball Notes," *Washington Post,* July 8, 1894, 15.
55. "Through His Bonnet," *St. Paul Globe,* March 20, 1895, 5.
56. Hugh S. Fullerton, "Odd Diamond Characters," *Chicago Daily Tribune,* April 8, 1906, A2.
57. "Browns Beaten Again," *Louisville Courier-Journal,* August 7, 1894, 5.
58. "They Need Strengthening," *Louisville Courier-Journal,* August 12, 1894, 16.
59. "Browns Beaten Again," 5.

13. After Baseball (1895–1899)

1. "Baseball Notes," *Washington Post,* July 20, 1899, 8.

2. Either Wagner's memory is faulty or Pete's bat was mislabeled, as the only home run he ever hit against St. Louis was in 1892. Like the label said, it was a ninth-inning walk-off homer, though it produced only two RBIs, not three.

3. "Baseball Notes," *Washington Post,* July 20, 1899, 8.

4. "Wagner's Mysterious Bat," *Baseball History Daily,* August 20, 2014, https://baseballhistorydaily.com/2014/08/20/wagners-mysterious-bat/.

5. "Browning's Bats Were His Mascots," *Paducah (KY) Sun,* January 30, 1907, 2.

6. "Through His Bonnet," *St. Paul Globe,* March 20, 1895, 5.

7. "Base Ball," *Bangor (ME) Daily Whig & Courier,* April 13, 1895, 3.

8. "Burglars with a Ladder," *Louisville Courier-Journal,* April 26, 1895, 6.

9. "Gladiator Pete's Opinion," *Louisville Courier-Journal,* May 19, 1895, 10.

10. "Browning," *Louisville Courier-Journal,* February 23, 1896, 9.

11. "Is Insane," *Louisville Courier-Journal,* June 8, 1905, 2.

12. "Four Right Handers," *Indianapolis Journal,* February 23, 1896, 6.

13. "Like Casey," *Louisville Courier-Journal,* April 10, 1896, 6.

14. "Kentucky Oolong: Effects of the Brew on Pete Browning, the Gladiator," *Chicago Inter-Ocean,* August 23, 1896, 11.

15. "Base Ball Notes," *Indianapolis Journal,* May 5, 1896, 5.

16. "Base Ball Notes," *Indianapolis Journal,* May 19, 1896, 3.

17. "From the Falls City," *Philadelphia Sporting Life,* January 30, 1897, 4.

18. "Sport up to Date," *Buffalo Enquirer,* November 10, 1897, 8.

19. "Sports," *Pittsburgh Press,* August 23, 1898, 5.

20. "Notes of the Game," *Louisville Courier-Journal,* August 10, 1887, 3.

21. "Baseball Gossip," *Louisville Courier-Journal,* January 9, 1897, 3.

22. "Brief Baseball News," *Decatur (IL) Daily Review,* March 9, 1897, 2.

23. "Gossip of the Diamond," *Louisville Courier-Journal,* June 1, 1904, 7.

14. Final Days (1900–1905)

1. "Tired," *Louisville Courier-Journal,* August 29, 1905, 8.

2. "News and Comment," *Philadelphia Sporting Life,* September 1, 1900, 3.

3. "Insane," *Louisville Courier-Journal,* June 8, 1905, 2.

4. Ibid.

5. "Pete Browning Hurt Here," *Indianapolis News,* September 21, 1905, 16.

6. "Jimmy Wolf Is Insane," *Louisville Courier-Journal,* July 12, 1901, 6.

7. "Phil Reccius Injury Fatal," *Louisville Courier-Journal,* February 16, 1903, 7.

8. "Old Pete Again," *Louisville Courier-Journal,* July 27, 1905, 4.

9. "Pete Browning Seriously Ill," *Baltimore Sun,* July 29, 1905, 4.

10. "Called Out," *Louisville Courier-Journal,* September 11, 1905, 5.

11. "Poor Old Pete Is No More," *Owensboro (KY) Messenger-Inquirer,* September 15, 1905, 2.

12. "Finds No Fault with Mr. Vogt," *Louisville Courier-Journal,* August 9, 1906, 1–2.

13. "Pete Browning's Funeral," *Paducah (KY) Sun,* September 13, 1905, 2.

14. "Line 'Em out Pete Dead," *Chicago Daily Tribune,* September 11, 1905, 8.

15. "Pete Browning Slugger," *Washington Post,* September 12, 1905, 2.

15. Legacy

1. Ross Barnes also earned three batting titles during this time, but two of them came in the National Association of Professional Base Ball Players, which is not recognized as a major league.

2. Jim Riggleman, interview with the author.

3. "As to Peter Browning," *Louisville Courier-Journal,* May 10, 1887, 2.

4. Four players whose careers began in the nineteenth century were elected by sportswriters prior to 1939: Cy Young, Willie Keeler, Nap Lajoie, and Honus Wagner.

5. Bill James, *Whatever Happened to the Hall of Fame* (New York: Free Press, 1995), 96–97.

6. Eugene Murdock, "The Pre-1900 Batting Stars," *SABR Research Journals,* http://research.sabr.org/journals/pre-1900-batting-stars (accessed January 27, 2022).

7. Jaime Aron, interview with the author.

8. "News of the Diamond," *Mansfield (OH) News-Journal,* September 3, 1904, 11.

9. "Pete Browning Slugger," *Washington Post,* September 12, 1905, 2.

10. Aron interview.

11. "Browning and Delahanty Greatest Hitters Baseball Has Ever Known," *St. Louis Globe Democrat,* December 2, 1910, 11.

12. "Pete Browning Slugger," 2.

13. "Pete Browning Responsible," *South Bend (IN) Tribune,* March 24, 1905, 3.

14. "Jimmy Collins Is the King," *Buffalo Enquirer,* March 17, 1903, 8.

Bibliography

Achon, Edward. *The Summer of Beer and Whiskey: How Brewers, Barkeeps, Rowdies, Immigrants, and a Wild Pennant Fight Made Baseball America's Game.* New York: Public Affairs Books, 2013.

Arthur, Rob. "The New Science of Hitting." FiveThirtyEight, April 13, 2016. https://fivethirtyeight.com/features/the-new-science-of-hitting/.

Bailey, Bob, David Ball, and Bob McConnell. "The American Association History Project." Society for American Baseball Research (SABR). https://sabr.org/research/article/the-american-association-history-project/. Accessed October 4, 2020.

Cook, William A. *The Louisville Grays Scandal of 1877: The Taint of Gambling at the Dawn of the National League.* Jefferson, NC: McFarland, 2005.

Curtis, Bryan. "In Search of Baseball's Holy Grail." Grantland, October 28, 2013. https://grantland.com/features/baseball-archaeologist-david-block/.

Dickson, Paul. *The New Dickson Baseball Dictionary: A Cyclopedic Reference to More than 7,000 Words, Names, Phrases, and Slang Expressions that Define the Game, Its Heritage, Culture, and Variations.* Boston: Houghton Mifflin Harcourt, 1999.

Faber, Charles F. *Baseball Prodigies: Best Major League Seasons by Players under 21.* Jefferson, NC: McFarland, 2014.

Felber, Bill, ed. *Inventing Baseball: The 100 Greatest Games of the Nineteenth Century.* Phoenix: Society for American Baseball Research, 2013.

Gordon, David J. "The Rise and Fall of the Dead Ball Era." *SABR Baseball Research Journal,* Fall 2018.

Hecker, Guy. *Hecker's Guide to the Art of Pitching.* Louisville: Hecker Base Ball Supply Company, 1885.

Hill, Bob. *Crack of the Bat: The Louisville Slugger Story.* Champaign, IL: Sports Publishing, 2000.

Hodges, Jeremy K., and Bill Nowlin, eds. *Base Ball's 19th Century Winter Meetings, 1857–1900.* Phoenix: Society for American Baseball Research, 2018.

James, Bill. *The New Bill James Historical Baseball Abstract.* New York: Free Press, 2003.

———. *Whatever Happened to the Hall of Fame.* New York: Free Press, 1995.

Jewell, Anne. *Baseball in Louisville.* Charleston, SC: Arcadia, 2006.

Keenan, Jimmy. "Cupid Childs." Society for American Baseball Research (SABR). https://sabr.org/bioproj/person/cupid-childs/. Accessed June 18, 2021.

Kirsch, George B. *Baseball in Blue and Gray.* Princeton, NJ: Princeton University Press, 2003.

Koppett, Leonard. "During the Brotherhood Revolt the Mood in Baseball Wasn't Fraternal." *Sports Illustrated,* June 1, 1981.

Levine, Peter. "Business, Missionary Motives behind 1888–89 World Tour." *SABR Baseball Research Journal* archives. http://research.sabr.org/journals/business-missionary-motives-behind-1888-89-world-tour. Accessed February 20, 2021.

Magee, David, and Philip Shirley. *Sweet Spot: 125 Years of Baseball and the Louisville Slugger.* Chicago: Triumph Books, 2009.

McLaughlin, Dan. "What Happened the Last Time Baseball Moved Back the Pitcher's Mound." *National Review,* May 29, 2021. https://www.nationalreview.com/2021/05/what-happened-the-last-time-baseball-moved-back-the-pitchers-mound/.

Mitchell, Eddie. *Baseball Rowdies of the 19th Century: Brawlers, Drinkers, Pranksters and Cheats in the Early Days of the Major Leagues.* Jefferson, NC: McFarland, 2018.

Morris, Pete. *A Game of Inches: The Story behind the Innovations that Shaped Baseball.* Chicago: Ivan R. Dee, 2010.

Murdock, Eugene. "The Pre-1900 Batting Stars." *SABR Baseball Research Journal* archives. http://research.sabr.org/journals/pre-1900-batting-stars. Accessed January 27, 2022.

Nemec, David. *The Beer and Whisky League: The Illustrated History of the American Association—Baseball's Renegade Major League.* Guilford, CT: Lyons, 2004.

———. *Major League Baseball Profiles, 1871–1900.* Vol. 2, *The Hall of Famers and Memorable Personalities Who Shaped the Game.* Lincoln: University of Nebraska Press, 2011.

———. *The Official Rules of Baseball Illustrated: An Irreverent Look at the Rules of Baseball and How They Came to Be What They Are Today.* Guilford, CT: Lyons, 2020.

Nesbitt, Stephen. "'It's an Epic Saga': An Exotic Beetle, Barry Bonds, Joey Votto and the End of Ash Baseball Bats." *Athletic,* January 3, 2022. https://theathletic.com/3043389/2022/01/03/its-an-epic-saga-an-exotic-beetle-barry-bonds-joey-votto-and-the-end-of-ash-baseball-bats/?source=dailyemail&campaign=601983.

Okrent, Daniel, and Harris Lewin, eds. *Ultimate Baseball Book.* Boston: Houghton Mifflin, 2000.

O'Malley, Mimi. *It Happened in Kentucky: Remarkable Events that Shaped History.* Kearney, NE: Morris Book Publishing, 2011.

Orem, Preston D. *Baseball (1882–1891) from the Newspaper Accounts.* Phoenix: Society for American Baseball Research, 2021.

Roer, Mike. *Orator O'Rourke: The Life of a Baseball Radical.* Jefferson, NC: McFarland, 2005.

Schenin, Richard. *Field of Screams.* New York: W. W. Norton, 1994.

Seymour, Harold. *Baseball: The Early Years.* Oxford: Oxford University Press, 1960.

Shieber, Tom. "Road Trip." Baseball Hall of Fame. https://baseballhall.org/discover-more/stories/short-stops/spalding-road-trip. Accessed June 23, 2022.

Silva, Chris. "The Fascinating History of the Game." Post Game, July 12, 2011. http://www.thepostgame.com/blog/throwback/201107/fascinating-history-baseball-glove.

Skal, David J. *Dark Carnival: The Secret World of Tod Browning.* New York: Anchor Books, 1995.

Smith, Robert. *Baseball: A Historical Narrative of the Game, the Men Who Have Played It, and Its Place in American Life.* New York: Simon & Schuster, 1947.

Sullivan, Dean A. *Early Innings: A Documentary History of Baseball, 1825–1908.* Lincoln: University of Nebraska Press, 1995.

———. *The Growth of Sport in a Southern City: A Study of the Organizational Evolution of Baseball in Louisville, Kentucky, as an Urban Phenomenon, 1860–1900.* Fairfax, VA: George Mason, 1989.

Tarvin, A. H. *A Century of Baseball: 1839–1939.* Louisville: Standard Printing Company, 1939.

———. "History of Baseball in Louisville." Unpublished manuscript, n.d. A. H. Tarvin Papers, 1838–1949, National Baseball Hall of Fame, Cooperstown, NY.

———. *Seventy-Five Years on Louisville Diamonds.* Louisville: Schumann Publications, 1940.

Thorn, John, ed. *Total Baseball,* 8th ed. Sports Media Publishing, 2004.

Tieman, Robert L., ed. *Nineteenth Century Stars.* Phoenix: Society for American Baseball Research, 2012.

Vasile, Joe. "Black Players in Organized White Baseball in the Pre-integration Era." Beyond the Boxscore, February 15, 2016. https://www.beyondtheboxscore.com/2016/2/15/10991906/black-baseball-players-history-before-jackie-robinson-negro-leagues.

Von Borries, Phillip. *American Gladiator.* St. Petersburg, FL: BookLocker, 2007.

———. *The Louisville Baseball Almanac.* Charleston, SC: History Press, 2010.

Wiser, Steve. "Digging into the Legendary Origins of Hillerich & Bradsby's Louisville Slugger Baseball Bat." Broken Sidewalk, September 22, 2015. https://brokensidewalk.com/2015/louisville-slugger-origins/.

Index